D0984321

Engendering Motherhood

PERSPECTIVES ON MARRIAGE AND THE FAMILY
Bert N. Adams and David M. Klein, Editors

ENGENDERING MOTHERHOOD:
IDENTITY AND SELF-TRANSFORMATION IN WOMEN'S LIVES
Martha McMahon

WIFE BATTERING: A SYSTEMS THEORY APPROACH
Jean Giles-Sim

COMMUTER MARRIAGE: A STUDY OF WORK AND FAMILY
Naomi Gerstel and Harriet Gross

HELPING THE ELDERLY: THE COMPLEMENTARY
ROLES OF INFORMAL NETWORKS AND FORMAL SYSTEMS
Eugene Litwak

REMARRIAGE AND STEPPARENTING:
CURRENT RESEARCH AND THEORY
Kay Palsey and Marilyn Ibinger-Tallman (Eds.)

FEMINISM, CHILDREN, AND THE NEW FAMILIES
Sanford M. Dornbusch and Myra F. Strober (Eds.)

DYNAMICS OF FAMILY DEVELOPMENT:
A THEORETICAL PERSPECTIVE
James M. White

PORTRAIT OF DIVORCE:
ADJUSTMENT TO MARITAL BREAKDOWN
Gay C. Kitson with William M. Holmes

WOMEN AND FAMILIES: FEMINIST RECONSTRUCTIONS
Kristine M. Baber and Katherine R. Allen

CHILDRENS' STRESS AND COPING: A FAMILY PERSPECTIVE
Elaine Shaw Sorensen

WHEN LOVE DIES: THE PROCESS OF MARITAL DISAFFECTION
Karen Kayser

FAMILIES BEFORE AND AFTER *PERESTROIKA*:
RUSSIAN AND U.S. PERSPECTIVES
*James W. Maddock, M. Janice Hogan, Anatolyi I. Antonov,
and Mikhail S. Matskovsky (Eds.)*

METAPHORS OF FAMILY SYSTEMS THEORY:
TOWARD NEW CONSTRUCTIONS
Paul C. Rosenblatt

FAMILIES IN MULTICULTURAL PERSPECTIVE
Bron B. Ingoldsby and Suzanna Smith (Eds.)

Engendering Motherhood

Identity and
Self-Transformation
in Women's Lives

MARTHA McMAHON

The Guilford Press
New York   New York

To My Late Mother

© 1995 The Guilford Press
A Division of Guilford Publications, Inc.
72 Spring Street, New York, NY, 10012

Printed in the United States of America

This book is printed on acid-free paper.

Last digit is print number: 9 8 7 6 5 4 3 2 1

Library of Congress Cataloging-in-Publication Data
McMahon, Martha
  Engendering motherhood : identity and self-transformation in
women's lives / Martha McMahon
    p.   cm. — (Perspectives on marriage and the family)
  Includes bibliographical references and index.
  ISBN 1-57230-002-7
  1. Motherhood—Canada—Psychological aspects. 2. Gender
identity—Canada.   3. Middle class women—Canada—
Attitudes.   4. Working class women—Canada—Attitudes.
5. Sociology
I. Title. II. Series.
HQ759.M425   1995
306.874'3—dc20   95-16209
                                                        CIP

Preface

This book is based on the research I did for my Ph.D. in sociology. Although qualitative research encourages the researcher to get close to the lived experience of those she studies, for a long time I did not really question the assumption that the story I was writing was about others and not also about me. This assumption of separateness of researcher and participants is reflected even in conventions of writing. For example, the copy editor for this book struggled to get me to use the word "the" with reference to the women in this study. But I felt it to be objectifying, as falsely distancing, and author-itative to be referring repeatedly to "the" women. Yet in not using the definite article I risked slipping into another objectifying tendency of research reports, that of communicating the impression of speaking about a whole category of people, for or about all mothers. This book is a story based on what participants in the study told me about their lives; it is a story grounded in my personal and sociological engagement of these women's accounts.

Writing about other women's experiences of motherhood drew me into reflecting on my own biography and the implications of what participants told me about motherhood for my own life as a childless woman. In some ways, my thinking about childlessness, maternal bonds, and of not becoming a mother myself has the character of a counter story to the story I wrote of the participants' experience of motherhood. Before I started the research I had not realized the ways in which the subjects of my research could come into my life, talk to me, tell me about myself. I had long said that I did not want to have children, having felt little pressure or desire to do so. But rejection of motherhood had not been central to my identity either. Doing this research made me revisit that decision. What was particularly unsettling for me in this research was the ways in which many women's stories of motherhood as connectedness confronted me with the implication that being childless might mean being disconnected. Participants' talk of connectedness later took on sad shadow meanings for me when, shortly after my initial writing up the research, my own mother died. Perhaps because I am an immigrant and my family of origin lives elsewhere, or perhaps because of the particular way in which my own mother had held together the world of my past, I felt torn apart by her death. Thus the theme of motherhood as symbolizing special social bonds of connectedness became a stronger one in the revisions for this book. In practice, idealized bonds of motherhood may be neither realized nor realizable, but the evocative image of motherhood can continue to provide a culturally powerful metaphor with which to think about social life.

My concern with the nature of social bonds has more pressing relevance at the time this book is being published than when I started the research. Increasingly, in the name of balanced budgets or deficit reduction, public political discourse imposes the logic of neoclassical economic models of the individual on the diversity of human relationships. I wonder about the implications for women like the young, alone, working-class mothers who took part in this study. How could Helen, Kathy, or Tina have managed to hold full-time jobs and support their children without publicly funded daycare? How could Renee or Kimberly have gotten off welfare without the government programs to help single mothers? What does it say about dominant social values if we design the social world so that it meets the needs of private business or industry but is inhospitable to women who are raising children? Both from my own life and my commitments as a feminist sociologist I find it more and more important to point to the value of caring and supportive human relationships and the work that women do in producing and holding up the social world of caring connections. For me, personally, this is what motherhood symbolizes. Doing this research has made me think about being a woman who has not and will not have children, and has led me to think of family in terms of the features of mutually supportive social relationships rather than as the idealization of presumed bonds between genetically related persons in the private sphere. I would like to think of family more as community. When I think this way, I see attempts to shape the world in the image of a competitive market place, and the unwillingness to provide public support for those who care for others—whether it be mothers caring for children, children caring for elderly parents, or people caring for and about others—as both antifamily and destructive of the possibility of community.

—MARTHA McMAHON

Acknowledgments

Many people helped in the creation of this book. It was built on borrowed stories generously shared by the women whose experiences of motherhood are discussed herein. Their contribution to the process of doing the research and to the final work cannot be adequately expressed in an acknowledgment.

Much of this book is about bonds between mothers and children. In doing the research I came to a deeper appreciation not only of these bonds but of the creative power of the bonds of friendship. I want to thank Sherryl Kleinman for her advice and encouragement and also for the kind of wonderful friendship that makes intellectual commitment to sociological analysis alive and exciting. My deepest thanks also to Greg Nicholls, my dear friend and partner, who tirelessly read drafts, who patiently produced food, and who tactfully encouraged me to write my ideas clearly. Thanks also to Marie Boutilier and Brenda Camitz for their help and support through our writing group.

I would like to express my gratitude to Ralph Matthews, who supervised the dissertation research out of which this book came. I was lucky to have an advisor who provided critical but positive responses to my work but also allowed me the freedom to make the work my own. I am grateful also to Dorothy Pawluch and Susan French for their assistance as committee members.

I would particularly like to express my deep appreciation to the

National Council on Family Relations and The Guilford Press for their support for this book through their Student/New Professional Book Award. I also wish to express my sincere thanks to Bert N. Adams and David M. Klein, editors of the Perspectives on Marriage and the Family series, for their kind assistance and patience in the project of turning a dissertation into a book.

Contents

1

Introduction

This book is about the experiences of motherhood among 59 mothers in Toronto, Canada. It looks at how these women came to have children and how they felt themselves changed through being mothers. The study explores the meanings of motherhood and what these women saw as the rewards and costs of having children; it also analyzes the impact of motherhood on women's identities. Although motherhood is often presumed to be a largely personal and private matter, disputed meanings of motherhood and family are central to some of the most hotly debated social and political issues in contemporary North America. Motherhood is contested terrain.

Contested meanings of motherhood need to be understood in their social context. Social structural and demographic changes have transformed men's and women's experience of adulthood (Smelser, 1980; Swidler, 1980). Such changes affect not just the decisions individuals make but also the development of self and the ways in which people make sense of their own and other people's lives (Bellah et al., 1985; Berger and Kellner, 1977; Turner, 1981). Adulthood no longer represents a period of stability of self but is fraught with uncertainty in a changing world (Smelser, 1980; Swidler, 1980).

Social change raises new issues about the social meaning of adult identity for women. Many women are marrying later, having fewer children, and having them later in life than their mothers or grandmothers did.[1] More women are having children outside of marriage, and there is more talk of childlessness as a valid option for women.

Most mothers, even those with young children, now work outside the home. Delayed childbearing, a permanent attachment to the labor force, and increased life expectancies mean that women are spending less of their lives involved in either childbearing or childrearing than ever before (Eichler, 1983, p. 38). But this picture of social change and the problems of identity it raises mask profound differences in women's experiences. What social identity of woman is rendered problematic? Poor and minority women have long worked outside the home. For many, their central social identities as domestic servants or low-paid industrial workers overshadowed their maternal identities, leaving such women with minimal resources with which to nurture children. Similarly, although the decision to have or not to have children is perceived by many to be a matter of a "modern" individual woman's choice (Currie, 1988; Gerson, 1985), it is not necessarily experienced or represented as such when the "wrong" women choose motherhood.

Many women now have greater occasion to develop and vest themselves in nonfamilial identities than did women in the past. But many of the cultural changes that have accompanied economic and demographic changes make the question of how to live as an adult problematic in new ways for such women (Gerson, 1985). Parental roles are no longer taken to define the meaning of a woman's adult life or of a couple's relationship (Swidler, 1980). Current cultural rhetorics of individualism mean that, among the middle class, it is no longer appropriate for adults to sacrifice themselves for their spouses or their children; instead the individual is offered cultural images of self-realization and of "finding one's self" as guides to identity and the meaning of life (Bellah et al., 1985; Swidler, 1980). Such changes in the meanings of womanhood and motherhood, however, are contested. Luker (1984) points out that conflict over the social representation of motherhood as optional rather than central in women's lives lies at the heart of the political debates on abortion in the United States.

At the same time, according to Berger (1977, pp. 72–80), the individualism and secularization of modern society has created a world in which it is increasingly difficult for people to feel at home and where public institutions now confront the individual as immensely powerful and alien. Thus, ironically, the same pressures that appear to threaten traditional family bonds and many women's commitments to children may also function to make family relationships and bonds with children more personally important than before. Relationships with significant others have become central to modern individuals' search for meaning—a form of modern religion (Bellah et al., 1985; Berger and Kellner, 1977; Schoenfeld, 1988). According to Turner (1981), we seem to be witnessing a significant transformation in the basis of self-conception in modern society: a shift in the locus of the experience of "real self" from institutional role to impulse, from role to feelings and sentiment.[2] In many ways the research questions about motherhood explored in this study are also questions about the social psychology of self.

There is, of course, no single meaning or given experience of motherhood. The experience of black single mothers in Rickie Solinger's *Wake Up Little Susie* (1992), a study of race and unwed pregnancy in the period before *Roe v. Wade* in the United States, stands in sharp contrast to the experience of white alone mothers in this study. Toni Morrison's novel *Beloved* (1987) tells a story of motherhood under slavery that is worlds apart from the motherhood of the white, English Rosamund in Margaret Drabble's *The Millstone* (1965), even though both women lived in poverty. The very term "motherhood" connotes a falsely static state of being rather than of a socially and historically variable relationship.

This study is about the meaning of motherhood in the lives of a sample of white, middle- and working-class Toronto women who have preschool children and who work full-time outside the home. The empirical focus is on how these women's sense of themselves was transformed through the process of becoming mothers. Analytically the study is about the process of personal change in adult life and the socially produced nature of gender identities. I invert the conventional idea that mothers produce children and look instead at how children produce mothers. I analyze motherhood as a gendered and an engendering experience. That is, the analysis goes beyond conceptualizing motherhood simply as an expression of female identity, to expose the ways in which the experience of motherhood *produces* a gendered sense of self in women. We will see how the production of gender in intimate relationships, even in those as seemingly private as a woman's love for her child and her domestic arrangements with a partner, reproduces social structure. Ironically, although biological reproduction is taken to reflect the "essential" differences between men and women, we will see how the social organization of biological reproduction provides a particularly rich opportunity for producing gender so that it appears unquestionably grounded in some essence of the individual or in nature. Motherhood in this sense is an "essence-producing" process.

RETHINKING THE RESEARCH PROBLEM

Research reports often begin with a statement of the problem: why one studied what one did. However, in this instance producing such a statement is not so simple. It is first necessary to explain how the research process transformed the conceptualization of the problem.

Originally I set out to study the relationship between the meaning of work and of motherhood in women's lives. Shortly after I started my interviews, however, I realized that the whole mood of the interview shifted when women discussed motherhood. They were more engaged in discussing motherhood than work; answers were much longer, more detailed and personally disclosing. I realized that while respondents and I talked about both work and motherhood, of the two, motherhood was the more salient issue in the interview.

At a theoretical level, I had long understood that to analyze social experience I needed to start with participants' understandings and meanings (Blumer, 1969). But in practice it was as though I had forgotten that message until the experience of making sense of interviews forced me to remember. The study's focus on women's identity transformations through motherhood grew out of my acceptance of respondents' definitions of what was important in their lives as a starting point for analysis.

As I gathered and analyzed the data for this study, my understanding of the problem under investigation began to shift. I had begun by asking how social structural changes in women's work and in the social organization of motherhood were affecting women's experience of motherhood. In formulating the research problem initially, I think I had unreflectively conceptualized the experience of motherhood, and by implication women's maternal behavior and ideas, as "dependent variables" of social structure. My hypotheses had been derived from both feminist and general sociological theory on motherhood and work in women's lives. However, as I collected, coded, and analyzed the data, I rediscovered the limitations of a logicodeductive approach for my research problem. For example, women's actions and ideas did not fit neatly into such categories as "traditional," "transitional," "nontraditional," or "feminist," which I had theoretically derived and whose usefulness I had felt I was "testing" in some qualitative way.

I also fairly quickly realized that I had operationalized the effects of change in women's lives in a way that led me to an overly narrow focus on conflicts between work and motherhood. While such conflicts do exist, role conflict is not exhaustive of what is personally or sociologically interesting about motherhood in women's lives. The research project had from the beginning been conceptualized and designed within an interpretive sociological framework that emphasizes the centrality of subjective meaning. However, my commitment to sociological explanation that goes beyond the social psychological to social organization had led me to attend *seriously* only to the social structural side of the dialectical process between human agency and social conditioning that Giddens (1984) refers to in his concept of "double hermeneutics." What this concept means for interpretive sociologists is that social actors already experience their own actions as meaningful, and it is the analyst's task to understand both these meanings *and* the larger social context simultaneously (Berger and Luckmann, 1966; Currie, 1988; Giddens, 1984; Stone and Farberman, 1981).

By attempting to resolve these types of issues in my own empirical work I came to appreciate to what a great extent qualitative research involves a dialectical process of going back and forth between theory, data, and concepts, and that my "problems" were a normal part of this research process (Currie, 1988; Glaser and Strauss, 1967). Findings that seemed puzzling and contradictory became more sociologically intelligible when I came to appreciate the dialectical relationship between data and theory. I found I had to confront the methodological implications of what has long been an interactionist maxim but has by now become a feminist research tenet: that the participants' experience provides the empirical starting point from which the subjective can be linked to social organization.[3]

Thus I came to put motherhood at the center of my analysis rather than treating it as a "dependent variable" or using it primarily to support or challenge preexisting sociological or political theories about women's lives. For example, I had intended to look at whether motherhood was still an important source of identity for women. I found it was. Had I stopped there I would have perhaps reaffirmed recent sociological findings about the persistence of a "motherhood mandate." However, I would not have been led to look so closely at the different accounts of transformations in women's self-conceptions or to explore women's feelings for their children, each of which later came to be a focus of the research. Originally I dismissed these data as of minor interest. How can one write a research piece that discovers women's identity is vested in their relationships with their children?

Or that they feel deeply connected to their children? Had there not been enough critiques of "the ideology of motherhood"? Women are expected to experience motherhood in that way. If they didn't, that would be news. Yet I felt almost haunted by the data, which repeatedly pointed to the tremendous significance of children and motherhood in women's lives. At the time it seemed as though the data on women's feelings and self-conceptions were forcing me to rethink, albeit a little late in the research process, how I should approach the study of motherhood.

HOW TO STUDY MOTHERHOOD

My study raised issues I had not foreseen. Until recently there had been relatively little research on women's experience of motherhood. Boulton (1983), in reviewing the literature on motherhood, concluded that it was dominated by biological conceptions of maternity. In the past women's maternal behavior was seen (by those with the power to speak definitively on such matters) as largely instinctual and as adaptively tailored to the needs of the uniquely dependent human infant.[4] Traditional psychoanalytically oriented theories, Boulton explained, expanded instinctual explanations to include the notion of psychosexual development by which maternity was taken as the normal expression of mature female identity, while women's dissatisfaction with motherhood constituted maladjustment and personal developmental failure.

The representation of motherhood as primarily a biological relationship concealed the gendered politics of social and "natural" relations. In Western cultures, women's "embodied humanity," most clearly symbolically expressed by their biological capacity to mother, has been used to exclude them from "true humanity"—to relegate them to a sphere perceived to be outside history, society, and reason: that is, "to nature" (Kahn, 1989; O'Brien, 1981). Nature and woman were both culturally associated and empirically devalued.

Feminist analyses, however, draw even deeper implications from these cultural associations and dualisms. Ecofeminism, for example, exposes the ways in which gendered constructions of "human" (masculine) and "nonhuman" nature have been embedded in the emergence of modern sciences and the associated political–economic relations of industrialization and colonization.

Patriarchal conceptions of woman and nature, they argue, are at the heart of destructive ecological practices as well as of the oppressive gender, class, and race relations on which they are built (Merchant, 1980; Shiva, 1989). Not surprisingly, many contemporary feminists are rethinking motherhood. For the analysis of motherhood, as Maroney (1986) points out, has the potential to challenge not just the political order but the deeper cultural images of human nature and the links between society and nature on which the social and political order rests. Thus the politics of motherhood extends beyond issues of reproductive choice.

The sociological conceptualization of motherhood as a role that varies according to how reproduction and childcare are socially institutionalized represented an advance over biologically based theories. Ahistorical "natural" explanations were replaced with sociological ones that pointed to the social nature and historical malleability of motherhood. The popularized image of mothering built on women's exclusive care for children in isolated, nuclear-family households, we learned, was unique to modern Western societies and was not very good for either women or children. Although such accounts were potentially more emancipatory for women, empirically the neglect of women's subjective experience of motherhood continued.[5] As a model for explaining women's behavior, mainstream sociology stressed the role of early childhood socialization. Gender socialization, through the internalization of norms and values, instilled in girls both the capacities and motivations to mother.[6] Research tended to focus on role behavior, role strain, role conflict, and so on. Sociological analysis emphasized the social system as the ultimate determinant of values and action.

The reemergence of feminism in the 1960s and 1970s led to a new interest in social conflict and structural coercion theories of women's experience and behavior. Motherhood, as institutionalized in the role of housewife, became perceived by many feminists as oppressive to women (Allen, 1984; Firestone, 1971; Luxton, 1980; Oakley, 1974). Some feminists attempted to distinguish between the *work* of motherhood (which was socially organized in ways that were stifling, overwhelming, and oppressive) and the *relationship* of motherhood (which was seen as potentially rich and rewarding to women) (Bernard, 1975; Oakley, 1974; Rich, 1976). For some time the conceptualization of motherhood as (unpaid) reproductive and caring labor came to dominate feminist theory and research, and motherhood as relationship remained largely unexplored. The domestic-labor debate within Marxist feminism attempted to give theoretical articulation to the oppression of women within the nuclear family that other feminists had described. Although theoretically interesting, this debate continued the by then well-established tradition of focusing on women's oppression and the coerciveness of social structural arrangements.

The difficulties of beginning with theoretical assumptions about the oppressiveness of motherhood and women's domestic work were among the first problems I faced in my research. If I adopted a theoretical stance that focused on the oppressiveness of motherhood, then I was led to interpret as ideological much of what women described to me and to see women as passive accomplices in their own subjugation. On the other hand, if I adopted the theoretical assumptions of the socialization model and interpreted women's commitment to motherhood as gender-role conformity, I would trivialize and neglect what women were telling me about their lives and the meanings of their actions, and I felt I would misrepresent the empirical reality I was studying. Moreover, the socialization model made political analysis of women's experience difficult. While both approaches were "valid," neither theoretical approach seemed adequate to help me understand and explain women's experience.

TENSIONS IN MOTHERHOOD

My difficulties in studying motherhood, of course, are not unique. Motherhood is an unsettling issue for feminist analysis.[7] It raises troubling questions about the meaning of gender differences and their political implication for women's struggle against inequality (Scott, 1988). Motherhood is clearly at the center of what Ann Snitow (1990) calls a key tension in feminism between the need to claim the (different) identity "woman" and give it a "solid political meaning, and the need to tear down the very category 'woman' and dismantle its all-too-solid history" (Snitow, 1990, p. 9). Thus feminism has attempted both to *validate the hitherto devalued identities and experiences of being a woman and mother and to reject and transcend the restrictions and oppressiveness of those identities.* This tension surrounding equality and difference is mirrored historically in changes within feminism and also in the contemporary feminist debates on essentialism (see Chapter 7). Understanding the tension helps explain the "tightrope" between alternatively offensive and defensive positions on motherhood that the women's movement in North America often seems to walk (Maroney, 1986).

On the one hand, some late 19th- and early 20th-century women's movements in Canada and the United States have been descibed as maternal feminist. Such movements invoked women's "difference," their distinctively "feminine" identities, to ground women's demands for social reform and political participation. Womanly virtues (or virtuous women?) were often presented as solutions to a variety of social problems—including vice, disease, alcohol abuse, poverty, and social decay.

On the other hand, second-wave feminism of the 1960s and 1970s often took a more cynical view, seeing the institution of motherhood as one of the prime means by which women were excluded from full participation in social and economic life. Biology is not destiny, it was argued. Feminist analysis exposed the "feminine mystique"; the motherhood "myth"; the real work of housework and childrearing; the compulsory nature of childbearing; the lack of access to abortion, contraception, and reproductive health information women faced; and so on. Snitow (1992) argues that the "demon texts" of this period of feminism are falsely read as antimotherhood. The target, she emphasizes, was patriarchy, not mothers.

The early analysis of the oppressiveness of motherhood was followed by feminist analyses that validated women and their work, qualities, and experiences. Negative conceptualization of motherhood, it was felt, reinforced a masculinist cultural devaluation of all things feminine and did a disservice to women, to the goal of gender equality, and to the need to transform society into a more caring place. Ruddick (1984a) talked of a type of maternal practice that could generate alternative values and human actions capable of resisting oppression. Although I am understating the breadth and divergences in North American feminist analyses of motherhood, feminist texts are increasingly including studies of reproduction, birth, midwifery, childcare, women's experience of birth, maternal thinking, and women's different voices. Maroney (1986) and Snitow (1992) tie this shift in feminist analysis of motherhood to broader demographic, political, and cohort issues facing U.S. and Canadian women in the late 1970s and the 1980s. Feminism attempted a revalorization of maternity that was both radical and feminist (Maroney, 1986), but in practice and implication, Snitow (1992) suggests, much feminist analysis of motherhood became pronatalist. The challenge facing feminist analysis became one of valuing women's social capacity to care and/or their biological capacity to give birth, while resisting having these capacities considered definitive or "essential" or best in what it is to be a woman.

The difficulty of juggling negative and positive interpretations of motherhood in feminism, Stanworth (1990) explains, reflects the empirical paradox that motherhood can be simultaneously women's weakness and women's strength. There are often heavy material, social, and psychological costs associated with having children that can "lock women into institutional and psychological structures of dependence and powerlessness" (Stanworth, 1990, p. 297). At the same time most women do become mothers and, as this study shows, many find much to value in the experience. Thus women's standpoints, women's realities, women's ways, and maternal thinking have all been offered as *positive* grounds for theorizing about society and women's lives and for resisting patriarchal oppression or constructing a better world. However, it is difficult to analyze motherhood without seeming either promotherhood or antimother (Snitow, 1992; Stanworth, 1990).

Is being a woman a liability within patriarchal society? And if so, are women who mother more "woman-like" and therefore in greater danger of being locked into subordination? Does resisting patriarchy mean resisting what is patriarchally defined as the "essence" of womanhood—motherhood?

Or does resisting patriarchy mean rejecting masculinist devaluation of women and motherhood, not womanhood and motherhood themselves? Can these identities be valued or defined in positive and woman-centered ways? Do they not offer a source of alternative (even better) social values and skills—a positive model of caring and connectedness to provide an empowering counterimage to patriarchal masculinity?

The terms of the questions, of course, are falsely posed. "Woman" itself is a social construction, and gender oppression cannot be easily separated from other forms of social inequality. No woman is *only* a woman (or mother)—she is socially located by race, class, age, sexuality, motherhood or nonmotherhood, abilities, and so on, which do not simply shape but constitute the meanings and experience of being female and of mothering. One's gender identity is the gender identity appropriate to one's ethnic, class, national, and racial identity (Spelman, 1988). Dominant groups are often unaware they carry privileged identities. For example, to the white majority in the United States and Canada, black (not white) constitutes a visible social identity. The women in this study were white women, and white mothers of white children, not simply women and mothers. In a racially unequal society, being white as well as being nonwhite organizes identities, even if one is not conscious of bearing such racially based identities.

Even feminist analyses of motherhood can be personally understood in dramatically different ways. For Ann Snitow (1990), feminism represented freedom not to be a woman (under patriarchy): free to *not* become a mother. For her friend it meant the opportunity to be a woman and mother and not feel humiliated by it. Motherhood, family, and paid work can have quite different meanings to different women. It is the context of poverty or racism in which many women mother, not motherhood itself, that oppresses many women. There is no single personal meaning of motherhood; and there is no unified feminist position.

What makes the debates on motherhood and, more recently, on the new reproductive technologies so engaging? Could it be, as Stanworth (1990, p. 297) wonders, that what is really at issue in these debates is mothering in the symbolic sense—the fear of a society where caring and tenderness is replaced by individual interest?

The tensions in feminist analyses of motherhood may well be irresolvable. The issues are often metaphors for a range of broader social issues. What we need to understand, K. Davis (1992) explains, is how the debates about the meanings of motherhood and gender identity function rhetorically to express concern about the political consequences of claiming "different" identities for women.

"WHAT'S A RESEARCHER TO DO?"

How was I to study motherhood in an empirical context fraught with such theoretical and political complexity? In recent studies, some feminist researchers have employed an explanatory model of women's decision making about work, motherhood, and domesticity that emphasizes the structured opportunities, rewards, and constraints, as well as the competing goals and values, within which women, as social actors, construct their lives and make commitments (Gerson, 1985; Luker, 1975, 1984; O'Donnell, 1985).[8] This cost–benefit analysis perspective is useful in analyzing women's behavior because it conceptualizes women as social actors who construct meaningful acts. The perspective also recognizes structural determinants of women's actions in the ways in which opportunities and resources relating to

marriage, work and domesticity are socially organized. Thus it helps
explain patterns in women's behavior that are otherwise puzzling. For
example, women frequently make difficult decisions about motherhood within a context of value ambiguity and structural contradictions (Currie, 1988). Women's adult options are socially organized to
produce ambivalence: typical male value orientations and life choices
are seen as of greater social worth than those that are typically female
(Gilligan, 1982). Women have to choose between structurally incompatible goals in ways that men do not (Currie, 1988; Gerson, 1985;
Hochschild, 1989).

Cost–benefit models have also been applied to trends in women's
fertility behavior. It does seem that historically a negative correlation
exists between North American women's labor force participation
and their fertility. Although the association is not clear, nor the pattern
consistent, birth rates have been falling as labor force participation has
been rising. Baber and Allen (1992) estimate the U.S. birth rate at
approximately 2.0 children per woman. Similarly, Canadian women's
total fertility rate has dropped to almost half that of the baby-boom
peak of 1959 and has remained fairly stable at about 1.7 children per
woman since the mid-1970s (Statistics Canada, 1990a, p. 11). As
Eichler (1983, p. 36) points out, until recently, declining fertility has
not necessarily meant that fewer women are having children; rather,
each woman on average has fewer children than before. What is clear
is that U.S. and Canadian women are delaying motherhood—some
permanently. In 1970, only 9% of U.S. women aged 35 were childless;
by 1989 this number had risen to 20%, although, no doubt, some of
these childless women later gave birth (Baber and Allen, 1992, p. 107).
What is also clear is that more women are having children outside the
context of legal marriage (see Chapter 2).

But cost–benefit analyses of fertility and childlessness, Nock
(1987) argues, have limited explanatory value. Changing reproductive
technologies account for some of the decline in unwanted fertility,
but current low fertility rates and increasing rates of childlessness need
to be understood in the context of changing symbolic meanings of
motherhood and childrearing in women's lives rather than simply the
economic opportunity costs of children (Nock, 1987, p. 373).

However, it is difficult to estimate current rates of permanent
childlessness, whether voluntary or involuntary, among U.S. and Canadian women. Rates are often given by age categories and may represent
deferment rather than permanent childlessness. Data often do not
distinguish voluntary from involuntary childlessness—nor is this dis-

tinction always an easy one to make. Data based on women who are now past childbearing age tell us about past, not present, trends.

Historically childlessness among North American women has shown fluctuations by historical period. Seccombe (1991, p. 191) estimates that in the United States in 1940, for example, 17% of married white women between the ages of 35 and 39 were childless; by the 1970s this figure had dropped to only 7% of that age group but rose again to 17% of women in that age category by 1986. Grindstaff et al. (1991) estimated that in 1984 11% of all Canadian women between ages 35 and 49 were permanently childless. Like U.S. researchers (Houseknecht, 1987), they found that childless women tended to be better educated. Among Canadian permanently childless women, nearly 19% of women with more than 14 years of education were childless, in contrast to only 6% of the least educated women. But the association, they concluded, was not between education and fertility; it was between education and timing of first birth.

Veevers (1980) estimated that 5% to 7% of all couples in the United States and Canada were *voluntarily* permanently childless and expected this figure to rise to at least 10% in the near future. Houseknecht (1987) and Jacobson and Heaton (1991), on the other hand, point to a continued pronatalist pattern and put voluntary childless rates lower, arguing that, contrary to popular belief, these rates are *not* rising.[9] Different estimates are in part explained by wide differences in definitions of voluntary childlessness and in measurement strategies (Houseknecht, 1987).

The expansion of alternative opportunities to motherhood and domesticity was a frequently cited reason for the apparent decrease in women's enthusiasm for motherhood and their increased propensity to delay childbearing (Gerson, 1985; Veevers, 1980). However, recent increases in first births to older Canadian women and the data from the middle-class women in this study suggest that some of the expected increase in childlessness may in practice translate into deferred motherhood.[10] A Statistics Canada (1990a, p. 11) report argues that whereas Canadian women are delaying both marriage and childbearing, when they do marry, they appear to catch up on at least some of the births that were "postponed." Whether or not the predicted rise in voluntary childlessness materializes, it remains clear that most people still expect and want to have children (Gormly et al., 1987; Machung, 1989).

A strictly utilitarian analysis of women's behavior regarding motherhood has its limitations. My research indicates that women in this sample were *not* simply pushed into motherhood by the absence of alternative rewarding options or pulled away simply because they found work more satisfying, though rewards and costs were important. The process of recruitment to motherhood in this sample was far more complex. As I will show, women's sense of identity was deeply implicated in their transition to maternity, and the process was experienced in moral rather than simply in utilitarian terms.[11] Motherhood has far more meaning in women's lives than simply a satisfaction-maximizing option.

The fact that the majority of women have children does not make either the process of becoming a mother or the experience itself non-problematic. Although my research was not designed to explain women's decisions to become mothers, the data I gathered show that women follow very different and often quite tentative paths to motherhood. From these women's perspective, it was far from predetermined that they would have children. But they did. Indeed, sooner or later, intentionally or otherwise, the vast majority of women become mothers. The sociological question for me became, How is it that, in pursuing what they experience as private and personal choices and decisions, many women come to follow apparently similar patterns? As Turner (1981) comments, the question is an old one:

> [Is the experience not] like [that of] the Plains Indians who sought purely personal visions to establish the basis of each individual's authority but faithfully replicated their culture in the form and content of their visions. (Benedict, 1943, cited in Turner, 1981, p. 219)

Indeed, this issue became one of the theoretical challenges of my work: to analyze women's experience of motherhood in a way that captured women's agency but at the same time recognized the persistence of shared patterns of meaning that emerged from women's experiences and actions. This, then, became a study of the subjectively creative production of identity and the social reproduction of cultural meanings associated with gender identity and motherhood.

THE THEORETICAL PERSPECTIVE

To better understand the social processes through which the women in the study become mothers, I heuristically divided the experience into two analytically distinct phases. The first phase, discussed in

Chapters 3 and 4, pertains to the social processes through which women became pregnant and sustained their pregnancies through to motherhood.

The second phase, discussed in Chapters 5 through 8, refers to the processes whereby these women developed conceptions of themselves as mothers. These two phases are not necessarily empirically separate or temporally sequential. A woman may develop a self-conception as a mother long before she becomes a mother, or she may not acquire such a self-conception even after she has given birth. The paths to both biological conception and social psychological self-conceptions varied among women in this study.

Both phases may be seen as part of the women's moral careers (Goffman, 1963). The changes women experienced in their self-conceptions can be seen as "moral" in two separate but related ways. The conventional use of the concept "moral" has an ethical or evaluative referent, and as I will show, many women felt themselves changed in that sense of the word. However, Goffman has used the concept "moral" to refer to the experience of the self or self-conceptions. Persons who share similar changes in self-conceptions share "moral careers," which in turn may become both cause and effect of commitment to a similar sequence of personal adjustments (Goffman, 1963, p. 32).

Socialization, and gender socialization in particular, is frequently invoked to explain the enactment of adult roles and the embracement of gender-role identities. Socialization has been conceptualized as the link between culture and conduct (Stokes and Hewitt, 1976). Socialization, simplistically conceived as the internalization of the norms and values of a culture so as to provide a blueprint for living, has been convincingly critiqued as inadequate to explain the improvisational, creative, problematic, and negotiated nature of social interaction in general (Blumer, 1969; Goffman, 1959; Turner, 1962) and the complexity of decisions facing women in modern society in particular (Bernard, 1975; Gerson, 1985). To argue that gender roles exist in society tells us little about the process whereby women are motivated to embrace or come to take on these roles. Neither roles nor culture should be conceptualized as conditioned responses (Fine and Kleinman, 1979). Indeed, what was remarkable about women in the present study, for example, is not that they all became mothers but that they followed quite different routes to motherhood and that many had considered voluntary childlessness. Motherhood had the paradoxical character

of appearing both socially determined *and* personally contingent
in women's lives.

Symbolic interactionism provides the major sociological perspective informing both the methodology and theoretical analysis of this
study. This perspective places meanings, identity, and experience of
everyday life at the center of its explanation of the social world
(Blumer, 1969). It conceptualizes individuals as creative social actors
whose conduct is oriented toward situations and objects on the basis
of meanings these have for them. Meanings, however, are conceived
of as neither private nor psychological but as arising through and being
embedded in social relationships and processes. Identity is seen as a
central dimension of meaning involved in social interaction. As
meanings and identity are understood in processual terms and as being
sustained in and through social relationships, the perspective is particularly suited to the study of changes in meaning and identity as
social relationships change, as they do when a woman becomes a
mother.

RETHINKING THE CONCEPT OF CULTURE

However, while the symbolic interactionist perspective used in this
study is well suited to an analysis of the negotiation of roles and
identities, it needs, according to Stokes and Hewitt (1976), to reclaim
the concept of culture to explain enduring meanings and patterns of
behavior. Indeed, what emerges from this study is that women,
pursuing what they experienced as their private and personal choices
and decisions, reproduced many of the gendered patterns of their
culture. The past tendency for symbolic interactionism to treat culture
in little more than a cognitive sense (knowing the rules) conveyed an
image of virtually limitless creation of culture (Stokes and Hewitt,
1976, p. 840). As we know, however, social objects frequently confront
us with preexisting meanings—as a taken-for-granted social reality. As
Berger and Luckmann (1966) point out, our relationship with our
social world is a dialectical one of mutual determination in which
existing meanings confront us as a legacy to which we must respond.
For Stokes and Hewitt (1976), both the problem of culture and the
persistence of meanings, as well as the creative nature of social action,
can be conceived in terms of the metaphor of alignment. Social action
can be understood as a process through which persons orient their

conduct toward each other and a common set of social objects (Blumer, 1969). But culture also provides resources with which to make sense of situations: People align conduct with culture by defining actions in culturally known terms. Vocabularies of motives, accounts, and disclaimers are among such cultural resources (Mills, 1940/1981; Scott and Lyman, 1981).

Thus culture itself can be conceived as a set of objects—ideas, knowledge, beliefs, roles, institutions, and norms, as well as ways of feeling, may all be designated and acted toward as objects (Stokes and Hewitt, 1976, p. 843). Culture in complex societies, Stokes and Hewitt conclude, must no longer be viewed as internalized and carried in the personalities of individuals, although some lines of conduct are shaped by normative structures internalized at an early age. Rather, culture needs to be reconceptualized as a "field of objects that are environmental to action" (Stokes and Hewitt, 1976, p. 487), that is, a set of cognitive constraints—objects—to which people must relate as they form their lines of action. As such, culture constitutes *one* of several conditions within which conduct is formed (Stokes and Hewitt, 1976, p. 847). Such a conceptualization of culture allows both for the continuation of normative culture and enduring meanings and for the empirical flexibility of human behavior and creativity of interaction. This conceptualization of culture as providing the resources through which people interpret both others' conduct and their own prospective or past actions, thus making sense of their lives, will become central to understanding the role the cultural motif of love plays in symbolically structuring women's experience of motherhood, which is discussed in Chapter 5.

CONCEPTUALIZING THE SELF

The concepts of self and identity are central to feminist analysis of women's lives. But these concepts can have different meanings. For interactionists, self and identity are *social processes*, rather than psychological phenomena. This conceptualization follows from Mead's (1934/1962) theory of the self as a reflexive process. The essence of the Meadian notion of the self is the ability to engage in self-interaction or indication: the self is both subject and object, knower and known (Mead, 1934/1962, p. 137). Among the most important objects of self-indication is the self itself: A person can be the object of her own reflectivity, an object to herself. Self, as object to itself, or self-concept, has been defined by Rosenberg as "the totality of the individual's thoughts and feelings having reference to himself as an object" (Rosenberg, 1979, p. 7). Identities, therefore, or selves as social objects, are a central component of self-concept. Although self must be understood as a process, we can also understand how persons can be the object of their own and others' acts, that such objects (identities) can be situated in both immediate and biographical contexts and that, as social objects, identities evoke not merely cognitive responses but affective and evaluative ones (Hewitt, 1976, p. 75). Thus the concept of identity expresses the notion of self as social object (Stone, 1981). Identity is not identical with self, but it locates the self in social terms; it refers to the social meaning of the self. Identities are variable and are transacted in interaction by "announcements" and "placements" (G. Stone, 1981). Announcements are the identities we claim for ourselves; placements are the identities in which we are cast by others. Identity is socially validated through the coincidence of placements and announcements.

As identities are sustained through interaction, appropriate identities must be established in order to enter into different social relationships. The social relationship of mothering a child, for example, has been generally restricted not simply to those who established their identity by giving birth (or satisfying the requirements of an adoption agency) but to those who displayed the proper conventions of heterosexuality by being married.[12] Not all women who give birth have their (potential) identities as mothers socially validated. In a wide variety of ways, as Solinger (1992) documents, post-World War II U.S. society structured maternal identities through class, race, and heterosexual identities and, in doing so, constructed many white unwed mothers as "nonmothers" and many unwed black mothers as "problem mothers." Indeed, many of the debates over the new reproductive technologies are implicitly about establishing social claims to parental identities, often couched in the language of biology.

MULTIPLE IDENTITIES

The interactionist conceptualization of identity as located in interaction implies the notion of multiple identities, not all of them active or invoked in any one situation. Women in this study, for example, were not simply mothers but held other occupational and interpersonal identities that were also important to them. McCall and Simmons (1978, pp. 73–74) develop the notion of multiple role identities by explaining that identities are not randomly collected but, at any one time in an individual's biography, are organized within the self in a prominence hierarchy, or the ideal self. The prominence of any particular identity in the hierarchy, they explain, is shaped most importantly by commitment to or personal investment in that identity, the degree of self and social support for the identity and the rewards associated with it (McCall and Simmons, 1978, p. 76). Thus the exchange of social support for valued identities becomes a central feature of social interaction as we strive to legitimate our self-conceptions. Rosenberg (1979, p. 53) employs a similar concept of psychological centrality to explain why certain components of a person's self-conceptions are more important for self-esteem than others.

Whereas the prominence or the psychological centrality of an identity refers to the personal importance of an identity to an individual, the concept of *salience* refers to the probability of its behavioral enactment. As McCall and Simmons (1978, p. 84) explain, we must be careful to distinguish the very fluid hierarchy of identities in terms of salience (the situated self) from the relatively enduring hierarchy in terms of prominence (the ideal self) in which a person's more enduring sense of self may be located. Thus situated selves or salient identities need to be understood as the properties of situations rather than exclusively of individuals (Maines, 1981, p. 474). One may observe, for example, that maternal identities appear less salient among women who are employed full-time, for work situations frequently preclude the invocation of maternal or family identities among employees. But this does not necessarily mean such identities are less central to these women's more enduring sense of self or identity prominence hierarchy.

The notion of multiple identities must not be taken to imply essentially shallow and fleeting selves who lack stability and integration. Although we recognize that identity is often situational, the concept of the ideal self or identity prominence hierarchy allows us to understand much of the stability and continuity in the experience of self. Commitment to identities provides a coherence to biography: It allows one to make sense out of life. Motherhood, as we will see, provided many of the women in this study with symbolic resources that not only contributed to the integration of personal biography but also allowed them to link individual biography with a collective biography of past and future generations. As Stryker (1968, p. 563) points out, individuals committed to different identities will seek opportunities for their profitable enactment. People seek out those who can significantly validate valued identities. Partners and children can be important validators of women's maternal identities. We must not assume, however, that they provide validation for the same identities or in equally significant ways. The identity of mother sustained in interaction with a child is not the same as the maternal identity sustained in interaction, for example, with the child's father or the school principal. Children, I will argue, carry unique significance as validators not just of women's maternal identities but, by implication, of their characters as well.

SELF-CONCEPTIONS AS A FRAME
OF REFERENCE: IDENTITY AND MOTIVATION

We can see, therefore, that self-conceptions and identity provide the conceptual basis for a theory of motivation that conventional role theory lacks (Foote, 1981) and a theoretical basis for the integration of the processual nature of self. The concept of identity provides a key theoretical link between conduct and both culture and social structure in the interactionist framework. McCall and Simmons (1978, p. 230), for example, argue that to understand what persons are likely to do we must look at their self-conceptions, in particular their role identities, for it is through these that the demands of the social structure are filtered. Similarly, Burke et al. (1988, p. 274) and Rosenberg (1979, p. 53) argue that identities provide fairly stable sources of motivation, leading people to behave in ways that are consistent with their identities. Indeed, Rosenberg (1979, p. 59) concludes that the motive to protect and enhance one particular dimension of self-conception, one's self-esteem, is among the most powerful motives in the human repertoire.

Thus, in analyzing the experience of women in this study it is important for one to understand how women's self-conceptions can provide, as Rosenberg (1979, p. 59) puts it, a fundamental frame of reference, the foundations on which actions are predicated. But how do children become so important to women's self-conceptions?

IDENTIFICATION WITH:
THE APPROPRIATION OF OTHERS
INTO THE SACRED REALM OF THE SELF

Traditionally, interactionism has used "identification of" as an important concept in explaining behavior. The term "identification *of*" refers to the establishment of the meaning of social objects. Before we know how to act toward something, we must identify it; that is, we must establish its meaning or implications for our plan of action (Blumer, 1969, p. 2). Children, as Zelizer (1985) points out, have become social objects of great cultural worth. They carry, I will argue, the symbolic power to transform women's identities.

Individuals, as we also know, act toward situations on the basis of their definitions of those situations. However, the basic meaning to be identified in any situation is ourself: Who am I in this situation? What is my identity? Stone and Farberman (1981, p. 318) point to the guiding role of identity in forming conduct: "If I am so and so, then I will want such and such, and accordingly I will do this rather than that." In looking at how identity provides a motivational basis for motherhood, therefore, it should be emphasized that a woman makes decisions about motherhood on the basis of her conception of who she is, rather than in terms of conformity to social roles.

Not all identities are appropriated as being central to a person's real self. Sociology professors may practice role distance from their academic identities; soldiers accused of brutality may claim they were following orders; and deviants may claim that troubled backgrounds, not defective character, led them to their crimes. Persons can thus be understood to appropriate certain roles as their own on the basis of *who they feel they really are.* This process of appropriation, or taking as one's own, is central to the concept of "identification *with*," or commitment to an identity (Foote, 1981, p. 336). The concepts of "identification *of*" and "identification *with*," therefore, are analytically separate but related.

The appropriation of identities makes social order possible without physical coercion. Not all social identities are appropriated in the sense that an individual vests some valued sense of herself in the associated social relationships. But some identities, like motherhood among women in this study, *are* so appropriated. Although some "external" observers may define women's commitment to the conventional role of mother as ideologically based and ultimately oppressive of women (Wearing, 1984), it is important to remember that the appropriation of identities also makes possible what we regard as our most human experiences:

> In fact, we will carry this so far as to say that only full commitment to identities shared with others makes possible the grand human phenomena of love and grief. . . . [The concept of appropriating identities] enables us to rephrase such imponderable speculations as "What are the psychological functions of love?" into definitely researchable forms, such as "How does this person acquire his [sic] identity?" or "How does he [sic] get committed to particular identities which tie him [sic] constitutionally as a self to other persons?" (Foote, 1981, p. 340)

Maternal love, I suggest, can be conceptualized as commitment to an identity and sense of self that a woman vests in her relationship with her child. That is, the identity established and validated in the social relationships associated with motherhood is appropriated by the self as constitutional of self. This idea is developed in Chapter 5.

The concept of *propriation* is central to understanding maternal commitment. It is a concept that, according to Turner (1981, p. 205) has been a neglected dimension of our understandings of self and self-conceptions. It allows us to capture that "realm of the self [that] is characterized by possessiveness, privacy and sacredness" (Turner, 1981, p. 205). This conceptualization of the self provides an *affective* and *moral*, rather than an overly cognitive, basis of self and self-concepts. In love, one can argue, the other is appropriated as constitutive of self, and the "loved one" acquires the character of the sacred through association with self. As we will see in the Chapters 3 through 6, a recurring theme in women's accounts of motherhood was that becoming a mother was experienced as a moral transformation. The notion of moral experience, as Goffman (1963) insightfully shows, has to do not merely with issues of ethics: It pertains more profoundly to the experience of self.

GENDER IDENTITIES AND GENDERED SELVES

Gender, within an interactionist perspective, is conceptualized not as a role or an individual property but as something evoked, created, and sustained in day-to-day interaction (Goffman, 1987). Women and men participate in the construction of the meanings of gender and distinguish themselves from each other *as* women or *as* men (Thompson and Walker, 1989, p. 865). Gender involves more than simply learning masculine or feminine behavior. It involves "the entire person in the process of *becoming human*" (Deegan, 1987, p. 4). The development of gender identity can be understood as a central aspect of the development of self (Cahill, 1987, pp. 89–94). It is, according to Goffman (1987, p. 51), the prototype of all social classification. Like other forms of social identification, it defines the nature of social objects and how self and others should be acted toward.

Gender identity, like other identities, locates an individual in social terms. It indicates to others (and one's self) how an individual is to be acted toward, establishes claims for entry into certain relationships, and provides a relatively unquestioned vocabulary of explanations to which both past and future behavior can be referred in socially plausible terms. We can, according to Goffman (1987, p. 55), see gender indentity as a process by which persons build up a sense of who and what they are by referring to their "sex class" and by which they judge themselves according to the ideals of masculinity or femininity. Social environments are routinely designed to evoke or allow the display of gender identities, and audiences are purposefully sought out to validate our gender claims (Goffman, 1987, p. 71). Situations, Goffman insists, do not allow so much for the expression of gender differences as for the *production* of such differences that legitimate our identity claims.

The relationship between biological sex and social gender is historically variable. The centrality of sex-based gender identities to the experience of self seems to be peculiarly modern. Laqueur (1990) argues that the radical separation of the male and female body that occurred in the 18th century "invented" sex as we know it today. Whereas previously women's bodies had been seen as inferior versions of men's, the emerging importance of biology in shaping social thinking resulted in the "differences" of women's bodies being seen as expressing women's absolute difference from men. As Laqueur (1990) points out, this new certainty of essential differences of "nature" arose at a time when egalitarian enlightenment philosophies were shaking the certainty of the old order; it allowed the reestablishment of patriarchal authority on secular rather than on divine grounds. Sexually defined inequality and difference became an increasingly important, but naturalized, basis of the new social order of industrial capitalism. Since the 19th century, Weeks (1981) argues, sex, with its "essential" expression in gender identity, has been seen as the defining aspect of the individual, socially and morally, as the truth about the self (Weeks, 1981, p. 12). The biologization of bodies (and gender identities) was particularly coercive in its application to women, as their reproductive capacity became defined as the essence of their personhood and nature. Motherhood was constructed as the expression of women's natural, social, and moral identity—or, rather, the identity attributable to moral women, that is, married white women.

The real significance of gender identification, therefore, is not just that it underlies many other forms of social identification but that it becomes deeply constitutive of self-concept and informs our deepest feelings about our own and others' essential natures (Goffman, 1987). Thus, at a deeper level, gender comes to inform not just our social identities but also what we experience as our essential natures, or "real selves." What persons come to vest their feelings of real self in, of course, is deeply gendered. Self is a gendered process.

The conceptualization of gender, therefore, must go beyond the notion of role identity. Role identities are learned and enacted in specific contexts, but men and women "do gender" all the time, in all contexts (West and Zimmerman, 1987).

But it is precisely the social context of gender that is often neglected. Even feminist analyses of the patriarchal context in which women's gender identities are constructed often neglected the race and class realities of those contexts (Spelman, 1988). As argued above, a woman is never only a woman; multiple other social relationships of race, class, ethnicity, or sexuality shape the lived meaning of being female. The gender identities of the women in this study cannot be separated from the reality of being white in a racially unequal society. Thus gender is both an interactional and a political process. Gender, race, and class relationships are thus implicated, albeit not always consciously so, in our deepest senses of our selves.

GENDERED SELVES: SYMBOLS AND STRATEGIES

The notion of self as a gendered process must *not* be taken to imply that there are innate or essential differences between male and female self-conceptions or psychosocial developmental trajectories. Rather, self can be partly understood as an expression of "culture in action" (Swidler, 1986). Culture, according to Swidler, influences action not by providing the ultimate values toward which action is oriented but by shaping the repertoire, or "tool kit," of habits, skills, and styles from which people construct "strategies of action" (Swidler, 1986, p. 273). Like all resources, cultural resources can be understood to be differentially available to society's members. Maccoby (1990), for example, argues that communication skills and interaction strategies are differentially distributed to men and women. While men and women may show little difference in individual-based measures of personality traits and ability, she notes, in interaction they display distinctive "cultures" of relationship and communication styles.

Like the interactionist conceptualization of culture, therefore, Swidler's understanding of culture as a set of resources includes not only a tool kit of habits, skills, and material artifacts but also the symbolic vehicles of meaning such as language, beliefs, gossip, rituals of daily life, love and other mythologies, popular art forms, and so on (Swidler, 1986). Motherhood, I argue, provides such a cultural resource. It provides a central cultural motif that functions to symbolically structure female adult biography. Feminist critiques of the ideology of motherhood draw attention to the power relations embedded in such cultural processes. Thus although a woman is the subject of her own life as a mother (or nonmother), she is also in a sense "simultaneously the object of her culture's script" (O'Barr et al., 1990, p. 3). That is, whether women do or do not become mothers, or mother in ways that veer from the dominant script, cultural images of motherhood provide coercive prescriptions for gender behavior that influence most women's lives.

However, the intersection between self and culture is far more contingent and subtle than is often suggested. Women are not merely victims of patriarchal ideology. Rather, they build lines of action from their cultural "repertoires," calling on their diverse cultural resources selectively, often in surprising ways.[13] Instead of seeing action as determined by values (or ideologies), we need to understand the empirical process whereby action and values are organized to take advantage of cultural competencies (Swidler, 1986, p. 275).

The notion of culture in action can be usefully extended to include people's familiar or preferred ways of thinking about self and the relationship between self and others that have been so central to recent feminist controversy (Gilligan, 1982). Breytspraak (1984, pp. 15–18) reminds us that the very idea and experience of a self varies by culture and historical period. Ways of experiencing the self can also vary by gender. Sampson (1988) shows how the socially constructed self is reflected in cultural modes of self-reflectivity and in ideas about individualism. We can compare cultures, he argues, by the indigenous psychologies of individualism that achieve dominance: In America, "self-contained individualism" is dominant. This psychology is characterized by sharp boundaries between self and other, belief in internal personal control, and an exclusionary concept of the person (Sampson, 1988, p. 16). However, even in America, Sampson points out, many people, especially women, operate within a mode better described as "ensembled individualism," which is characterized by more fluid self–other boundaries, field control, and an inclusive conception of self as defined in and through social relationships (Sampson, 1988, pp. 16–18).

Evidence for the effects of gender on the development of self also comes from Gilligan (1982, 1986). Gilligan argues that in American society there are different ways of thinking about moral issues. One way is associated with, but not necessarily restricted to, women; the other way is typically associated with men. Men's moral thinking, she argues, tends to be characterized by abstract principles of justice and rights, women's by an ethic of care and responsibility (Gilligan, 1982, 1986). The different styles of thinking, Gilligan emphasizes, are identified by theme, not by gender.

Developing the notion that ways of thinking about self and others are gendered, Lyons (1983) argues that individuals show a preference for using one of two distinct ways of describing the self in relation to others. Women, she notes, tend to define themselves in terms of connectedness with others; men more frequently use characterizations of a separate/objective self. Men and women seem able to employ either mode of self-definition but show a preference for one mode rather than the other. Interestingly, Lyons discovered that regardless of gender, individuals who described themselves primarily in terms of connectedness with others used an ethic of care and responsibility in making moral decisions. Those who describe themselves in separate/objective terms more often use an ethic of justice and rights in their moral thinking (Lyons, 1983, p. 141).

In thinking about women's experience of motherhood, therefore, we need to recognize not only that gender is a socially constructed phenomenon but also that self and self-conceptions are likely to reflect the gendered structures and processes of the worlds in which they arise.

GENDER IDENTITY
AS A SOCIOHISTORICAL PROCESS

I have argued that identity and self are social processes that express the social relationships in which they arise. For feminist analysis, the personal is more clearly political. Social constructions of women's selves and motherhood embody political processes. When motherhood, or a particular image of motherhood, is defined as constitutive of femaleness, political processes can be imported into the self, there to structure consciousness and desire.

The culturally idealized image of motherhood as involving an intense emotional relationship and exclusive maternal care of children in nuclear family households is recent and historically specific. Even in its heyday in the 1950s, this image reflected a culturally privileged model of mothering from which the experience of those who lay outside a white, Western, and patriarchal model of the nuclear family—poor women, single mothers, women of color, lesbian mothers and others—may have been largely excluded (O'Barr, 1990). It is ahistorical in that it disguises the ways in which reproduction, family, bonds with others (including children), and gendered subjectivities are themselves shaped by economic, racial, and gender relationships. But in what ways can the self, and women's experience of themselves as mothers, come to express sociopolitical processes? Part of the answer lies in the social construction of "proper" family relationships, which organize and elaborate practices of good mothering and which can even define who is a mother at all.

The industrialization of 19th-century North America and the growing influence of an urban-based middle class were historically associated with the emergence of smaller, more child-centered families. Declining infant mortality and fertility rates, together with transformed social understandings of both the nature of childhood and appropriate childrearing, led to a changed experience of motherhood for women. Emerging professions and public policy spheres of medicine and education helped articulate the socially redefined nature of childhood and motherhood. Children in the 19th century gradually acquired a culturally sacred value (Zelizer, 1985). At the same time, however, the often quite brutal social treatment of "wayward" women and their children suggests the empirical reality was frequently quite different. In many ways the social worth of a particular child depended on the social worth of the parent to which it was (or was not) attached. The child, however, also became the symbolic key to the future (Maroney, 1986)—an avenue of social mobility for the individual or family and an expression of hope for a perfectible social order. That women were increasingly "attached" to children allowed them to be regulated in the name of child welfare (Smart, 1992). Motherhood became identified as a specific kind of caring and the expression of proper and true womanhood. The "cult of true womanhood" and domesticity in an emerging idealization of motherhood emphasized not only women's private role of nurturing children but also their indirect roles as moral guardians of society. Women (and female sexuality) were regulated through discourses of precious children and proper motherhood. The idealized images of mothers' lives were unattainable by poor or minority women; gradually, however, their (inappropriate) mothering and sexuality became the object of a variety of social and medical reform movements (Smart, 1992; Valverde, 1991).

But the social regulation of motherhood can provide the occasion of its active cultural engagement or resistance. Analysis of motherhood must go beyond looking at how social control is imposed on given subjects (e.g., women) to looking at how subjects are constituted in gendered, raced, and classed ways—and the ways in which these subjects themselves are active cultural agents (Smart, 1992, p. 3). Various 19th-century women's movements used cultural assumptions about the virtues of motherhood to limit (some) men's sexual access to (some) women; to increase (some) mothers' rights to children; and to ground (some) women's claim to public participation on the basis of the qualities, skills, and virtues associated with the private sphere (Smart, 1989, 1992).

"Woman," as Smart (1992, p. 15) points out, is constructed not simply through discourses of gender but of race and class: Class is gendered and sex is raced. Valverde's (1991) analysis of the moral representations of motherhood and gender in Canadian social purity movements, for example, showed that they carried clear messages of white racial superiority. These movements sought to create or maintain, at least at the symbolic level, a white, Protestant Canada. Similarly, Sandelowski (1990) locates the emerging medical and social concern with women's reproductive health and fertility in turn-of-the-century America in its race and class context. Between 1800 and 1900 in the United States, total white fertility rates decreased by about 50%; by the period from 1870 to 1915, the difference in fertility rates by class and race became the object of public concern (Sandelowski, 1990). White women's motherhood became linked to the welfare of society

(Sandelowski, 1990): Their heterosexual fertility was seen as protecting (white) society from "decline and extinction." White women's sexuality was biologically redefined (and thus socially regulated) through idealized representations of motherhood such that other activities or intellectual pursuits were seen to threaten both women's essential social role and their natural fertility (Sandelowski, 1990). In consequence, "The failure to become a mother became the failure to be female; the nonmother is, by nature or will, a bad mother" (O'Barr et al., 1990, p. 5)—a nonwoman. Thus the multiple symbolic links between motherhood and female morality established in the white, bourgeois family became embedded in a culturally privileged model of mothering. Images of motherhood, I argue later, carry "shadow images" of immoral women (nonmothers) and bad mothers (nonwhite, nonmarried, or improperly sexualized women).

For many feminists, the sentimental ideal of motherhood that is the presumed pinnacle of appropriate gender behavior expresses a male-defined paragon of woman that is oppressive to women (O'Barr et al., 1990, p. 2). But women, as I argued earlier, are not merely victims. Individual women experience motherhood in terms of their own situated but interactive relationship with their social worlds and the material and cultural resources available to them. That is, they engage, rather than merely express, the circumstances of their existence. Women (like other persons) also engage their worlds collectively and politically—sometimes "as women," at other times as members of other political categories. Although the present study is one of participants' personal engagements of motherhood, the personal and political in motherhood cannot really be separated. Motherhood, as I have said earlier, raises far more political questions than I had expected.

OUTLINE OF THE CHAPTERS

Chapter 2 describes the research methodology used in this study. Chapters 3 and 4 look at accounts of how the women in this study came to be mothers. In analyzing these women's accounts we see that change in adult life is not simply a superficial building on established identities and that motherhood has the paradoxical character of appearing as both socially determined and personally contingent in women's lives.

Women describe their experience primarily in personal terms, but it is important to recognize how *social class* and other social structural relationships shape women's lives as mothers (Bernard,1975; Komarovsky, 1962; Rubin, 1976; Wearing, 1984). In a class society, women's opportunities and constraints are unequally socially organized, and my data show this condition affected the sorts of options women faced. Thus the data presented in Chapters 3 and 4 are organized by social class. These chapters look at how middle- and working-class women respectively came to have children. The meaning of race, however, is "obliquely" present in all the chapters, potentially capable of exposing the assumptions of whiteness in much of what is taken for granted and what is experienced—by participants and me. And so, much of the time it remains oblique. Much is *not* told through the stories of motherhood in this book.

Chapters 5 and 6 look at how women's self-conceptions are transformed by the experience of motherhood, albeit in class–specific ways. These chapters explore the meaning of children in the lives of the women in this study and the ways in which children come to be constitutive of these women's identities. I show how women experience themselves as not merely changed by becoming mothers but as being morally transformed. In a social psychological sense, children create mothers.

Chapter 7 focuses on women's everyday, practical lives as mothers. It explores the rewards and costs of motherhood and looks at how women combine paid work and motherhood in their lives. Chapter 8 analyzes parenting as both a gendered and an *engendering* experience for women. That is, I show how the social organization of parenting is a profoundly socializing experience and produces, rather than merely reflects, a gendered experience of self. Women do not simply become parents when they have children—they become mothers. The identity these women claimed as mothers was quite different from that which they ascribed to fathers.

Chapter 9 summarizes findings and analyzes the implications for understanding motherhood and its social meanings.

2

Methodology

As a methodology, the symbolic interactionist perspective used in this study requires that we make the "meanings things have for [those we study] central in their own right" (Blumer, 1969, p. 3). Thus the research was designed to gather in-depth, qualitatively rich data that captured the social world as experienced by the women interviewed. Through a "grounded" (Glaser and Strauss, 1967) approach, the theoretical categories and issues that became the central focus of my study were those generated by my engagement of the data.[1] As discussed in the introductory chapter, the focus of analysis grew out of the issues and meanings that were salient for the participants in the study, which were different from what I had expected. The analysis of women's experience goes beyond the description of their points of view to provide a sociological explanation of personal experience in terms of the social organization and social processes that shape it.

The data for this study were gathered in 1988–1989 through in-depth interviews with 59 mothers living and working in the metropolitan Toronto area. All were Canadian educated, were employed full-time, and had at least one preschool child who lived primarily with them. The sample was purposefully restricted in this way for theoretical and methodological reasons. The study was limited to the investigation of identity and the meaning of motherhood under specific social circumstances. The findings do not apply to all women or all stages of motherhood. As social circumstances change, so do identities and meanings. The sample included only full-time employed mothers of preschool children for several reasons. First, this population represented the most obvious challenge to the traditional image of motherhood, in which women stayed home to nurture children (Wearing, 1984). Mothers of preschoolers had experienced a particularly rapid increase in their labor-force participation rates in the 15 years prior to this study (Parliament, 1989). Also, the experience of motherhood changes with different stages of the family life cycle; mothering preschoolers represents a clearly identifiable and particularly demanding stage of motherhood (Bernard, 1975, pp. 73–75; Wearing, 1984, p. 13). In general, restricting a sample provides a more homogeneous group to study. Although it is not possible to fully control for ethnicity in a Canadian sample of this size, by including in the sample only women who had been educated in Canada (from grade 1), I hoped to reduce potential variations in the experience of motherhood that were specific to immigrant women. All the women in the sample were white.[2]

Research on motherhood based on white women's experience can be criticized for communicating an impression that it represents *all* women's experience or for implying that nonwhite women's experience is *so different* that it cannot be included in the same study. Both impressions are false. In racially unequal societies such as Canada and the United States, unequal race relations connect white and nonwhite women's experiences of being mothers. Race relations are often implicit in many cultural representations of motherhood and in public discourses on who should or should not have children. "Other" women's motherhood provides shadow images that shape the dominant meanings of motherhood and thus the experience of motherhood among the white women in this study.

I limited the sample composition because a small sample could not sufficiently represent or capture the diversity in women's experiences. The demographic and ethnic composition of Toronto's population at the time of this research suggests just how great this diversity might be. In 1986 approximately 36% of the population had been either born outside Canada or were not citizens of Canada at the time of birth (Statistics Canada, 1990b). Of a total population of 3,399,680 in the 1986 Census Metropolitan Toronto area, 827,940 of those who gave a single-language response to the census question on language gave *neither* English *nor* French as their mother tongue (Statistics Canada, 1990b). Approximately a half million of Toronto's population were classified as "visible minorities." Although the diversity of Toronto's immigrant and ethnic populations would have made it difficult to adequately appreciate the differences in women's experience of motherhood in a small sample, it may have been possible to speak of shared experiences of racism or discrimination.

An interview schedule that contained structured, semistructured, and open-ended questions was used. The open-ended, in-depth questions allowed the collection of rich, descriptive, and detailed data through categories grounded in the respondents' own meanings and experiences. Unless stated otherwise, the tables summarizing participants' responses were built from unprompted responses to open-ended questions, and participants may have given more than one response. Closed questions in the schedule provided tools for the collection of more standardized and background information on these women's lives, such as household income, ages of children, and hours of work. Some of the questions were adapted from research schedules used in other studies of mothers in order to facilitate comparison.[3] Pilot interviews were also carried out to assess and refine the schedule. Responses were recorded in writing at the time of interview, and a microcasette recorder was also used. Interviews were usually conducted in the respondent's home and without other adults present to facilitate the uninhibited expression of ideas.[4] The average interview lasted approximately 2.5 hours; overall, the interviews ranged from 1.75 to more than 3 hours.

INTERVIEW DATA

Interview research is often seen as a lesser form of qualitative research (Kleinman et al., 1994). It relies heavily on what respondents say rather than on what they are observed doing. But the distinction is false if it implies that observed data are better or "more real" than participants' accounts. Neither field observations nor interview data can be treated as real in the positivist sense; that is, as a true representation of an objective "reality." The social world to which the data refer and participants' and sociologists' representations of that world need to be understood as social constructions. Mothers' accounts, therefore, are not merely one side of the picture, potentially to be balanced against fathers' accounts or outsider observation, and whose true meaning is to be revealed by sociological analysis. Rather, interview data from mothers allows interpretive access to respondents' self-reflexivity, feelings, identities, and meanings, which, like the sociologist's story, are representations. Interview data, like all data, must be interpreted against the context in which they are produced. The data on biography in this study, for example, express interpretive procedures and conversational practices that were present in the interview setting. However, the generation of biographical accounts is appropriate to a study of identity, because biography is one of the social mechanisms through which the experience of self as a unitary subject is produced. And it was this experience of self that was the focus of this study.

The "constitutive authority" of the subject's perspective in qualitative research does not make sociological explanation impossible. Interview data, as Silverman (1985, p. 157) argues, display cultural realities and practices. The data, therefore, are neither biased nor accurate but are "real" in the sense that they express social structures, meanings, relations, and practices. They can display, for example, how the identity of mother is appropriated as personally meaningful in different ways by women from different social classes or by women who are themselves critical of the institution of motherhood. The social structural relations embedded in the interview may be expressed in respondents' accounts but at the same time be hidden from their reflective awareness (Silverman, 1985, p. 157). Interview data, therefore, can allow interpretive access to the relationships between social organization and lived experience.

THE SAMPLE DESIGN

The sampling design was purposive or theoretical sampling. Purposive sampling is distinguished from types of random sampling in that it does not use probability estimates to approximate population representation. Purposive sampling looks for representativeness by "purposefully" choosing a sample that typifies the population, the theoretical category, or phenomenon to be studied. Thus it does not allow one to make statements about the general population from this type of sample, but it enables one to learn a great deal about the particular phenomenon or theoretical issues under study. The sample was chosen in order to investigate typical phenomena pertaining to theoretical issues of identity, *not* to represent the population.

Purposive sampling was combined with quota sampling so as to fill the sample. Quota sampling methods require that first the population be classified in terms of the theoretical phenomena, characteristics, properties, and so forth that are deemed to be relevant to the issues to be studied. Classification may be on a theoretical or empirical basis. The literature on motherhood and employed mothers indicated that social class would be an important variable (Bernard, 1975; Komarovsky, 1962; Lopata, 1971; Luxton, 1981; Rubin, 1976; Wearing, 1984). Komarovsky (1962) and Oakley (1974), for example, argue that working-class women do not share middle-class women's discontent with domestic roles. Kohn (1977) and Bernstein (1971) found class differences in attitudes to children and childrearing patterns, and Wearing (1984), in the ideology of motherhood. Stack (1974) documents the distinctiveness and resourcefulness of the social organization of childrearing and kin-like relationships among the urban black poor families she studied.

Social class also emerged from the data as an important analytical category. There were class differences in both the qualitative and standardized data gathered about participants' experiences of motherhood. Social class provided not just a theoretical basis for classifying respondents but also an empirically relevant way of organizing the substantive chapters of the study and analyzing data. The sample included an almost equal quota of working-class (48%) and middle-class (52%) mothers.

The sample selection attempted to limit diversity by controlling for employment status and ethnicity; however, neither middle- nor working-class women in this sample were homogeneous groups. As research on both U.S. and Canadian families reveals, there is a great deal of diversity not just between working-class[5] and middle-class[6] families but within each category (Baber and Allen, 1992; Bernard, 1975; Eichler, 1988; Hochschild, 1989; Komarovsky, 1962; Lopata, 1971; Luxton, 1980; Rubin, 1976; Stack, 1974). Although class is often treated as an independent variable in sociological research, we will see how class and gender interacted to shape the lives of those interviewed and how gender also crosscut class to produce some shared experiences of motherhood.

All mothers worked full-time. Full-time work was operationalized according to the Statistics Canada convention, that is, as being employed 30 hours per week or more. I also included the criterion of normally working, or expecting to work full-year, to exclude women who were employed for only part of the year, and could be considered part-time workers.[7]

The research was designed to explore women's experience of

motherhood; thus the sample included mothers with (75%) and without (25%) permanent partners. Having a partner was operationalized to included mothers who were living with partners whom they perceived as permanent, whether legally married or not. Alone mothers[8] included previously married women who were divorced, separated, or widowed as well as never-married mothers, all of whom who were *not* presently living in a permanent relationship with a partner.

ALONE MOTHERS: THE INTERACTION
OF CLASS AND GENDER

I argue in Chapter 4 that the experience of becoming an alone *young* mother described in the following chapters is typically working-class, not a middle-class, phenomenon, although it is clearly not typical of all Canadian working-class women in that most such women do not give birth at such a young age. This study looks at women's experience of motherhood *by social class*, not by whether women were alone or partnered. The latter research focus would have led to a different research design and sample selection. The analysis explores the inter-action of gender and class in shaping women's experience as mothers. Thus the comparisons that can be made by marital status within the sample are limited.

Alone parenting is a far more common experience of parenting than cross-sectional analyses of family structures might suggest. Al-though at any one time about 10% of Canadian families with children are headed by females, in 1984, for example, 27.7% of Canadian mothers aged 40 to 49 years had been alone parents for part of their maternal careers (Moore, 1989, p. 432).

Being an alone mother has concrete implications. For example, in Canada the average income of alone-parent families headed by women is less than half that of two-parent families, and in 1985 60% of alone-parent households headed by women had incomes below the Statistics Canada Low-Income Cut-Offs (Moore, 1987, pp. 34–35).

Being an alone mother can be seen as a temporary state many mothers move in and out of. Alone motherhood in Canada typically lasts about 5 years (Moore, 1989, p. 349), but the consequences depend on *how* and *when* a woman becomes an alone mother. Although most Canadian women who become alone mothers do so through separation and are usually in their early 30s (average age of 31.6), an increasing percentage of those who become alone mothers do so through out-of-wedlock births (Moore, 1989). Such women are typically younger and less educated and have less work experience than other mothers.

The consequences of early childbearing for women's later lives is the subject of much debate (Chapter 4).[9] Many argue that the costs of early childbearing are both high and enduring, especially in terms of education and employment (Grindstaff, 1988; Grindstaff et al., 1989; Moore, 1987, 1989).[10] Writing of the United States, however, Furstenberg (1992) and Genonimus (1992) both reject the simple characterization of teenage motherhood as determining a woman's later life. Childbearing must be placed in its social context. Age at first birth appears to be associated with life circumstances; women from working-class and disadvantaged backgrounds, in particular those with less education and higher rates of unemployment or poverty, have first children at younger ages than more socially advantaged women (Furstenberg, 1992; Geronimus, 1992; Grindstaff, 1988; Rubin, 1976; Wearing, 1984). The pattern also seems to hold at societal, not simply individual, levels. Zimmerman (1992, p. 427) points out that U.S. states that have higher teen birthrates are those that also have higher rates of poverty, unemployment, and divorce and lower rates of school completion. Adolescent childbearing in the United States, Furstenberg (1992) and Geronimus (1992) argue, is associated with persistent poverty.

However, whereas Geronimus (1992) sees the "costs" of adolescent childbearing as relatively low for women who are already extremely disadvantaged, Furstenberg (1992) argues that although adolescent childbearing does not cause poverty, delaying childbearing can increase a woman's chances of avoiding it.

The sample of mothers in this study clearly displayed socioeconomic-related differences in the timing of childbearing—perhaps exaggeratedly so. Working-class women were on average 22.1 years old when they became mothers (see Table 3.1). Middle-class women, on the other hand, were on average 30.5 years old when they first became mothers.

Overall in Canada there has been a trend toward deferred childbearing in recent decades. The median age of Canadian mothers giving birth has risen: In 1987 it was almost 26 years (Statistics Canada, 1990a, p. 11). Indeed, one out of three children born in 1987 was born to a mother 30 years of age or older (Statistics Canada, 1990a, p. 10).

ADOLESCENT PREGNANCY AND UNWED
MOTHERHOOD: PERCEPTIONS OF PROBLEMS

The makeup of the sample of mothers in this study raised issues I had
not originally intended to address. Almost half (46%) of the working-
class women I interviewed had become pregnant with their first child
in their teens. Most Canadian working-class women, of course, do not
become mothers at such an early age. Although adolescent women
are now widely seen as too young for the responsibilities of motherhood, it is important not to take for granted the public perception of
adolescent motherhood as inherently beset with problems. It is
necessary to put birthrates by age and marital status and the public
concern (especially in the United States) about teen pregnancies in
their social context. For the United States, Nathanson (1991, p. 27)
argues, this context includes demographic and social changes such as
the "surplus" of teenagers in the population of the 1960s; the relative
decline in fertility both of older women and of married adolescents;
changes in marriage patterns and an increase in births to single
women, particularly *white* single women; the declining appeal of
adoption to single mothers; and the legalization of abortion.

Historically young motherhood was often considered not only
appropriate but desirable. In Canada in the decades before this study,
however, there was a clear trend *away* from young motherhood. In
1971, the fertility rate for first-order births to women 15 to 19 years
was 33.0 per 1,000 women; by 1986, this rate had fallen to 19.0: The
same magnitude of change was recorded for the 20 to 24 age group
(Statistics Canada, 1990a, p.11).

What is "new," however, is that although the rates of teen
motherhood have declined, more of the women giving birth in
their teens are unmarried and more of these unmarried teenagers
are choosing to keep their babies than in the past. In Canada
between 1951 and 1985, out-of-wedlock births more than quad-
rupled, growing from about 14,000 in 1951 to 59,600 in 1985
(Moore, 1987, p. 32). The increase was not just in absolute numbers.
During this period out-of-wedlock births as a percentage of *all*
births increased from less than 4% in 1951 to more than 16% in
1985 (Moore, 1987, p. 32).[11] Indeed, in the period from 1975 to
1986, the overall fertility rate for single (never-married) women
almost doubled, increasing from 15.2 per 1,000 in 1975 to 29.0 per
1,000 in 1986 (Statistics Canada, 1990a, p. 11). The largest increase
was among women aged 20 to 24.

Adolescent birthrates in the United States also fell during the period under consideration. Some commentators, for example Thompson (1994), estimates they fell by almost 20% between 1970 and 1984 although they started to rise again more recently. Nathanson's (1991) comparison of adolescent birthrates between 1920 and 1987 shows these rates are not unique. Adolescent birthrates in the United States followed a historical pattern of change very similar to that for women aged 20 to 24—falling in the depression; peaking in 1957; and declining rapidly until about 1976, when they plateaued and remained relatively stable. Part of apparent recent increases in teenage childbearing is attributable to the cohort effects of increasing proportions of teenagers in the general population (Zimmerman, 1992). Indeed, if one were to consider the lowering of the age at first menstruation (by 6 months for every 10 years in this century), teenage fecundity would make the percent of teenage pregnancies seem surprisingly low. Some recent upward trends in U.S. teen birthrates raise questions about future direction of these rates. Thompson (1994), suggests that rising rates may reflect an increased stigmatization of, and greater restrictions on, abortion in the United States. Yet whatever the explanation for demographic patterns, as Nathanson (1991) argues, neither the rates nor the patterns of adolescent childbearing explain its recent sociopolitical reconstruction as a major social problem.

Again, as in Canada, U.S. birthrates among unmarried women have increased as birthrates in general have declined. Since 1940, the birthrate for U.S. unmarried women 15 to 44 years of age has more than quintupled; between 1980 and 1987 alone, the percentage of births to unmarried women aged 15 to 44 increased 33%, from 18.4% to 24.5% (Zimmerman, 1992, p. 424). Whereas historically in the United States black women have had higher rates of nonmarital births than white women, the gap has narrowed considerably, from being almost seven times wider in 1970 to being only three times wider in 1989 (Zimmerman, 1992, p. 424). Between 1970 and 1988 in the United States, when the trend in birthrates for unmarried white women was upward, the trend for black unmarried women was generally *downward* (Zimmerman, 1992, p. 424). Despite popular misconceptions, in absolute terms most teen births in the United States, Sidel (1990, p. 128) emphasizes, occur to white teens.

The historically downward trend in overall birthrates in the United States has been accompanied by increased birthrates for single women and especially for unmarried adolescent women. Birthrates to *unmarried* adolescent women (girls 15 to 19 years of age) increased from 22.4 per 1,000 in 1970 to 36.8 in 1988 (Zimmerman, 1992, p. 424). Relative to all births, however, the percentage of births to teen mothers *declined* by 20% between 1980 and 1988, from 15.6% to 12.6% (Zimmerman, 1992, p. 424).

As will be discussed in Chapter 4, public debates over adolescent pregnancies are often codes for public concerns about unorthodox female sexuality; unwed motherhood; race relations; and a host of perceived related social problems such as school dropouts, welfare, and poverty (Griffin, 1992; Nathanson, 1991). Ironically, as Nathanson (1991, p. 25) points out, unwed teen motherhood became the object of intense public concern and professional interventions at a time when teen birthrates had been *falling* but birthrates for unmarried women generally, and white unwed women in particular, were *rising*. Unwed motherhood challenges the patriarchal gender order. Conservative political interests, therefore, have attempted to forge links between teenage pregnancy, race, family disorganization, and welfare dependency (Griffin, 1992; Phoenix, 1991b; Nathanson, 1991).

Birthrates among U.S. adolescents appear to be noticeably higher than in other developed countries, including Canada. Sidel (1990, p. 127) notes that the 1981 birthrate among U.S. teenaged women was twice the Canadian rate, nearly double that of England and Wales, and nearly four times the Swedish rate.[12] However, Nathanson (1991, p. 26) explains that higher adolescent birthrates in the United States have been a historical pattern since 1950; the trend, she suggests, will be toward convergence.

SAMPLING STRATEGY

Both the sample size and the purposive sampling design mean that the research findings are not representative of all mothers' experiences. On the other hand, the qualitatively rich data allow the development of a deeper understanding of women's experience of motherhood and the processes of identity transformation. They also allow one to explore the ways in which subjective processes may reflect changes in social structural circumstances. Paid work is increasingly coming to dominate the objective structures of Canadian women's lives (Duffy et al., 1989). Like women in this study, the majority of Canadian mothers, even those with young children, now work outside the home. In 1988, 57% of mothers of children under age 6 whose husbands were employed were themselves employed, as were 42% of alone mothers of preschoolers (Parliament, 1989, p. 4). The shift in family patterns has been so great that between 1967 and 1986, the proportion of two-parent families with children, which were "traditional" in the sense of the husband being the sole breadwinner, fell from 61% to 27% (Moore, 1989, p. 24). These changes also mean that women's earnings are becoming increasingly important to their families' economic welfare. By 1986, wives' earnings amounted to 29% of family income in dual-earner families, but this proportion was higher among women who were better educated; women with university degrees earned 35% of their dual-earner family incomes (Moore, 1989, p. 25). Thus women in this study are part of the growing proportion of women who are, according to Eichler (1983, pp. 245–260), creating a new pattern of motherhood.

THE WOMEN IN THIS STUDY

All the participants in this study were mothers with at least one preschool child living with them. To help locate the voices of the women who speak in this study in their family contexts, information about their marital/partner status and numbers and ages of children are given in Appendix 1. In all cases mothers' preschool children were theirs by birth. Most of the mothers interviewed (77%) each had just one child, 20% had two children, and 3% had three children. In all but five of these cases, these second and third children were also preschoolers.

Most of those interviewed expected to have another child. Fourteen percent were pregnant at the time I interviewed them, and a further 46% planned to have one or more additional children.

The sample was designed to allow the analysis and deeper understanding of issues pertaining to identity and the meanings of motherhood. Some unplanned-for characteristics of women in the sample provided a particularly interesting opportunity to achieve these aims. The majority of middle-class women (77%) described themselves as feminists, and another 13% said they both "were and were not" feminists. Only 21% of working-class women described themselves as feminists, while 25% said they were not; many did not understand the meaning of the term. The ideological composition of the sample, therefore, provided a very interesting context in which to study issues of gender, identity, and motherhood.

When I interviewed them, the median age of the middle-class women was 35 years and that of the working-class women was 27. About half the sample claimed some religious affiliation, usually Christian. All the women in the sample had grown up and been educated in Canada. Most had grown up in large cities; many, especially working-class mothers, in the metropolitan Toronto region.

SOCIAL CLASS

As indicated earlier, the existing literature suggested that class would be an important determinant of the women's experience of being a mother. But the concept of class is a difficult one whose meaning varies according to different views of the nature of social structure and the object of research (Giddens, 1973). The concept is particularly problematic when applied to women's lives and their experience of motherhood (Boulton, 1983, p. 42). We know that the prevailing economic system creates differential life experiences for those who are differentially located in its structure, but traditional theories of class and stratification have had very little to say about gender. In response to this neglect, feminists have pointed out that gender itself is an element of stratification (Acker, 1988; Eichler, 1977). Men and women experience the world differently, they argue, and gender may create shared experiences among women that crosscut male-derived class positions. And social class distinctions developed with reference to the situation of men may not always reflect meaningful distinctions among women (Acker, 1988; Boulton, 1983, p. 43). The tradition of studying class differences in women's experience using male-derived conceptual schemes and measures has come under increasing criticism (Acker, 1988; Bernard, 1975; Boulton, 1983; Murgatroyd, 1982; Rapp, 1978; Wearing, 1984). Indeed, Oakley (1980b) stresses that the tradition of categorizing women by "husband rather than by self can be seen as participation in the cultural typification of women that relegates them to a second-class status." Such a practice rests on the assumption that the family is the unit of stratification and that inferences can be made about all family members on the basis of the husband's class position. It denies the relevance and importance of employed women's direct relationship to the social structure in favor of a derived relationship. It makes the class position of women who support households difficult to conceptualize. And it neglects the impact of gender itself as a dimension of stratification in our society. As Acker (1988, p. 33) puts it, "stratification theory has been a theory of white males." We can no longer assume a male work world (Murgatroyd, 1982, p. 574). With greater and greater numbers of women in the labor force, the determination of all family members' socioeconomic status by reference to a male "breadwinner" must be questioned (Blishen et al., 1987). Whatever the justification for categorizing unemployed married women according to their husbands' class positions in the past, the practice would be problematic in this study, in which all the women interviewed are employed full-time. The women were classified according to their own class position rather than according to male-derived indicators of class. The decision to operationalize social class in terms of women's direct, rather than derived, relationships with the social structure provided an empirically relevant, pragmatic, and consistent classification criterion in this sample, where all the women in the study had full-time jobs and 25% of them were not currently living with partners. In order to look at contrasts and similarities in women's experience of motherhood, a consistent measure of class that allowed comparison between married and unmarried women had to be employed. Using husbands' class position for some women but not for others would have made comparison difficult and trivialized the significance of women's employment as well.

   This study looks at how women became mothers. As Gerson (1985, p. 40) points out, class position powerfully influences women's decisions regarding work and motherhood by determining their options and constraints and shaping how they will evaluate their choices. A full analysis of women's experience requires that we look at how both middle-class and working-class women build their lives from the different raw materials they are offered (Gerson, 1985, p. 40). This research uses class as a way of talking about the different life situations in which women find themselves. The concept of class is used because it captures the notion of different worlds of experience in ways the concept of socioeconomic status does not. Indeed, this is the tradition in which class has been used in family sociology—to convey the different worlds in which women live (Boulton, 1983; Kohn, 1977; Komarovsky, 1962; Rubin, 1976; Wearing, 1984)—and its use will facilitate comparison with existing research findings.

   In this study I use Giddens's (1973) approach to class. Giddens attempts to integrate conceptually the Weberian and the Marxian traditions of class analysis using the concept of market capacity. He sees the market in capitalist society as intrinsically a structure of power in which the possession of certain attributes advantages some groupings of individuals relative to others (Giddens, 1973, p. 101). Market capacity, for Giddens (1973, p. 103), refers to all the relevant resources and attributes an individual may bring to the bargaining counter of the marketplace. There are three sorts of market capacity that Giddens considers important in this respect: ownership of the means of production, possession of educational or technical qualifications, and possession of manual labor power. These distinctions yield, albeit in complex manners, the basic three-class system in capitalist society— upper, middle, and working class (Giddens, 1973, p. 107). Educational qualifications or recognized skills are, according to Giddens (1973, p. 103), a major factor influencing market capacity. The returns gained through market capacity go beyond merely income and may include security of employment, prospects of career advancement, pension rights, benefit packages, safe work conditions, and so on. Through differences in their bargaining power in the market place, therefore, some women have access to greater resources than others. While the notion of market capacity does not include all the differences among the women in this study, or suggest that the women in one class category form a homogeneous group, it is a useful way of indicating their different relationships to the economic system.

Mothers' level of education was chosen as the primary criterion for operationalizing the concept of class and classifying respondents (Appendix 2). While educational level is not identical to class position, it is a good indicator of the sorts of class differences in options and life circumstances that are looked at in this study. Gerson (1985) explains the relevance of using education as an indicator of class to study women's decisions about work and motherhood:

> Educational attainment is, of course, not an exact proxy for class level, but it is closely linked to class background, life chances, and ultimate class position. Even more important, as the most powerful determinant of occupational access, educational levels affect the work and thus indirectly the family decisions women make. (p. 41)

Participants' education level, rather than income, was chosen as an indicator of class because education also best fits both the theoretical conceptualization of class as market capacity and the research concern with identity. Education can be understood as a means of accessing resources in modern society—in particular, as a means of accessing occupational identities and structurally generated opportunities. At least for men, occupational identities have come to replace kin (or tribal group) in providing the central public identities claimed by modern persons. One of the issues looked at in this research is the extent to which a family-based identity (motherhood) has remained salient among women. Income may have provided an adequate indicator of class differences among women when the only resources and differences under consideration were material, but this is not the case in this study. The other limitations of using income as an indicator of class for women in this study arise from the fact that the association between income, class, and education does not operate the same way for women as for men (Boyd, 1986; Murgatroyd, 1982). Using income as such an indicator also would have created the problem of whether to use total household income or individual income and would have made the comparison of women in single- and dual-income households difficult.

While women's education was taken as the primary indicator in assigning women to one class or other, the decision to assign a woman to the working- or middle-class sample was cross-checked with her occupation as validation (see Appendix 2). Women with a university degree or a 3-year community college diploma, for example, were classified as middle class. Typically these women held professional occupations. Women with grade 12 or lower education were assigned to the working-class sample; these women typically held unskilled or semiskilled manual, clerical, or service jobs or were doing or had done an apprenticeship. Most cases fell readily into one of the two class categories; however, a few cases were difficult to classify. One woman whom I decided to classify as middle class had a grade 13 education and no postsecondary education. However, she held a managerial occupation, had an annual income of between $30,000 and $34,900, and lived in a household in which the total annual income was over $90,000. Another woman had completed a 4-year apprenticeship and was earning more than other women in the working-class sample. However, as an apprenticeship is typically connected with a working-class occupation, I decided to classify her as working class. This woman's husband held a semiskilled manual job, so their household income did not differ greatly from that of other working-class women.

THE WOMEN'S JOBS, EARNINGS, AND EDUCATION

The middle-class women in the study worked primarily in professional, semiprofessional, and administrative occupations. Working-class women, on the other hand, worked in predominantly clerical and service occupations, but a small minority (18%) worked in skilled or semiskilled trades or manual jobs (Appendix 2).

Eighty-one percent of the middle-class mothers had had a university education at the level of a B.A. or higher. Twenty-six percent had completed an M.A. or graduate-level education, and another 13% were currently working on an M.A. or Ph.D. Only one middle-class woman did not have any postsecondary education.

The working-class women had less formal education. Sixty-one percent of the working-class sample had finished grade 12; the rest had not. Few had received any formal training or education beyond secondary school. Those who did included 11% who had some formal secretarial education. Eleven percent were either in or had completed an apprenticeship, and another 6% had received some short-term vocational skills training that prepared them for their present occupations.

A quick look at the women's biographies also reveals class differences. The middle-class women had entered the full-time labor force at a median age of 21 years. Most (70%) also gained some formal postsecondary or graduate-level education after they first entered the labor force.

Working-class women, on the other hand, started their working lives much younger, at a median age of 17.5 years. For them, any further education or training typically involved night school to try to finish their grade 12, for example, or for typing or wordprocessing classes. Twenty-eight percent either had gone to or were attending night school for such reasons.

All the women interviewed worked full-time and full year. Their median annual income from work was $25,000–$29,999. Middle-class women had a median annual income of $35,000–$39,999. Working-class women earned a median income of $20,000–$24,999 (Table 2.1).

TABLE 2.1. Respondents' Median Earned and Household Incomes

	Middle-class women	Working-class women
Median earned income for all women	$35,000–39,999	$20,000–24,999
Median earned income for alone mothers	$30,000–34,999	$20,000–24,999
Median household income (all women)	$70,000–74,999	$35,000–39,999
Median household income for mothers with partners	$75,000–79,999	$45,000–49,999
Median household income for alone mothers	$30,000–34,999	$20,000–24,999

Note. N = 59.

The median income from work for alone working-class women was the same as that for working-class women with partners, but middle-class alone mothers earned less than middle-class mothers with partners. Their median income was $30,000–$34,999, compared with $35,000–$39,999 for those with partners.

Most women in the sample lived in dual-income households. All but one of the 75% of mothers with partners said that their partners also worked full-time. This fact explains why the median income of these households at first seemed relatively high when compared, for example, with the 1986 Canadian average income of dual-earner families of $50,000 (Moore, 1989, p. 25). However, this national average also included families in which household members worked part-time. The relatively high incomes among families in this study must be interpreted within the context of two full-time family earners and the high cost of living, especially of housing, in Toronto in 1988.

The median annual household income for the middle-class women was $75,000–$79,999, but for alone middle-class women it was only $30,000–$34,999. The median household income for the working-class women was approximately $35,000–$39,999, but within this group the median income for those with partners was $45,000–$49,000 and only $20,000–$24,999 for alone working-class mothers.

48 ENGENDERING MOTHERHOOD

WOMEN AS FAMILY-INCOME PROVIDERS

Because these women worked full-time, their earnings constituted a significant proportion of their household incomes, and they should not be considered as supplementary income earners. Forty-four percent of the middle-class women earned *as much* as if not more than their partners; another 22% earned only 10% to 15% less than their partners. Thus most middle-class women's earnings were not significantly different from what their partners earned. Indeed, only 11% of the middle-class women earned 60% or less of their partners' income.

There was greater variation in the relative earnings of men and women in the working-class couples. Only 12% of the working-class women earned more than their partners, whereas 22% of the middle-class women did so. Thirty-one percent of the working-class women earned about the same as their partners. In total, 43% of the working-class women earned as much if not more than their partners. At the same time, however, 37% of the working-class women earned only 60% or *less* of their partners' earnings, and 19% earned half, or less than half, of what their partners earned.

Alone mothers' earnings constituted most or all of their household incomes. A third of these mothers were receiving some child support, but in most cases the amounts were relatively low. Only one mother received more than $300 a month in child support. Many of the alone working-class mothers had received welfare benefits for some time after their babies were born, but at the time they were interviewed all were in full-time employment, supporting themselves and their children. Several had been assisted in the transition from welfare to full-time employment by government-sponsored programs. Perhaps significantly also, most had government subsidized daycare for their children.

FINDING THE SAMPLE

Originally I had planned to recruit women to the study by randomly selecting from the client lists of several daycare centers in both working- and middle-class areas. However, I realized that this method might introduce a systematic bias in the sample, because approximately 80% of children in daycare are in unlicensed or informal settings (Duffy, 1989, p. 56). Instead, women were recruited for inclusion in the sample by an adapted form of snowball sampling and personal referrals. Although these sampling methods have an established tradition in the sociological study of women (Boulton, 1983; Wearing, 1984; Duffy et al., 1989), I was anxious to avoid the problems of bias associated with them, in particular the problems of self-selection and overrepresentation of the characteristics of a particular network. To minimize possible network bias I used multiple starting points for contacting women, and I strictly limited the number of women contacted through any one original source. My starting points for accumulating a pool of potential respondents were diversified, including day-care centers and home day-care providers, places of employment, community college programs and associated networks, sole-support mothers' groups, coordinators of women's training programs, literacy programs, preschoolers' playgroups, and personal acquaintances and their friends. Once identified, potential respondents were sent an explanatory letter, followed by a phone call to determine whether they fit the three eligibility criteria and, if so, whether they were willing to participate. This strategy limited the possibility of self-selection and also provided me with records of referrals, contacts, and refusals. Only one mother who received a letter and subsequent phone call refused to be interviewed. Another three indicated that they did not wish to be contacted about the study prior to having received the explanatory letter or phone call.

To protect their anonymity, the names of the women who took part in the study have been changed. The names of family members referred to are also altered. Where it was felt that they might violate anonymity, occupational titles have been modified slightly.

SUMMARY

The research methodology directed the study to an investigation of the social processes that shaped these women's experience of motherhood rather than to causes. The focus of the analysis grew out of the issues and meanings that were salient for the women in the study. However, the research was designed to analyze the description of women's personal experience in terms of analysis of the social organizational context in which it was located.

3

Paths to Motherhood:
Middle-Class Women

This chapter looks at midde-class women's accounts of how they came to give birth to their first child. As explained in the introduction, I found it useful to distinguish between how these women came to have children and how they developed self-conceptions as mothers. This and the next chapter look at recruitment to motherhood. The participants' self-conceptions as mothers are analyzed in later chapters.

Concepts such as motherhood mandate (Russo, 1979), gender socialization, or choice do not capture the complexity of the process through which the women studied came to have children. Central to this process was the construction and reconstruction of biography and the negotiation of circumstances. Although like most women in our society all these women became mothers, this shared outcome should not obscure the diverse meanings of the process. The data show how many women did not step easily or deliberately into the role of mother. On the contrary, their paths to motherhood were often tentative, unanticipated, and difficult and their experiences did not fit dominant notions of motherhood as choice. Many of the women had once thought they would choose to be permanently childless. Others had wondered if they would find the "right relationship" in which to have children or if they would be able to conceive. If the analysis focused on *outcome* rather than *process*, it would miss much of these women's experiences.

This chapter shows how conceptions of self, time, and adulthood; implicit meanings of motherhood and childlessness; and relationships with significant others were all implicated in these women's maternity. We will see how the women's identities as mothers are better understood as products of interaction rather than of gender-role conformity. Becoming a mother is not simply about having children; it is also about engaging available cultural identities.

MOTIVES FOR MOTHERHOOD

It is popularly held that motherhood has become a matter of individual choice. But becoming a mother did not have the character of choice in the lives of many who participated in this study. Choice suggests, for example, that the women reflected on options or weighed the costs, benefits, and consequences of having or not having children. Yet most middle-class women interviewed in this study found it difficult to give their reasons for why they had, or had wanted to have, children.[1] The problem was not simply that they could not remember why but that they had difficulty applying the common-sense notion of "reasons" to having children. Some of the women did not choose to become pregnant or to terminate a pregnancy; for others, the notion of reasons is inappropriate.

Where childbearing is culturally normative, women do not need to explain why they want children—only why they do *not*. Thus Jean, an archivist, could give no "reasons" for having wanted a child except "just really wanting to have children, you know. . . . It wasn't really [discussed] very [much] in depth at all." Similarly Fran, a lawyer, had been trained in rational decision making; yet a request for reasons didn't fit her experience.

I don't know. Now that's the funny thing about it. I'm not sure what it was. I don't know what it was. Why was it that I wanted to have children? I don't even know. (Fran: Lawyer)

Susan had "always wanted to have a child." Her reasons expressed her commitment to motherhood rather than grounds for a choice:

I don't think it is a rational decision. It's much more emotional. I'd just always wanted to have a child. I'd worked with disturbed kids and I just thought I could do a much better job than other people do. . . . It's something you want to do and you feel you can do it very well. (Susan: Social Worker)

Rachael too "always wanted" children. Although she gave reasons, her commitment to motherhood was experienced as given, as so constitutive of herself that she described it as instinct:

> I always wanted children, I knew that. . . . First of all, it was just expected, so I never really had to discuss it. And my husband, he really wanted to have children as well. So it was never really a question. We both knew we wanted to have children. It was something we talked about before we got married. . . . I really felt this, whatever, maternal instinct, wanting to nurture, and I wanted that life-style and I certainly wanted the experience of what being pregnant was all about. (Rachael: High School Teacher)

Articulated reasons should not be confused with causes. And absence of articulated reasons does not indicate a lack of meaning or reason. Scott and Lyman (1981) remind us that, whether claimed or imputed, reasons do not necessarily lead to behavior but function as after-the-fact accounts that make problematic behavior intelligible or legitimate. Reasons are called for when behavior needs explaining: the "choice" of motherhood generally does not.

In contrast, people pursuing adoption or infertility treatment are frequently called on to articulate their reasons for wanting children. Their accounts expose many of the normative ideas about motherhood, adult identity, implicit meanings of biological ties, and the stigma of infertility in our culture (Matthews and Matthews, 1986; Sandelowski et al., 1993; Woollett, 1991).[2]

Voluntarily childless women in Veevers' (1980) study, on the other hand, often held negative images of motherhood, associating it with personal incompetence, martyrdom, loss of freedom, and reduced marital satisfaction. Not surprisingly, such women developed a variety of strategies and accounts to challenge normative assumptions about parenthood and to cope with being asked to explain their childlessness (Campbell, 1985; Veevers, 1980). Even in such cases, a commitment to childlessness often does not come from a rational assessment of reasons. Rather, reasons and cost–benefit analyses often constitute post hoc explanations of *prior* decisions that are offered as justifications for nonconformity (Campbell, 1985). Research suggests that a minority of permanently childless married women have an articulated commitment to childlessness before marriage. Most become childless through postponement, default, or by discovering that they (or their partners) really do not have a strong commitment to parenthood (Campbell, 1985; Veevers, 1980).[3]

Yet motherhood is represented as a choice. Societies typically supply members with vocabularies of motives with which to make sense of the choices people are expected to make (Mills, 1940/1981). Thus motives can become "causal" by becoming implicated in individuals' decision making: We act *toward* them rather than *from* them. Motherhood, as Luker's (1984) analysis of the abortion wars shows, has the dual character of being both a taken-for-granted part of being a woman *and* constructed as a choice. Thus, although motherhood may be culturally normative, it is also, especially among middle-class women, culturally held that children are a matter of individual choice, not of biological destiny. Therefore motherhood can require accounting for. Unlike working-class women, for whom "no reason" or "I don't know" satisfied as an account, many middle-class women, usually after some reflection, offered personally meaningful accounts of how they came to have children. What remain culturally unavailable, according to Stanworth (1990, p. 292), are viable justifications for *not* having children.[4]

THE PROBLEM WITH REASONS

Forty-five percent of the middle-class women interviewed had "always wanted" or assumed they would have children (see Table 4.1). Asking such people why or questioning the taken for granted is usually seen as nonsense: It makes no sense.

> Why does anyone ever want to have children? [responded Nina]. It wasn't a *decision*, it wasn't a question. We didn't try to decide to have a child or not to have a child. . . . It was taken as given. (Nina: Director, Nonprofit Organization)

The notion of "always wanted" represents a particular kind of identity claim. Women who had "always wanted" a child were emphasizing the noncontingent nature of their maternal desire and locating it in something unchanging in themselves.

In contrast, Anna had had to articulate her reasons. As an unattached woman of 39 years, she had been called on to account for having given birth to a child outside a relationship.

> [I started thinking about it when I was] 37—well, actually probably 30, off and on. But when it was off, it was very off . . . well, say 34 . . . say up to 37, and then it became something I thought about a lot. . . . I have never really been attracted to them [children]. I'm not a person who will rush over and play with children, but I felt that this was the answer to what I wanted. . . . [I talked about having a child] a lot. It was mostly all verbal. Over those years I was thinking about it, I talked it over with various male friends I was considering being the father—this was when I would do a very planned [pregnancy]. And they were very good in terms of relating in an objective way. And I talked about it with female friends. . . . (Anna: Community College Teaching Master)

For Anna, having a child represented an opportunity for an enduring, committed relationship in ways that male partners had not. Although her motherhood was unorthodox, Anna's account articulated many of the themes of connectedness and relationship that recurred in women's reflections on motherhood:

> I had felt that I had lived too long in a place where I hadn't put down any roots. It was time for me to think about my roots and my future. I hadn't met anyone I had wanted to share life with, but roots are very important and . . . I started to think about making my own roots with a child. . . . [I wanted a child because] I wanted there to be someone very important in my life with whom I could share the [life] experience and still be around in 20 years, or 10 years, because there has never been anyone long term, and I have always traveled alone, so I really wanted *continuity.* (Anna: Community College Teaching Master)

The question Why? creates the need for an ideological response, especially among those who assume that their choices govern their lives. But there is little ideological consensus on motherhood from which middle-class women can generate accounts (Luker, 1984;

Harding, 1981). Much feminist reflection on motherhood, for example, has been deeply ambivalent.

Middle-class women in the study also had difficulty in giving
reasons for pregnancies because children are not simply the products
of reasons but of social process whereby individuals or couples come
to make sense of their lives or to jointly construct biographies (Berger
and Kellner, 1977; Campbell, 1985). Children were socially, not simply
biologically, conceived. As Wendy recalled:

> We thought we would make a nice baby. It was a joint project.
> We were both at a stage of life where we wanted it. [I once
> thought I would choose to remain childless.] I hadn't wanted any
> [children]. I hadn't thought I would have the patience and
> dedication. And you have to have a relationship in which you are
> settled and very comfortable going into it. I hadn't had that. So
> it's all of a package, I guess. (Wendy: Research Advisor)

Having children is not simply the outcome of a desire to parent:
It has to do with what is seen as conceptually appropriate rather than
simply biologically possible. Both Wendy and Debbie (below) once
thought they would remain childless. Both later came to want
children. Wendy located the possibility of motherhood in a particular
"settled," "comfortable" relationship with a man—it was "all of a
package." By being part of a "package," as Grogan (1992) argues, the
construction of motherhood is closely bound into the construction
of heterosexuality such that, without a man or marriage, having a child
is "inconceivable" or deviant.

This presumption of heterosexuality had once excluded Debbie
from motherhood. For this lesbian woman, motherhood had not been
taken for granted. Having a child felt like receiving an amazing gift:

> I didn't really expect to have children. I "came out" at a very early
> age. . . . Childlessness seemed to me one of the real impoverish-
> ments of the [lesbian] life-style that seemed to be available to me.
> So [now, having a child] it feels like an amazing gift to me.
> (Debbie: Accountant)

Debbie continued:

> [I had lived with a woman who had a child.] I really enjoyed
> having this child in my life for the 5 or 6 years that she was there.

The other relationship I'd been in, the plan was the other woman was going to have a child. So I'd been planning on *us* having a child, but I hadn't really thought about *myself* having a child until I left her, or *she* left me, to be more precise. . . . [I started thinking about having a child myself when] I was putting myself back together after a relationship had broken up and I was starting a new one and starting life all over again. And that's when I found a method of getting inseminated I could live with. (Debbie: Accountant)

We conventionally think of motherhood as an expression of a heterosexual female gender identity. But Debbie's, Anna's, and Wendy's experiences suggest the meanings are more complex. Implicit meanings of motherhood are made visible, not in the observance of norms, but in their breach: the lesbian mother who "*knew*" motherhood assumed heterosexuality; the alone mother who "*knew*" it was about connectedness; the mother, once committed to childlessness, whose heterosexual relationship *produced* the desire for children. Rather than seeing motherhood as the expression of heterosexual female gender identity, we need to understand how the social production and organization of heterosexuality itself, through the institution of "the couple," generates and regulates the production of children.

Although many women talked about the decision to have children as emerging from their relationship with male partners, some did not. Rebecca, a once-married, currently alone mother, reflected on her desire for children:

I always wanted to have a family. A white-picket-fence sort of mentality and looking forward to being a grandparent. I remember I used to talk about it—my children having children, stuff like that. There was never any question in my mind that I wanted to have kids. I never knew if I wanted to get married. I never quite saw myself as much of a wife, but I did see myself as a mother. (Rebecca: Counselor)

Rather than being naturally associated, Rich (1976) argues, motherhood and heterosexuality are oppressively linked in patriarchal societies. However, in everyday thinking, as Campbell (1985, p. 76) points out, marriage and children are so associated in popular imagery that they function to provide legitimation for each other—marriage functions as a reason for children and having children as grounds for marriage.

PREGNANCY ACCOUNTS: PLANNED
AND UNPLANNED PREGNANCIES

Research on motivation for parenthood often relies on family inten-tion surveys—a prior accounting for anticipated behavior.[5] Women's pregnancy accounts, on the other hand, are after-the-fact interpreta-tions of experience. Pregnancy accounts are, perhaps, as good indica-tors of present meanings as they are of past events; recollected accounts will be interpreted as guides to meanings rather than as objective facts.

Although most women in this study said they had always wanted or always assumed they would have children, a surprising number did not. In women's own experience, motherhood is *less* taken for granted than it may once have been. For some period of their adult lives almost half of the middle-class mothers (48%) thought they would choose to remain permanently childless (Table 4.1).[6]

Some of these women had simply not been strongly committed to parenthood:

I did [think I would never have children because] . . . of never *really* wanting them that badly. . . . I think it was something if I didn't have them, I could deal with it. I didn't feel [I had to have children]. . . . I think it's the kind of thing that unless you've had a child, you don't know what you're missing, because you've never had it. (Jill: Marketing Manager)

Others were not attracted to the life-style:

I thought kids would be an infringement on [my] life-style. I saw . . . mothers with children, you know, shuffling the kids to parties and I felt sorry for them. . . . It did not look like my cup of tea. (Alice: Graphic Designer)

Voluntary childlessness, however, is not easily defined (House-knecht, 1987); it raises questions of social context and the degree and permanence of commitment.

The commitment to motherhood might seem clearer for the

middle-class women who always assumed they would have children (see Table 4.1), but this was not necessarily so. "Always wanting" a child did not mean a child was wanted at any time: 71% (and 46% of working-class women) described their pregnancies with their first child as having been planned (see Table 4.2). Unplanned pregnancies carried various meanings: Some were unanticipated but welcomed. Others were unwanted but became acceptable or wanted. A small minority remained unwanted. Still others appeared to have been the result of contraceptive risk taking and resolved irresolvable questions. Maternal careers that ended in abortions were not represented in this study.

The rate of unplanned pregnancy noted above brings into question the notion that fertility is under women's control and is primarily a matter of choice and technology. Rates of unplanned pregnancy and abortion must be understood in terms of how class, race, age, education, gender inequality, and social support structure both the circumstances in which women become pregnant and their responses to pregnancy (Baber and Allen, 1992, pp. 121–124; Sidel, 1990, p. 129). These rates vary greatly between comparable industrialized countries with similar fertility technologies but with different social arrangements. Canadian women, Sidel (1990, pp. 127–129) points outs, have an abortion rate and teen birth rate approximately half that of U.S. women.

Unplanned pregnancies are not limited to teenaged women. Fewer than half the babies born to older mothers (40+) in Berryman's (1991) British study were planned. Perhaps unplanned pregnancy and abortion rates are relatively high for older women because they change contraceptive practices for health reasons, because they assume that pregnancy is unlikely (Berryman 1991, p. 113) or because of how contraception and motherhood decisions are made. Unlike the women in Veever's (1980) study, for whom pregnancy scares encouraged a clearer commitment to childlessness, unplanned pregnancies in this study often led to motherhood.

The notion of planned and unplanned motherhood is, therefore, a problematic one. Several women who described their pregnancies as planned, for example, were *surprised* when they became pregnant. As Luker (1975) shows, women may plan to accept a risk of pregnancy or plan to stop using contraceptives. This, however, is not the same as planning motherhood. Beth explained:

> We decided to cease [using] birth control. We probably started discussing it, made the decision, and I got pregnant [all] within 6

months. . . . In the abstract it was great, [but] when I actually got pregnant . . . it was a month of sheer panic . . . partly because I always thought that people spent a long time trying to get pregnant. It was really fast. It took me by surprise. I had a month of real panic. (Beth: Management Board Officer)

Luker (1975) shows how women's assessment of the conse-quences, cost, and benefits associated with contraceptive practices and of the prospect of motherhood vary before and *after* conception; the actual outcomes in terms of pregnancies, abortions, and births are situationally contingent.

Some of the middle-class women's pregnancies were neither planned nor unplanned. As Anna put it, "I hadn't planned it, but I hadn't *not* planned it. . . . Fate gave me a little push." Joanne, who was not in a stable relationship at the time, was clear that her pregnancy was not planned, but "felt great" when she learned (at the age of 32) that she had accidentally become pregnant:

I felt great [when I found out I was pregnant]. I had absolutely no doubts about it at all. And I think it's partly when I was around 27 I decided that if I ever did get pregnant accidentally I would accept it and do whatever I need to do in order to have a child. (Joanne: Elementary School Teacher)

Women who are ambivalent about pregnancy may describe themselves as just "falling pregnant" (Luker, 1975; O'Donnell, 1985). For Currie (1988), contraceptive risk taking is a way not only of handling ambivalence about having children but also of attempting to reconcile the structural contradictions that women who mother must manage.

The middle-class women in the study who had planned their pregnancies included among their reasons for having children the desire for a relationship with their own child, in particular a relation-ship of love or nurturance (32%). They also spoke of a maternal instinct or natural drives (23%). About a third of these women mentioned difficult-to-code but loosely related themes about children enriching life, motherhood being part of a pattern, or making sense of things. Not uncommonly, pregnancy accounts were idiosyncratic and diffi-cult to code, supporting other research findings that, among middle-class women, maternity decision making is often difficult and ambiva-lent (Gerson, 1985; Currie, 1988; O'Donnell, 1985).

IS IT TIME?: TIME CONCEPTIONS AND
PREGNANCIES AMONG MIDDLE-CLASS WOMEN

When we shift our attention from the participants' reasons for having children to descriptions of how they became mothers—to what they thought and talked about and what was happening in their lives when they became pregnant—a clearer pattern emerges. Time was a dominant theme in pregnancy accounts. Eighty-two percent of the middle-class and 61% of the working-class mothers who planned their pregnancies invoked some concept of time in their accounts (see Table 4.4). On the surface a reference to time seems to explain *when*, not *why*, it was seen as desirable to have children. However, as I will show, it has to do with both.

The women organized explanations of their pregnancies around time in two ways. They talked of chronological age and a "biological clock," but they also talked of a temporal flow of meaningful events in their lives, which I call biographical time.

It is tempting to see time or age as an independent variable. What can appear more given? But time and age were experienced through personally significant frames of meaning and through social categories of class and gender (Chapter 4). Class-specific time frames, for example, help explain how working- and middle-class women became mothers at different ages (Table 3.1). Middle-class mothers' average age at the birth of their first child was 30.5 years; their median age was 32 years. Working-class women were much younger; on average they were 22.1 years, and their median age was 22 years.[7]

Half (50%) of the middle-class women who planned their pregnancies indicated that consciousness of their chronological age or "the biological clock" helped them decide to become pregnant (see Table 4.4). But the personal meanings of time, as we will see, are complex.

TABLE 3.1. Average and Median Ages at Birth of First Children

	Middle-class women	Working-class women
Average age at first birth (all)	30.5	22.1
Median age at first birth (all)	32	22
Average age at first birth among *presently* alone mothers	31.25	21.1

Note. N = 59.

Another 9% said their partners' age also meant that "time was running out." Marie was 32 when her first child was born; her partner was 9 years older:

> Well, I felt like time was running out—I felt I was getting older. Frank was getting older—[I thought,] "We'd better do this." And I didn't ever feel I would be necessarily ready to have a child. But I came to terms with it. "All right, I'll do it," even though not everything is perfect; because nothing will be perfect. I had been waiting for the perfect time. Well, on and off. I think for 4 to 5 years I didn't want to have a child. Then, you know, the biological clock started ticking. And I felt, "I want to do this, and I want to do it sooner than later"; a little sooner because Frank is 40, you know. (Marie: Education Consultant)

For some, the biological clock raised the issue of not only whether they would but whether they *could* have children. Twenty-three percent of women said they had been unsure they would be able to conceive:

> I think probably on and off for 5 or 6 years it was "Do we? Don't we?".... We were feeling that we were handling all the finances well. We had accomplished most of the [house] renovations. I was feeling that I was beginning to have made some career advances.... The pulls were equally strong in both directions. There were many positive things for the double income, no kids [life]. ... Yet I figured [that] further down the road, when it would probably be too late, I would probably have so many regrets. ... I had a miscarriage . . . and [I feared,] "Maybe there's something wrong with me . . . maybe, physically, I won't be capable of it." (Mary Lynn: Policy Analyst)

When Susan was about 33, she became aware of "the biological clock." From Susan's account, however, we see that time refers not simply to biological time but to the time women need to socially arrange motherhood.

> The biological clock was ticking away. I said we got married to have children—I think they were synonymous—the decision to get married was a decision to have children. And I definitely wanted children. . . . It was either [he agreed] or . . . I would have

found *another relationship*. [Having a child] was something I wanted to do, and I had reached the point where I realized I only had a small amount of time in which to do it. (Susan: Social Worker)

But contrary to common sense expectations, the women who "heard" the biological clock most often were those who were ambivalent or who had *not* "always wanted" children, rather than those who had. For some time Sandra thought she would not ever have children; at the same time she did not want to lose the option to choose:

[I once thought I would not ever have children]. I thought I would be a terrible parent. But when I thought about it seriously I thought, "This is not the time, I don't have to think about [children] now." . . . In my 20s I realized I wanted to think carefully about having a child because I didn't want to end up without the opportunity—biologically. I guess by the time I was 30 I decided I wanted to have a child, and the case was when and who. (Sandra: Civil Servant)

Almost half (47%) of the women who once thought they might choose to be childless felt aware of, or pressure from, "the biological clock." Given the commitment of those who always wanted to be mothers, one would have expected a greater awareness of time pressures among this group. But this was not the case. Could this be explained by the different ages at first births among the two categories? Older women could be expected to "hear" the ticking more loudly. However, the average age at first births among those who always wanted and those who did not were quite close, 31 years and 32.6 years, respectively.[8] The pattern of biological time awareness is better explained by listening to *how* women made decisions about pregnancy.

THE CHANGING CONTENT OF WOMEN'S OPTIONS: HOW "WHEN" BECOMES "WHETHER"

At first glance the "biological clock" appeared to be an issue of *when* to have children, not *whether* to have children. However, for many women, when decisions became whether decisions. After being in a "solid" relationship where having children had not been considered, partly because of her partner's financial commitment to children of a previous marriage, Kim said she and her partner came to a "fairly spontaneous decision" to have children:

> My past had been—I've had a relatively happy life. Nothing traumatic has happened that would make me feel negative about having children. And probably the fact [was] that I was getting older and we [now] knew we wanted to have a child, so it was a matter of deciding whether we would or not. . . . [There were no reasons.] It was a fairly spontaneous decision. . . . The age factor, I guess. Many women at this point feel the clock ticking. The clock certainly helped the decision along. (Kim: Librarian)

Jill had thought she would never have children, partly because she "never really wanted them that badly." She and her partner "knew [they] didn't want children before they were 30."

> [When Jill was 30, she and her partner] just figured—well, we're 30 and we'll slowly try to get pregnant, and if we do we do, and if we don't we don't. . . . [I] wasn't really excited about the whole thing. I didn't have, you know, the great maternal urge. I didn't even really like babies. (Jill: Marketing Manager)

When she reached 30, no longer having a reason to not have children, Jill became pregnant:

> We were almost so *laissez faire* about it. We really didn't have a reason for wanting a child other than we thought if we were going to have one, we wanted to have one before we were [in our] mid-30s. . . . I think we knew we didn't want children before we were 30. And then when we hit 30 we said, "Gee, if we are going to do it, we should do it now." But it was never, sort of, you know, we want to have a little baby in the house. (Jill: Marketing Manager)

Running out of reasons for postponing children, as Veevers (1980, p. 33) notes, forces couples to face the decision to commit either to children or to childlessness. Wendy, who had previously intended to remain permanently childless, explained:

[Later on] I wanted a child, that's all. And the main reasons I wanted a child? It was time to get on with it, that's all. The time was tick, tock, tick, tock. . . . (Wendy: Research Advisor)

The biological clock invoked by middle-class women was flexibly biological. Women constructed and readjusted biological age as subjective make-up-your-mind times or cutoff dates for considering pregnancy. "My new cutoff date is 40," explained Sandra, who was undecided about having a second child. As the public perception of biological cutoff ages changes, the time frame in which fertility decisions are made expands accordingly.

The "biological clock" did more than urge women in this study to make up their minds about having a child. It faced them with a new decision: that of remaining permanently childless. During their adult years, these middle-class women, although childless, had retained a potential identity of mother. Neither women who had earlier thought they would remain childless nor those who were ambivalent had taken irrevocable steps in *rejecting* motherhood potential—for example, through sterilization. Whether it was perceived as a desirable option or not, women retained a *potential* claim to motherhood identity and the attendant relationship with a child. Thus for years women could be nonmothers but potential mothers at the same time. This balancing act made motherhood temporarily a "nonproblem" for both those who "always wanted" children and those who did not.

The "biological clock" threatened this balance by destroying one side of the equation—the future potential identity and relationship of mother. These women were faced with a new identity: that of *permanently childless woman*. This new identity, unlike previous childless identities, was irrevocable. Earlier in their biographies women could adopt a nonmotherhood identity with little cost. But time threatened to make lifelong and potentially costly commitments out of temporary decisions. As Mary Lynn put it:

[We were thinking about having a child] probably off and on for 5 or 6 years. It was, "Do we? Don't we? When do we?" . . . And I was feeling too that the biological clock was ticking and that we sort of had to get on with it if we were going to do it. (Mary Lynn: Policy Analyst)

Mary Lynn and her partner found it hard to decide to have a child until Mary Lynn realized she could not accept the idea of being permanently childless. Her decision was more a *rejection* of permanent childlessness than an *embracement* of motherhood at that particular time:

> At one point, when we were waffling so much [about having children] and forever changing our minds, I thought that perhaps during that time that the ultimate decision would be no. . . . But I felt sort of empty and at a loss [with that decision]. I wasn't happy with it for very long, and that's why I kept going back to [the idea of having children]. (Mary Lynn: Policy Analyst)

Marie also felt that time was running out. At 32 she felt ambivalent and "not ready" to have a child; but she could not commit herself to childlessness:

> You know, you have images of yourself. . . . Mine was never a childless one—not that it was necessarily one *with* a *child*, but it sure [wasn't being childless]. . . . While I didn't imagine myself with kids around me, I never imagined myself without them. . . . I thought I may not have children at certain times—I don't think I ever, ever, thought I wouldn't have one. (Marie: Education Consultant)

Motherhood is not simply about having children. It is about engaging identities and their attendant cultural meanings: mother or permanently childless woman. For example, Veevers (1980) found that the childless women in her study invoked the possibility of adoption to symbolically defer their final decision about childlessness. Such a strategy may neutralize the morally degrading implications of being someone who either did not like or would not be able to care for children. Voluntarily childless couples can thus claim to be not that different from parents (Veevers, 1980).

Women who reject or postpone motherhood do not necessarily welcome the cultural meanings of childlessness, with its implications of selfishness, immaturity, and aloneness. One attraction of motherhood to the infertile women Woollett (1991) studied was the release from the negative identities that childlessness carries.[9]

Although voluntarily childless women may successfully reject others' attempts to construct them as deviant or selfish, they must *also* resolve the issues of living without the significant cultural relationships and resources for making sense of adult life and personal identity that having children offers.

As Veevers (1980) and Campbell (1985) show, decisions to postpone pregnancy can, almost by default, lead to lifelong childlessness. On the other hand, difficulty in sustaining an identity of nonmother appears to have led some women in this study to become pregnant.

BEING "READY": MOTHERHOOD
AND BIOGRAPHICAL TIME

Independently of referring to chronological age or a biological clock, more than half the middle-class women (64%) who planned their pregnancies invoked *biographical* time in explaining their decisions to have children (Table 4.4). They located decisions about having children in a temporal flow of their lives that assumed a developmental or progressive character. Women spoke in terms of "*being ready* for children," or it being the "*right time*." "We were *ready*," Jenny, an executive secretary emphasized. "We were both at a stage of life when we wanted it," explained Wendy who, at 36 years, had recently had her first child.

Middle-class women talked about specific dimensions of readiness for children: financial readiness, employment readiness, personal and emotional readiness, and being ready in terms of their relationships. Loretta put it like this:

> We were mature enough. We had satisfied a lot of other needs. We were ready to make a commitment to children. We were very sure in our relationship. . . . Emotionally both of us were ready. . . . We both wanted to have a baby . . . the inevitable result of our relationship. We talked about it. . . . Our relationship had been established . . . there was obviously a commitment there. It seemed like the right thing to do. (Loretta: Elementary School Teacher)

Similarly, Marie explained the termination of a much earlier pregnancy as follows: "I didn't feel I was ready [then]—financially ready, emotionally ready, ready with another person to parent with."

The themes of readiness in the discussions of motherhood by these middle-class women had material and social psychological referents. The "right time" referred to the practicalities of having children, such as money, work, housing, and support with domestic tasks. Some women mentioned home renovations or owning a home as part of readiness. Others referred to being financially ready or ready in terms of their own or their partners' work. Even women who felt personally ready for children had to consider other dimensions of "readiness:"

> I wondered about how getting pregnant [would] affect my career advancement. Was I at a point where I should be changing jobs? And if so, getting pregnant was not a good idea. (Laura: Accountant)

Sandra, who at 34 knew she wanted children and planned her pregnancy, explained how she had to make the right circumstances:

> [I changed my job.] Part of the reason I got into this job was I knew I would get maternity leave and have the security to go back to it . . . and [have the] benefits. (Sandra: Civil Servant)

Tess, who was 33 when her first child was born, had to achieve readiness in terms of her career and finances, as well as her relationship, before she could contemplate having children:

> I always wanted to have a child, but I didn't seriously contemplate it until a few years ago, when I felt financially ready. Also, John didn't want to have children for a long time. So it was after we got married; I think we felt very comfortable with one another and thought maybe it would work. I had a permanent job; I had some work experience. . . . I'd established myself at work. (Tess: Senior Policy Advisor)

We often talk about women's hard choices between career and family. However, for Tess, career success was *not* seen as a substitute for motherhood:

> It's not like I could say to myself, well, yes, these are all as interesting, as inherently satisfying, [and] it's just a matter of choosing between this and having a child. It is *not* that way. Having a child was such a fundamental thing. . . . Had John not wanted to have a child . . . I don't think I would have kept a relationship with him. (Tess: Senior Policy Advisor)

Thus Tess, like other middle-class women whose commitment to children preceded their relationship, needed to organize the life circumstances in which she could have children. As Currie (1988) argues, the notion of the right time for children (among middle-class women) often corresponds to a configuration of material circumstances such as employment, shared parenting, housing, and finances, which women feel they must *personally* manage before deciding about having children. As many of these factors are outside their control, women face the problem of developing personal strategies to handle structurally generated problems. These strategies, Currie (1988, p. 249) notes, are often misinterpreted as ambivalence.

Work-involved women may attempt to engage male partners in family work in order to reduce the practical costs of children to themselves and to make maternity more viable (Gerson, 1985, p. 166; Hochschild, 1989, p. 193). Loretta's commitment to having a child, for example, was *contingent* on making such a bargain with her partner, *not* prior to it. Loretta said that she and Peter had reached a joint decision to have children but that a commitment to shared parenting had been part of that decision:

I think [the decision to have children] depends on your spouse and the type of commitment you are going to get from them. . . . We had a very equal relationship, and I wasn't going to get involved in having children unless that continued. . . . Peter does 50% of the childraising, and I know he is fairly unusual. . . . He does 50% of the cooking and 50% of the cleaning. . . . It didn't work out easily; it's something we worked at continually. (Loretta: Elementary School Teacher)

Work-oriented women may tend to marry men who profess similar egalitarian ideals. However, egalitarianism is often little more than a family myth disguising the persistence of a gendered division of labor (Backett, 1982; Ferree, 1984; Hochschild, 1989; La Rossa and La Rossa, 1981).

Like Loretta, Tess had tried to reduce the potential costs of motherhood to herself by making a joint commitment to shared parent work a part of the decision to have children. Although her partner agreed to have a child, his commitment to fatherhood did *not* involve a commitment to sharing the work. Her greater desire to be a mother put Tess in a weakened bargaining position:

> John was concerned about my career: how [having a child] would affect it. He wasn't in any hurry really to have a child. He wanted it to be the right time. We talked about how our relationship would be affected by it. . . . We talked a bit about how much responsibility he would take vis-à-vis [sharing the work]. There was no definite commitment in the sense that he was prepared to do half [the work]. (Tess: Senior Policy Advisor)

Some middle-class women found themselves in the right circumstances for deciding that they were ready to have children; others attempted to negotiate their circumstances; and others adapted their definition of readiness. Even those who broke with conventional timing were aware of the presumption of readiness:

> You think about having a child and you think it's not the right time, so [you don't] . . . [but] then it just seemed there would never be a right time, so we may as well go ahead and do it. (Jean: Archivist)

Although women referred to other aspects of being ready for children, especially their work or careers, their relationships with men dominated middle-class women's accounts of how they came to have children.

THE "RIGHT RELATIONSHIP"

A characteristic feature of biographical "readiness" for middle-class women was the presence of the "right relationship." When asked when they first started thinking about actually having a child, many women said it coincided with a particular relationship, "readiness" in a relationship, or replacing one relationship with another that they came to define as the "right relationship." Although women talked about relationships as having led them to pregnancy, the data show these women often invoked their relationship to explain or support their motherhood.

As with the commitment to childlessness (Campbell, 1985; Veevers, 1980), the commitment to motherhood can occur prior to, or emerge in the context of, a particular relationship. Identities, whether childless or maternal, are not simply chosen but emerge and are sustained or transformed in social relationships. Just as women who once assumed they would have children later "became childless" (Campbell, 1985), so participants in this study who had once thought they would remain childless later became "ready" to have children. In some cases the changed commitments of these women emerged, as it did for Loretta (below), as a joint decision—a product of the relationship. In contrast, Patricia's commitment to motherhood preceded, but was also contingent on, a relationship. Patricia had always wanted children but was 36 before she had her first child. Patricia had waited for the "right Dad":

> When I was 35 I found the right Dad. I had [a child] as soon as I thought I had the right father, and that was simultaneous to the marriage. I always wanted to have a child, but I couldn't have a child unless I felt I had a particular [partner] that I felt was the right person to have a child with. I've always had a very deep desire [to have a child]. (Patricia: Community College Teaching Master)

Patricia's account inverts the historical relationship between herself, her child, and her marriage. Her child "chose" her:

> Oh, we [my partner and I] think that she [our daughter] picked us to be her parents. We think David and I had to be together, and then she chose us [to be her parents]. (Patricia: Community College Teaching Master)

Thus motherhood and marriage were not merely expressions of Patricia's choice; they were proof that she had gotten things right.

Many middle-class women invoked their relationships with partners as a decisive factor in becoming a mother. Without the right relationship, becoming a mother appeared problematic. Women with partners often spoke of children as representing joint projects with a partner. Social psychology has long pointed to relationships with significant others as having a crucial relevance for establishing and validating identity (McCall and Simmons, 1978; Rosenberg, 1979; Hewitt, 1976), and for maintaining childless identities (Campbell, 1985; Veevers, 1980). Berger and Kellner (1977, p. 9), for example, maintain that modern marriage holds a "privileged status among the significant validating relationships for adults in our society." In a marriage, according to Berger and Kellner (1977, p. 9), the partners come together to redefine themselves and to build a private cosmos in which they can experience their lives as making sense.

What emerged from this study, however, was not that most couples consensually built biographies but that women often claimed or perceived the decision to have children as jointly made. Women *presented* readiness for children as mutually achieved. Loretta described how she and Peter came to reject childlessness:

> When we got married, we were definitely *not* having children. . . . . Peter was in grad school and I was working. He finished [school] . . . and I went back to school. Then we were both working while we were doing the house. We both found we were in jobs that weren't terribly satisfying, yet they were financially rewarding and could consume our [lives]. And yet we decided that the quality of life wasn't quite there. . . . It took us some time to realize that children were the next move we were ready for. (Loretta: Elementary School Teacher)

The romantic discourse of mutuality surrounding heterosexual parenthood, however, can obscure the power basis underlying motherhood that leaves women's responsibility for childcare unquestioned (Grogan, 1992, p. 496).

ACHIEVING THE "RIGHT RELATIONSHIP"

Middle-class women's notion of readiness for children corresponded to a set of material and personal achievements that were class specific. Those who wanted children typically felt they first needed to achieve success and stability in both a career and a relationship. They expected to provide, albeit jointly and partially, for their children. After all, supporting and raising children is usually thought of as a private responsibility. Having children outside class conventions about being ready could jeopardize a middle-class woman's class position and that of her children. It would also challenge middle-class notions of individual autonomy and private responsibility should a woman, by chance, find herself dependent on state support for her children.

But culturally embedding dominant images of motherhood in heterosexual marriage and private responsibility cuts women off from other women's (and societal) support for their mothering (Rich, 1980; Grogan, 1992). In one sense, therefore, the "right relationship" becomes a class and heterosexist practice that reflects both women's continued dependence on men for access to motherhood and the politics of liberal individualism that shapes the social organization of reproduction. Working-class women in this study, as we will see, were less likely to invoke occupational success, finances, or the right relationship as a precondition for having children.

Recent U.S. Census Bureau figures, however, indicate a steep increase in the number of educated and professional women who become mothers without marrying.[10] Women's *own* occupational achievement may be replacing the symbolic and practical importance of men and the right relationship in the construction of middle-class women's readiness for children.

As in other social relationships, definition and redefinition of identities within marriage involved negotiation, strategic interaction, and conflict, as well as consensus. For many of the women in this study right relationships were not found: They had to be achieved. For some, redefining themselves as mothers required that they strategically altercast partners into paternal identities that partners were reluctant to assume. Sandra explained:

We had never really settled it 'till I was in my early 30s. . . . We talked about it a lot, and he wasn't ready, and I was ready and sort of waiting. He finally just said to me, "Do you want to have a baby?" And I got pregnant at the same time. It was understood between us that I wanted to and it was up to him to decide to be ready, and that maybe he should hurry up. (Sandra: Civil Servant)

In contrast, Janette and her partner had "established" that they were not going to have children:

Sam had his children; he wasn't keen to start a new family. . . . He didn't really want to have children again. We'd established we weren't going to have children. (Janette: Manager)

However, Janette continued to feel some distance from that "joint" decision and claimed only a temporary commitment to a nonmotherhood identity:

I always figured I'd find a way [to have a child]. I figured I'd hang on 'till I was 30. . . . He definitely didn't want [to have children] with me or anybody else. And I thought "Well, . . . when I hit 30, I'll get serious.". . . Always in the back of my mind was that he might come round. (Janette: Manager)

The situation was resolved when Janette accidentally became pregnant: " . . . We went away for the weekend and I forgot my pills, and. . . ."

Twenty-three percent of women in the middle-class sample described how they achieved readiness to have children by transforming their reluctant partners' identities and negotiating their relationships into the right ones. Cindy chose a strategy of direct confrontation:

Well, I had been wanting to have a child, even before we were married. In fact, that was the thing our marriage hinged on. My husband wasn't particularly [keen]; he wasn't at all interested. We, in fact, started to not remain together before we were married. We split up over this issue because I knew I wanted to have a child so badly. Anyway, it all worked out that he. . . . We finally got back together again on the understanding we would have one child. I wanted to have a child from the moment we were married, which was 1980. But we waited for 5 years. (Cindy: Coordinator of Language Studies)

For women like Cindy, becoming a mother involved not some simple conformity to adult female role expectations but a tentative process characterized by strategic interaction and negotiation.

Alice recalled that before her previous marriage broke up,

I was not very happy. . . . My former husband . . . really wanted children [and I thought about having a child], and I thought I would *not* with that partner. I decided to leave and try again. (Alice: Graphic Designer)

When she accidentally became pregnant by the new partner with whom she had started living, Alice felt she faced the choice of becoming a single mother or having an abortion, because he did not want children:

[When I learned that I was pregnant] I felt, "Oh, shoot, now this." I also felt a little touch of aura—I felt apprehensive, excited, [and thought,] "What's Michael going to say? Oh! Oh!" But I decided I knew no matter what Michael said, I was going to *have* the baby. . . . [I wouldn't choose to be a single mother, but] if I was involved with the father, if I really cared for the father . . . I would carry through a pregnancy [even] if it were an accidental pregnancy . . . whether that meant becoming a single mother or whatever. (Alice: Graphic Designer)

The discussion between Alice and her partner led to a redefinition of the relationship as one that included the already conceived child but excluded future children.

The ability to sustain a childless relationship usually relies on acceptance, if not support, from partners (Campbell, 1985; Veevers, 1980). The commitment to childlessness, as with the commitment to motherhood, is often maintained or abandoned in the context of a relationship. Kate had decided never to have children, but her partner clearly wanted them. Despite her unhappiness with becoming pregnant, therefore, Kate did not terminate her unwanted pregnancy; but she remained ambivalent throughout.

[When I learned I was pregnant I was] unhappy. I didn't want to have a baby. I had just decided I wasn't going to, *ever*. And because it wasn't coming at a great time in terms of my career. If I could have waved a magic wand. . . . I felt like that for half the pregnancy, and I was still apprehensive through all of it. (Kate: Social Worker)

Her partner, she said, became an "incredibly involved father."

NEGOTIATING THE PATH TO MOTHERHOOD: ALTERCASTING MEN AS FATHERS

The paths to maternity followed by the middle-class women in the study sometimes involved altercasting men into fatherhood roles that they were reluctant to assume. For women, men's responses to pregnancies are often seen as a test of their commitment to the relationship (Gerson, 1985; Luker, 1975). In this study, the women whose pregnancies or desire for children cast reluctant men into parental identities risked transforming their relationships in unintended ways. Several women said, for example, that they were afraid their pregnancies would harm or destroy the relationship. Della felt that the fears she had had for her marriage when she accidentally became pregnant had been justified. She is now an alone mother:

> [When I learned that I was pregnant] my initial response was fear. I wasn't sure if the relationship was strong enough, and it wasn't. [Back then, however,] after we decided that everything would be OK . . . we were going to have this baby and everything would be fine [between us], I was ecstatic. (Della: Childcare Social Worker)

Cindy, on the other hand, remained with her partner after she, too, had successfully negotiated becoming a mother with a very reluctant partner. As we read earlier, she put the relationship itself on the bargaining table when they talked about having a child. Cindy was pregnant with her second child when I interviewed her. Her negotiations, however, may have weakened her subsequent claims to her partner's involvement in childcare, as theirs was a particularly unequal division of labor among middle-class couples.

Thus women who appear to want children much more than their partners do may find themselves strategically disadvantaged in the subsequent division of childcare work. Machung (1989) points out that popular notions about men's and women's commitment to parenthood place women in general at such a strategic disadvantage. Machung (1989) found that young men and women sustain the misconception that women typically want children more than men do. Thus women anticipate having to make career and other sacrifices for children; men do not. Describing this state of gendered pluralistic ignorance, Machung (1989, p. 49) notes that "missing from both [men and women] is the awareness that men often want families as much as women." The men and women in Machung's study differed, not in their desire to have children, but in the projections each gender made about the other's desire for children:

> Men see women as wanting children more, as having the instinctual capacity to care for them better, and therefore as having to make career sacrifices for them. . . . Women see men as not wanting children as much . . . and therefore as exempt from career sacrifices. (Machung, 1989, p. 50)

Thus, because children are perceived as wanted more by women than by men, women can be "legitimately" expected to bear more of the costs.

Kim was an exception to this pattern. Unlike Cindy, who had bargained with her relationship, Kim felt that risking her relationship was too high a price to pay for motherhood:

[Having a child] was something I would have wanted . . . and yet the relationship was such, and I valued the relationship [so much], that I wasn't prepared to trash the relationship in order to have children. (Kim: Librarian)

In spite of her partner's original reluctance, Kim's eventual pregnancy came to be defined not simply as being a joint decision but as something they *both* wanted. Having a child was presented as the product of their relationship, not as Kim's project:

We both wanted to have a baby—the eventual result of our relationship. We talked about it and thought it was something we very much wanted. [There were no reasons;] it was a fairly spontaneous decision. (Kim: Librarian)

This recognition of having an equal investment in parenthood may help explain the equal division of childcare that appeared to exist in their household.

But whereas Kim's pregnancy finally emerged as a joint project with her partner, other women's did not. Joanne, now an alone mother, had lived with a previous partner and his daughter for 8 years when she realized:

I thought, "Oh, gee, you know, not only do I like this [caring for a child] but I seem to be fairly good at it." It would be something I would definitely like to do. [Then] I knew definitely that I really enjoyed kids and I'd like to [have a child]. . . . [Then] it became clear to me that the commitment to the relationship wasn't equal any more. . . . I had made a request [that we have a child] and got no response one way or the other. . . . Tim didn't know what he wanted. I did. (Joanne: Elementary Teacher)

Things might have been different, Joanne reflected, "If I had known myself and if I had known that I would like kids. See, I didn't know [that I would want children] 'till I was near 27." Joanne's partner was unwilling to support her desire to have a child. In response, Joanne set out to effect her passage to motherhood by controlling what she saw as the determining circumstances of her life:

Partly [that is why I changed my job]. I got out of [acting] because I thought you can't have a family situation unless you have a regular job. I wasn't ever going to meet anybody [in theatre life]. I thought, "Nothing is going to happen here under these circumstances." In fact, that's basically what happened. I changed my life and I have met all my goals . . . by accident in a way. . . . I got it backwards, but it sort of *happened*. (Joanne: Elementary School Teacher)

Joanne perceived that she was ready for children. Although she lacked a permanent male partner, Joanne acted to control other contingencies of her maternal transformation. When she was "around 27," she decided that "if I did get pregnant accidentally, I would accept it and do whatever I needed to do in order to have a child." When, as a single woman, she unintentionally became pregnant, her interpretation of her relationship with the father as being, if not the right relationship, at least a right enough relationship, allowed her to sustain her identity transformation:

I chose not to terminate the pregnancy, which I suppose is a choice. . . . The fact that his father is the man that he is made a lot of difference because I knew him [the father] quite well, and I also knew he would be very supportive. I also knew that he would enjoy the child as well, so . . . that had a lot to do with it. He did provide me with a lot of security—emotional security. It turned out he helped me financially as well. . . . I'm sure if it had been somebody I didn't know, I may have rethought again. . . . It happened at a particular point in my life, too—when I was ready, and I knew I could cope, and I knew I was grown up enough. (Joanne: Elementary School Teacher)

In contrast, women who have an early commitment to maternal identities can try to avoid the contingencies of negotiating parenthood by making a potential partner's desire to have children a precondition not just to marriage but to a serious relationship. Laura put it like this:

I had made up my mind [to have children] a long time ago. . . . I discussed it with him [my partner] before we even got married;

before we even became serious. I wanted to be sure he wanted children, because it was very important to me. If he didn't, then let's not get serious. (Laura: Accountant)

However, such strategies are not always applicable. As we have seen, many women wished to present the decision to have children as a *joint* product of a relationship with a partner, not as a precondition of that relationship. In other cases, women presented their decision to have children as a private one but one that required them to renegotiate their partners' identities. Finally, women who could not find or construct what they defined as the right relationship found themselves doubly at risk. They faced the option of remaining not just partnerless but childless. It is not surprising, therefore, that women invested so much "relationship work" in their romantic attachments and in finding the right relationship.[11] They had a great deal at stake.

TIME FOR PARENTHOOD: CLASS AND GENDER

How is it that the middle-class women so often presented themselves as responsible for organizing their own and their partners' transition to parenthood? Barbara Ehrenreich (1983) suggests that modern men are revolting against the emotional and financial burdens of raising a family—as "fleeing commitment." Hareven's (1977) historical framework provides an alternative explanation. Hareven argues that men's and women's "family clocks" are no longer synchronized. Family time, she explains, has become dominated by industrial time: Occupational roles for men and women have come into conflict with family in ways not experienced in the past. Hareven's analysis, then, suggests that the apparent reluctance of middle-class men described in this chapter may have as much to do with the different cultural time frames within which men and women operate as with flight from commitment.

Similarly, Maines and Hardesty's (1987) research on young adults' career and family plans supports the notion of gendered temporality and its effect on women's decision making around motherhood. Men's anticipations of their futures, they found, reveal an image of temporally linear life in which their multiple roles in education, work, and family are seen as sequentially organized and nonproblematically related. Once the young men in their study had decided what they wanted in life, Maines and Hardesty (1987, p. 117) observed, they developed an almost taken-for-granted set of assumptions as to how they would realize their goals. The futures anticipated by the women in the study, on the other hand, were characterized by temporal discontinuities, contingencies, and a recognition that they had only partial control over their futures. The women envisioned the relationship between work and family in their lives as potentially difficult, and their thinking about the future was characterized by *how* questions. The consequences of these gendered temporal anticipations were far reaching in that the women, but *not* the men, made career decisions and plans based on the recognition of the potentially difficult relationship between work and family. Linearity is thus a masculine form of cultural engagement:

> The support systems, career symbols, and vocabularies of motives that are present in our culture contribute to linear futures for men. The "whats" and "hows" of their futures are provided for them. Linearity for women, however, is a form of *cultural disengagement*, because in order to be fully linear, they typically must sacrifice all or part of family participation. (Maines and Hardesty, 1987, p. 115)

Since women are believed to have a greater commitment to having children (Machung, 1989), they are expected to handle the problems associated with "their choices." Balancing work and family come to be seen as women's issues, not men's. And women face the problem of synchronizing their own and prospective partners' biographies. They must accomplish this task within a context in which men's lives are socially organized in ways that deny the reality of the competing commitments between work and family that have become structurally endemic to the temporal organization of women's lives. Men's commitment to the labor force is popularly perceived as an uncomplicated, progressive, and continuous attachment (Maines and Hardesty, 1987). Such easy attachments, however, are predicated on having support systems (such as wives) that allow men to concentrate on their work (Machung, 1989, p. 53). Becoming a parent, therefore, is quite different for men and women.

THE JOINTNESS OF PARENTHOOD

The middle-class women in this study often talked about the decision to have children as having been a joint one. The belief in the jointness of parenting, however, obscures the inequalities hidden in such "family myths" (Hochschild, 1989). No doubt many of the men talked about in this study were committed to becoming fathers. But the implications of a commitment to parenthood are quite different for men and women. The dominant ideological construction of motherhood casts women in the role of primary caretaker and characterizes fathers' participation as desirable, laudable, but optional (Grogan, 1992; La Rossa, 1988). Constructing parenthood as a joint project is one way in which women with demanding occupations can attempt to implicate men in the work of parenting—albeit not always successfully.

But the discourses of jointness and "couples becoming pregnant" can hide the unequal contribution of male and female bodies in reproduction. Having a child is constructed as an act of will, desire, or individual choice, rather than of women's bodies and labor. Marilyn recalled:

When I became pregnant I became aware in a much more concrete way of what the limitations were . . . and how being a mother was different from being anything else. . . . I had a very idealistic notion that being a parent would be a totally collective activity with my husband and myself. It immediately became apparent to me that *I* was the one who was pregnant. . . . The first part of my pregnancy wasn't very easy. I felt the inequality of the situation there, and I felt it was just going to get worse. (Marilyn: Literacy Coordinator)

Legal and medical definitions that conceptualize parenthood primarily as a genetic tie rather than a nurturing, physical, and social relationship, Rothman (1989) argues, have damaging consequences for women. In everyday life, however, parents construct their own claims to children. By presenting pregnancies as joint, for example, couples produce men's symbolic participation in pregnancy. Parental claiming rests, therefore, not simply on genetic ties but on an emotional commitment in which men and women can *appear* to be equally involved but remain *unequally* implicated in the practical and caring labor. Indeed, male identification with specifically female body experiences, whether of menstruation, pregnancy, or childbirth, as Douglas (1975) points out, is part of the cultural politics of (hetero)sexuality. In societies where men have little economic power over women, Douglas (1975, p. 65) observes, such identification provides men with the *symbolic* means with which to claim a relationship with a particular woman and her child. Couvade, for example, as Douglas explains, typically occurs where there is a weak definition of marriage and a strong interest on the husband's part in claiming a woman's child as his own. Douglas points to the parallel between modern men's attendance at births and tribal men's couvading. Both are forms of parental claiming: "The couvading husband is saying, 'Look at me, having cramps and contractions even more than she! Doesn't this prove I am the father of her child?'" (Douglas, 1975, p. 65).

In a society, therefore, where patriarchal fatherhood claims are contested, "jointness" ideologically grounds men's parental rights in *love* but *not in labor*. Although women may welcome involved fathers, the goal of gender equity and the quality of men's fathering may be better served if, as Rothman (1989) suggests, men's parental claims were also grounded in the practical work of nurturance and daily caring: love *and* labor.

WOMEN AS EMBODIED SOCIAL ACTORS: MOTHERHOOD, NATURE, AND TIME

Women's talk of chronological age or biological clocks should not be taken to mean that time or biology determines behavior—that the biological clock somehow "gets to women in the end." Talk of time implies that women take time into their reckoning in locating themselves in a social order, an order that itself rests on cultural engagements of temporality and nature. Although theories of adult development conceptualize life as a staged order of events, there is often a tenuous relationship between women's lives and their chronological age (Fisher, 1989, p. 143). Within outer limits, a dominant social clock, rather than a biological clock, organizes peoples' lives. The cultural association of life events with chronological age, however, makes our life patterns appear grounded in nature—and thus inevitable.

The women I interviewed were aged between 16 and 39 years when they gave birth to their first children. Although these women's fertility spans a period of nearly 35 years, the (different) culturally appropriate periods for childbearing are more limited. Culture mediates age. On the one hand, popular imagery may represent teenaged women as *too young* for motherhood. On the other hand, the medical literature often constructs many women as *too old* for childbearing—as

"problems" to be managed through sophisticated technology (Berryman, 1991). And although biological parents in their late 30s and early
40s have children, such couples would likely be rejected as *too old* to
become adoptive parents.[12]

Whether they reject, modify, or accept it, in their everyday lives
women confront a dominant social clock with its normative sense of
age-appropriate behavior. The dominant social clock carries hidden
gender and class interests in its notions of the right time (Fisher, 1989;
Berryman, 1991). The social messages women internalize about time
and their personal development often reflect patriarchal relations, as
in, for example, the way in which having a baby has been constructed
as the precondition for female maturity (Baber and Allen, 1992, p.
144).

On the surface the "biological clock" to which the middle-class
women referred appears linear and inevitable. But, as Fisher (1989, p.
144) points out, and as was supported in this study, it is usually women's
life circumstances—their class, marital status, and relational commitments, rather than chronological age—that are central to their major
life transitions and decisions.

Yet, although culturally mediated, the "biological clock" pointed
to a determinacy of nature in women's lives: the possibility of
permanent childlessness and a time of "no choice." Are women bound
by nature in ways men are not? Though male fertility declines with
age, men can father children even into old age. But to cast fathering
this way is to invoke a patriarchal construction that implies fatherhood
is primarily a genetic relationship. In contrast, if we see fathering as a
long-term social relationship of nurturance, responsibility, and practical care (Rothman, 1989), then men, too, face temporal limitations on
fatherhood. Culture shapes the meanings of biology. In practice, most
men are like women in that they become parents within a socially
appropriate period in their lives. About 7% of men have children when
they are 45 or over (Berryman, 1991, p. 104).

Yet only women become pregnant and give birth. Although the
meanings of these biological capacities are not simply given but
emerge from their cultural engagements and thus vary, do women's
bodies provide an opportunity for a gendered experience of nature
and time? For is it not women, rather than men, who, at a certain age,
face the prospect of losing access to both the symbolic and the
concrete social experiences available to those in a society who become
pregnant and give birth?[13] Even if we acknowledge the temporal
limitations to social fatherhood, the loss of the potential for biological

parenthood happens differently for men and women and may carry quite different implications.

For some women, the social and personal meanings they ascribe to the physical experience of pregnancy and birth are central to becoming a mother. And the absence of such an experience in life may signify a great loss. For others, the physical experience may be the unwelcome (even revolting) cost of motherhood (Rothman, 1989, p. 76). The contemporary social devaluation of pregnancy and women's physical and emotional contribution to the generation of a child, Rothman argues, is part of a patriarchal cultural devaluation of the body. Pregnancy itself, Rothman adds, should be understood as being a social relationship, not merely the prelude to a relationship. However conceptualized, both the capacity for pregnancy and giving birth and the relatively nonnegotiable time limits on these capacities suggest that men and women engage time and nature differently through the resources offered by their own bodies.[14] And such cultural engagements of time and nature, I suggest, were embedded in participants' accounts of having children and in their reflections on time.

"I WANTED CONTINUITY": MOTHERHOOD AND TIME

On the one hand, reference to the biological clock may help explain why some women in this study, especially those who always wanted children, became pregnant when they did. On the other, it might imply that neither the other women's earlier commitments to permanent childlessness nor their later coming to have children was authentic. It may imply that "nature" triumphed in the end. But for whom would such an interpretation be persuasive?

Our beliefs about nature are themselves products of social relationships (Douglas, 1975; Evernden, 1992). Not only tribal but also modern societies use dominant views of nature as mechanisms of social control. Nature, Douglas (1972, p. 137) explains, is seen to respond morally: "It is on the side of the constitution, motherhood, brotherly love, and it is against human wickedness." Thus we may invoke nature to explain what *must not be questioned*. Indeed, debates about nature are often implicitly debates about law and order—social law and order (Douglas, 1975, p. 6). Not surprisingly, representations of nature, motherhood, and women's bodies often reflect hidden gender, class, and race relationships (Merchant, 1980; Shiva, 1989).

In practice most cultures, especially modern ones, engage in massive transformations of nature. Nature is put to social use. But social engagements of nature transform *both* the natural and the social, making them in many senses inseperable. Thus to question the notions of time and nature embedded in representations of motherhood is also to question the broader social order.

Feminist philosophers point to how particular notions of time have been central to the historical tension between nature and culture in dominant Western thought (Forman, 1989a; O'Brien, 1981). Father Time, as a reminder of death and an orientation toward futurity, has been a crucial component of time consciousness—a masculinist time consciousness (Forman, 1989a, p. 6). Men, it is argued, have sought to transcend time through immortalizing deeds (Kahn, 1989, p. 20) or have striven for "authentic" existence through the awareness of death (Forman, 1989a, p. 6).

But why is death rather than birth so often taken as the ultimate orientating life event in Western culture? (Forman, 1989a, p. 7). Is it because reproduction is seen merely as an act of nature—physical birth from below rather than a spiritual or cultural birth from above (Kahn, 1989)? The former is dependant on women, the latter on a male God or (male) gatekeepers of cultural institutions.[15]

Rather than understanding women's experiences of time and nature as simply given through biology, therefore, we can see how the biological possibility of giving birth provides women with symbolic resources with which to challenge dominant linear and patriarchal representations of time. Birth, not just death, can locate the self in time and social space. Jenny, the mother of an infant girl, reflected on motherhood and its implications for the meanings of time, life, and death:

It's like knowing death, to never have a child—to experience your own death as you are living. It's not so much that *I'm* going on with her, it's just that *everybody* is going on. That life goes on. And that's important for some strange reason. I don't know why, but it is. . . . That's probably it, you know, knowledge of your own death. (Jenny: Executive Secretary)

Women's physical and emotional labor in building and sustaining the social world is often unrecognized or devalued. Yet for Jenny, it was part of the reason for pregnancy and birth:

[I had a child for] the fulfillment of the relationship with my husband. I think, as well, [for] recreating a relationship I had with my mother and my sister. . . . We talked for years. . . . You wonder what all this communication [will produce], you wonder what the result could possibly be. (Jenny: Executive Secretary)

Birth, or rather the meanings we attribute to the birth of a child, offers cultural and personal resources with which both men and women can respond to life crises. Twenty-nine percent of middle-class women located their pregnancies with their first child at a time of personal crisis or upheaval—half of these mentioned a death or impending death in the family. Penny recalled the timing of her first child, Pete, who was born when she was 32:

In my own life not a lot was happening. But my husband's father had died, my husband's sister died . . . when I was 31, so it was very important for him, you know, when there is death in the family you want to replace. . . . [For me] I just wanted to. I thought it would be a great adventure, and I was curious. . . . I think having a child is a really life-affirming sort of thing. It's not exactly a religious reason, but it would be if I were a practicing Christian or a practicing Jew. . . . If you really love life and you're able, you probably want to see it perpetuated in some form. (Penny: Managing Editor)

Historically in the West, a cyclical pattern of time modeled on the unity of life and death, of past and future, of growth and decline, has been replaced by "progressive time": time of endless growth, time made to yield profit (Rossetti, in Forman, 1989b, p. 186). The modern notion of career, for example, expresses a location of self in time that is both linear and progressive. Linear time is the dominant time in industrial societies, for both men and women. But pregnancy, birth, and an organization of time around the relationship with an infant, according to Kahn (1989, p. 22), makes a more organic social experience of time possible for women in industrial society. The meaning of time for participants in this study, I argue, was not simply given by biology or by nature but emerged through reflection on time and female biological resources.

Thus, in referring to the biological clock, women in this study were reflecting on the meaning of time, engaging its implications for their experience in the world as embodied social actors. The biological clock refers, not to a determinacy of nature or a coercion of linear time, but to a reminder of the opportunity to locate oneself differently in time through relationship, continuity, and connectedness that the possibility of giving birth symbolically offers. Many of the women talked about wanting to experience the connectedness of a relationship with their own child, but few were as articulate as Anna:

> [I wanted a child because] I wanted there to be someone very important in my life. . . . I really wanted *continuity*. It just came to me when I was . . . 36 or 37. I started to feel, "Why am I, what's the *purpose* of my life? Why am I here?" And I had done everything I had wanted to do and felt when I looked into the future it was more of the same. . . . I wanted continuity, roots, and shared experiences. (Anna: Community College Teaching Master)

Thus for Anna, who was once committed to childlessness, the symbolic meanings attached to the capacity to give birth to a child provided a way of relocating herself in the world.

INTEGRATING CHILDLESS
AND MATERNAL IDENTITIES

How did women who had once rejected motherhood later claim it as so central to who they were? Many, as we have seen, presented motherhood as an issue of readiness and maturity. Others disassociated themselves from past childlessness in ways that integrated past and present and thus constructed themselves as responsible and stable rather than as fickle or erratic. For example, Laura had come to interpret her earlier decision never to have children as "a cold one"; one not made by "me as a person." Motherhood, on the other hand, "turned out to be the thing that I had wanted." Other women explained their earlier rejection of motherhood by saying they would not have made good parents back then. Women often felt they had changed in ways that made children seem appropriate and desirable:

> It took us a long time to realize that children were the next move we were ready for. . . . Before I got married and for the first, I'd say, 5 years of our marriage, we were definitely not going to have children. . . . It took a long time to see myself as a feminist and a mother. So that I had to sort all that out for myself before I

could make a commitment to motherhood, because I knew I couldn't be a traditional mother. (Loretta: Elementary School Teacher)

Alternatively, a woman could come to terms with her earlier rejection of motherhood by realising that the motherhood she had rejected was not the only type of motherhood:

I had thought a mother had to be certain things. . . . One of them was that a mother had to be unhappy—my impression of a mother was that she was self-sacrificing and she was unhappy. And I discovered it does not have to be the case. . . . I thought I would have to become self-sacrificing and unhappy. . . . I found I didn't have to change myself. . . . I learned and I grew and the changes did happen, but I didn't have to force myself into any kind of mold. (Beth: Management Board Officer)

Becoming a mother provided an integrative biographical narrative in which change in a woman's life seemed to make sense.

BEING READY: ACHIEVEMENT
AND MIDDLE-CLASS MOTHERHOOD

Value, economists remind us, is established not simply by personal preference but also by scarcity. Highly valued social positions and commodities are generally those to which there is restricted access.[16] Unlike entry into high-status occupations, recruitment to motherhood is not formally regulated. The informal regulation of motherhood has also changed. A woman who can conceive can become a mother. Unmarried women now usually keep their babies. Some women, especially young, disadvantaged, or disabled women, may be discouraged from claiming motherhood, but access cannot be fully denied.

Easy access, however, can threaten a role's social worth. One response to a potential "debasement" of motherhood is to establish a notion of valid and invalid claims: fit and less fit mothers. In practice, the social rhetoric surrounding valid claims to motherhood, as A. Davis (1993), Griffin (1992), and Phoenix (1991b) point out, often carries class, heterosexist, or race priorities.

As we have seen middle-class women in this study presented

readiness for motherhood as an achievement. Women can become
mothers before they are "ready," but this situation was presented as
inappropriate, as was having a child for the wrong motives:

> [It's not right to have] . . . kids to keep you company, or to fill
> your life; to fill some kind of a void, or to make your marriage
> work, or something like that. I mean I think those are just the
> wrong reasons. So I think having kids for the wrong reasons is a
> poor parenting strategy. (Nina: Director, Nonprofit Organization)

Some women talked about some women being "too needy" or
"not having their own needs met" as leading to inadequate motherhood. Readiness for motherhood among many middle-class women
implied a claim to some degree of psychological and emotional
self-sufficiency.

Being a woman in itself did not represent adequate grounds for
becoming a mother. Rather, *achieved* social maturity was presented as
a precondition for motherhood among middle-class women. That is,
they had to be not just "grown up" but *appropriately* "grown up" before
they were ready to have children. Appropriate adulthood, however,
carried class imagery. Readiness implied accomplishments in career,
finances, relationships and emotional life. Middle-class women's biographical accounts had a self-evolutionary, developmental character.
They came to be the sorts of persons who could properly have
children. Their adult achievements were preconditions of readiness,
though not necessarily the source of their motivation.

Ironically, achievement is traditionally associated with a masculine model of adulthood. Similarly, achievement carries class imagery: middle-class, more than working-class, persons are expected
to achieve, whether educationally or occupationally. Not unexpectedly, few working-class women in this study associated achievement
and motherhood (see Chapter 4). In this sense, a class-based and
somewhat masculinist notion of adulthood, rather than a primarily
or exclusively female gender identity, constructed the preconditions
from which middle-class women felt they could legitimately become mothers. Unlike the childless women studied by Veevers
(1980), career-invested women in this study did not construct their
lives in terms of permanent dichotomous options, a choice of *either*
career *or* motherhood. Rather, they constructed their biographies
so that potentially incompatible ways of being in the world were
sequentially organized. For many, however, this organization of

biography was experienced not merely as an organization of linear time or a postponement of childbearing, as is commonly thought. Instead, it was experienced in terms of the development of self: becoming the sort of person who could properly have children and/or rejecting the cultural implications of remaining permanently childless.

SUMMARY

This chapter looked at *how*, not *why*, the middle-class women interviewed became mothers. The data show that it is too simplistic to see their transition to maternity either as conformity to gender-role expectations or as the outcome of individual choice.

Middle-class women often found it difficult to give reasons for wanting children. Many of the meanings of motherhood are implicit and become visible only in their counterimage. Aging, for example, confronted some women with the possibility of childlessness. Motherhood, I have argued here, is not simply about having children; it is about engaging identities and their attendant cultural meanings, mother and nonmother.

References to a biological clock were common. However, the data showed that what looked like a question of *when* to have children was often a question of *whether* to have them. Time did more than urge procrastinating or ambivalent women to make up their minds: It presented them with the possibility of a new and irrevocable identity—that of being permanently childless.

The middle-class women's accounts of their pregnancies had a self-evolutionary aspect. The "right time" was frequently presented in terms of maturational, social, and economic *achievements*. These women typically presented themselves as psychologically and financially ready and as having achieved readiness in terms of their occupational careers and relationships with partners. Talk of the jointness in becoming a parent, or of couples becoming pregnant, however, disguised the very different and unequal contributions of men and women in the love and labor of having children.

Ironically, being a *woman* in itself did not represent adequate grounds for claiming motherhood. Even for those who had always wanted children, becoming a mother had the character of a personal accomplishment. Women's adult achievements were seen as preconditions for readiness for children. That is, middle-class women had to *become* the sort of persons who could properly have children.

The accounts of these women put into question not only the sociological explanations of motherhood in terms of gender role conformity but also the political representation of motherhood as individual choice. I argue that the capacity of these women to give birth presented them with resources for cultural engagements of time, nature, and social connectedness. That is, women engaged their worlds as *embodied* social actors, and their references to time and talk about having children expressed this engagement.

4

Paths to Motherhood: Working-Class Women

In Chapter 3 we looked at how middle-class women came to be mothers. In this chapter we look at working-class women's paths to motherhood. Initially the most striking contrast between the two groups was the difference between the average age at which the women first gave birth (see Table 3.1). The differences in their experiences, however, ran far deeper than this aspect. We will see that time conceptions, positive conceptions of motherhood, the expression and claiming of adult identities, expectations of maternity generated by family and friends, and class-structured life options were all linked to how and when working-class women became mothers. As with the middle-class women, becoming a mother had to do with issues of adulthood. However, the meanings of adult identities and the relationship between motherhood and adulthood varied by class. Whereas middle-class women indicated they felt they had to achieve maturity *before* having a child, working-class women's accounts suggest that many of them saw themselves as achieving maturity *through* having a child.

The average age at which the working-class women in this study first became mothers was 22.1 years (see Table 3.1). Within this sample, currently alone mothers were slightly younger at the birth of their first child; their average age was 21.1.

ALONE MOTHERS: THE INTERACTION
OF CLASS AND GENDER

It is important not to categorize either unwed or alone motherhood as an essentially different or deviant form of parenting (Eichler, 1983). Rather, alone parenting often represents a temporary, but widely shared, experience or phase in women's maternal careers.[1] In recruiting women to the study I originally intended to have equal representation of middle- and working-class alone mothers to allow comparison. Alone mothers made up 25% of the total sample. However, I found it much easier to locate working-class alone mothers of preschool children than middle-class mothers. There was the danger that if the sample of working-class mothers contained a higher proportion of alone mothers than did the middle-class sample, it would limit comparison. I had intended to select the sample purposively to increase the proportion of alone middle-class mothers until I realized that the pattern of my sample reflected typical class differences in women's experience of motherhood. The experience of being an alone mother depends on *how* and *when* a woman becomes an alone parent (Moore, 1989). Women become alone mothers through separation, out-of-wedlock births, and widowhood. Separation is the most common antecedent to becoming an alone parent in Canada; for Canadian women separation typically happens at an average age of 31.6 years (Moore, 1989, p. 347). Out-of-wedlock births, on the other hand, tend to occur to *younger* women (average age of 20.6 years), the second most common way to become an alone mother.

Age at first birth, however, is itself associated with social class. All young women face pressures to conform to the social expectations of heterosexuality, marriage, and motherhood. However, as Griffin (1992, p. 493) points out, such expectations are experienced and negotiated in racialized and class-specific contexts that police young women's transition to adulthood. Thus becoming a *young* alone mother is typically a working-class, not middle-class experience.

Not only does becoming an alone mother tend to have different *antecedents* for women of different social classes, but, given women's different educational and income-earning resources and the lack of social support in raising children, it also has different *consequences*. Middle-class women do not typically give birth in their teens or early 20s, when they have little postsecondary education and limited work experience, and they do not typically become welfare mothers, as did most of the alone working-class women in this study.

Thus women's experience of motherhood is compared *by social class*, not by whether women were alone or partnered. The latter research focus would have required a different research design and sample selection. I chose, therefore, to explore how class and gender interacted in women's lives to shape their maternal career paths. In consequence, the comparisons that can be made by marital status between the two sample groups are limited.

"I ALWAYS WANTED TO BE A MOTHER"

Working-class women in this study were more likely than middle-class women to say they had "always wanted" or assumed they would have children (Table 4.1).

TABLE 4.1. Percentage of Women Who "Always Wanted" to Have Children

	Middle-class women	Working-class women
Always wanted/assumed would have children	45%	79%[a]
Once thought would choose to remain childless	48%	21%
Others	7%	0%

Note. N = 59. Table built from responses to directed questions on issue.
[a]Fourteen percent of these women gave birth by age 17.

TABLE 4.2. Planned Pregnancies of First Children

	Planned pregnancies
Middle-class women (all)	71%
Working-class women (all)	46%
Middle-class women currently with partners	74%
Working-class women currently with partners	70%
Currently alone middle-class women	50%
Currently alone working-class women	9%

Note. N = 59.

But the working-class women were less likely to describe their first children as having been planned: Only 46% did so (Table 4.2). The difference was associated with the interaction of marital status and social class (Table 4.2).[2] Currently alone mothers were less likely than those currently with partners to say their pregnancies had been planned, even if they had been living in a permanent relationship at the time of conception (Table 4.2). Only one alone working-class mother said her pregnancy was planned; 70% of working-class mothers with partners said their first child was planned.

MOTIVES FOR MOTHERHOOD AMONG WORKING-CLASS WOMEN

Like middle-class women, the working-class mothers also found it difficult to give reasons for wanting children. Wanting children did not seem to need accounting for. Working-class women often prefaced their replies with, "I don't know"; or, "No reason really, I just wanted a child"; or, "Why not?"

The most common given accounts for wanting children among those who planned their pregnancies were: just wanting a baby or wanting to get pregnant (46%); feeling ready (46%); the desire to establish a family (38%); feeling that their partners really wanted a child (31%); wanting to share something with, or wanting a closer relationship with, a partner (31%).

Again, if we look at *how*, not *why*, these women came to have children, the pattern is clearer. Motherhood was more taken for granted among working-class women: The issue of children was *when*, rather than whether. Fewer said they had once wanted to never have children, and those who did were more tentative about it and held the idea of childlessness for less time than did middle-class women. Judy, a mother of two, recalled her brief commitment to nonmotherhood:

Yes [I once thought I would never have children]. In 1977 I thought I was not going to get married and *not* going to have children. That was a fabulous year. . . . I had quit school under financial pressure from my stepfather. . . . [Later] I went back to high school and was the first girl to [take traditionally male shop subjects]. . . . I broke *all the barriers* . . . and thought I could do anything. . . . [It was a] crazy year. [That year] I was my real self. Next year I started work. (Judy: Apprentice Woodworker)

In spite of describing herself as having been ambivalent about having children and not wanting them when she married at 21, Judy also "knew" that she would have children:

> [I started thinking about having children] when I was about 21. I was just married. Shortly before we got married we decided we were going to have two children. [He had wanted a large family.] It seemed like a good idea [but] I was kind of neutral about it. I didn't want children, but I was a bit [ambivalent]. . . . *He* always wanted children. . . . He didn't want to wait too much longer because he is older than I am. It was more his age that we done it. We both knew we were going to have children. (Judy: Apprentice Woodworker)

Lisa also found it difficult to maintain an adult identity of nonmother.

> Oh, yeah [I didn't always want children]. When you see other [people's] kids and you see how bratty they are and how much they drive you up the wall! I thought, "No, I don't want any of this.". . . At first I thought, "No, I don't want any [children]," but then, like, it just goes away and you think, "I'm just being *silly*. Eventually I probably will have one or two.". . . [Then it became that] I said I wanted children. Eventually you *do* want children. (Lisa: Data Entry Clerk)

In contrast to the reluctant fathers portrayed by middle-class women, 31% of working-class women who planned their pregnancies, as against 10% of middle-class women, indicated that at the time it was more their partners' desire to have children than their own that was decisive in their pregnancies. Karen, who married at 19, described how she came to get pregnant:

> Well, I just got married, and children to us are very important to have. . . . But to tell you the truth, I really didn't think about it. . . . It was mostly [that] he wanted a child. Well, me too, but he was more [keen]. (Karen: Dry Cleaner's Shipping Clerk)

TIME CONCEPTIONS AND PREGNANCIES
AMONG WORKING-CLASS WOMEN

As we have seen, time conceptions were central to middle-class women's accounts of their pregnancies. References to time were less important in working-class women's pregnancy accounts, and the data suggest that time conceptions were differentiated by class (Table 4.3).

Class differences, however, were smaller among those with planned pregnancies (Table 4.4).

If we look more closely at how women spoke about time, however, we see that working- and middle-class women's conceptions of life stages and of biographical time were different. Fewer working-class talked about chronological age or biological time than did middle-class women. Of those who did, the middle-class women talked about not wanting to find themselves *too old* to have children, but working-class women were more likely to describe themselves as wanting to be *young* with their children.

TABLE 4.3. References to Time in Accounts of Pregnancies with First Child

	Middle-class women	Working-class women
Mentioned either chronological/biological or biographical time (positively or negatively)	71%[a]	39%[b]
Mentioned chronological/biological time	39%	16%[c]
Mentioned biographical time	45%[a]	25%

Note. N = 59.
[a]Fourteen percent of these women mentioned time negatively (e.g., not being ready).
[b]Eighteen percent of these women mentioned time negatively (e.g., being too young).
[c]Forty percent of these women said they were too young.

TABLE 4.4. References to Time among Those Who Planned the Birth of Their First Child

	Middle-class women	Working-class women
Mentioned either chronological/biological or biographical time	82%	61%
Mentioned chronological/biological time	50%	23%
Mentioned biographical time	64%	46%

Note. N = 35 planned pregnancies.

Working-class women mentioned few advantages to deferring childbearing; many saw childbearing associated positively with being young. Ramona decided to become pregnant at 21:

> Well, you know, you always dream about having children and what not. I think [we decided] about a year after we were married. . . . [We wanted] to start our family when we were young, so we could, you know, kinda all grow up together, kinda thing. . . . [We had waited] because we wanted to give ourselves at least a year to get to know each other living together. (Ramona: Bookkeeping Clerk)

Pam, who had the first of her two children at 24 recalled:

> I don't know [what our reasons for wanting children were]. My husband and I just didn't want to be too old when we had our children. [We wanted it to be] so we were young with our children. . . . I didn't want to be too old—I'm pushing 30 now. (Pam: Clerical Worker)

Kathy, an alone mother, had not intended to conceive at 18; she was single when she became pregnant. Later, when interviewed, she said she was glad she became pregnant when she was young:

> I hadn't yet [begun to think about actually having a child]. I always said I'd wait 'till I was 26, and by then I probably wouldn't want one. So I'm glad I was sort of unaware. I was thrilled to death when I found out. . . . I was [also] scared to death. I didn't know anything about babies. . . . As soon as I found out I was pregnant, I ran out and got a whole bunch of books. (Kathy: Accounting Clerk)

For the middle-class women, deferring pregnancy meant waiting until one was in one's 30s; for working-class women, deferring motherhood until they were 30 seemed unthinkable. Marg's husband had wanted to postpone children, but she made it clear that waiting until she was 30 was not an option:

> You've always wanted to have kids, and it's like, "I don't want to be 30 when I'm having my first baby," you know. . . . Well, he [my husband] is a year younger than me, and he thought, "I don't

want to have kids 'till I'm 30." And I thought, "There's *no way* I'm going to wait 'till you are 30, because I will be 31." (Marg: Accounting Clerk)

BEING TOO YOUNG FOR MOTHERHOOD: CONFLICTING IDEAS

It seems plausible that the reason fewer working-class women referred to age or biological time was that their youthfulness removed them from the impending prospect of being physically incapable of having children. However, few suggested they felt themselves as having been too young for motherhood. As Phoenix (1991a, p. 93) points out, although young mothers may recognize the social stigma attached to teen motherhood, for example, they do not necessarily consider that stigma as appropriate to themselves. Forty-six percent of working-class mothers in this sample became pregnant in their teens or had given birth by the age of 20 (Table 4.5).

Only two working-class women felt they had been too young when they had children. Tina, who gave birth when she was 16, said that was younger than she would have chosen; she had expected she would have been 20 before she became a mother. On the other hand, another young woman explained: "I had been putting off [having a child] since I was 16. . . . [By 19,] I didn't want to wait anymore."

Delayed childbearing is often associated with more positive

TABLE 4.5. Age at Conception of First Child

	Middle-class women	Working-class women
Women who conceived by age 19	0%	46%
Women who conceived by age 24	16%	75%
Women who conceived by age 29	39%	100%
Women who conceived by age 34	84%	100%
Women who conceived by age 39	100%	100%

Note. N = 59. Age at conception was estimated as 1 year younger than age at birth of child.

outcomes for women, in terms of income, education, career, and psychological profiles (Baber and Allen, 1992, p. 112). However, as argued in Chapter 2, the relationship may not hold in reverse: Early childbearing does not cause poverty. In the United States, Canada, and the United Kingdom, it seems, women who become mothers in their teens come predominantly from groups of women who are already economically, educationally, and employment disadvantaged (Grindstaff, 1988; Moore, 1987, 1989; Phoenix, 1991b). This was also the case in this study.

Recent research challenges the view that early childbearing necessarily has a negative effect on women's lives, especially the lives of those who are already severely disadvantaged (Furstenberg, 1992; Geronimus, 1992; Phoenix, 1991b). The disadvantaged social characteristics of early childbearers are often treated as though they are a *consequence* of early childbearing, when, in fact, they *precede* it. Early childbearing may be partly a response to, rather than a "cause of," many young women's social and economic disadvantage. Teens whose future is bleak, argues Zimmerman (1992, p. 427), may drift into parenthood before they are ready. In the United States, Lopata (1993b) argues, lack of education (e.g., rather than race) explains lack of career commitment in young women. Thus, even where women may not have a strong early commitment to motherhood, as was true of at least some of the young working-class women in this study who had had accidental pregnancies, the consequences of childbearing *come* to determine other interests and activities. Where there is little societal support for raising children, early childbearing makes a young woman *unavailable* for other commitments and involvements, such as education and career (Lopata, 1993b, p. 258). Therefore, in a societal context of structural gender (class and race) inequalities, early childbearing can "cost" young women, in the sense of limiting the options and resources with which they can *resist* the social patterns of disadvantage in their lives.

If early childbearing cannot be called the cause of poverty, neither can poverty be said to cause early childbearing. Most disadvantaged or working-class young women do not become adolescent mothers. Rather, Phoenix (1991a, p. 90) explains, poverty, unemployment, or disadvantage can be seen as the *context* for adolescent motherhood, not its cause. As we will see, the "choice" of motherhood for several of the young women in this study was less of a choice than a reflection of their (lack of) investment in avoiding or deferring early childbearing.

"BEING READY": DEFINITIONS OF THE SITUATION
AS CLASS CONSTRUCTS

In this study, working-class women were less likely than middle-class women to invoke the concept of "being ready" or the "right time" to explain their first child (Table 4.3). But among the minority who described their pregnancy as planned, almost half (46%) mentioned such biographical time conceptions.

However, "being ready" and the "right time" were different for working- and middle-class women. Middle-class women presented readiness in self-evolutionary or personal development terms. Readiness included specific material and psychological components and was seen as a personal achievement. Among working-class women, "being ready" referred, on one hand, to a readiness to *take on responsibilities*. On the other hand, it referred to fewer expectations about improved material conditions and control over life.

The social definition of *readiness* was shaped by class expectations. The working-class women seldom talked about having established themselves at work, about home ownership, or about home renovations (although home ownership was desirable) as preconditions to parenthood. Marg's definition of reality focused on what she did control, not on what she did not. She presented her desire to have a baby as taking precedence over the material aspects of life:

> I was ready. I was at that age, I was responsible enough to . . . bring up a baby. Our relationship was good and solid. I've always wanted one; I just couldn't wait to have one. . . . We had a bit of money in the bank but no house. . . . [My husband] wanted to have a house, [but] houses are so expensive. . . . He didn't really want to bring up a baby in an apartment . . . [but] I didn't ever thought we'd move into a house. (Marg: Accounting Clerk)

It was not that working-class women were indifferent to the issues of money, home ownership, or steady jobs: Rather, they did not have the same expectations about those material circumstances of their lives as did middle-class women. As Jackie put it when she became pregnant, "I didn't know how we were going to handle it." Lack of money was something to be handled, a given to which one had to adjust; having money or an established career was not a prerequisite for having children.

Waiting for what the middle-class women would define as

readiness appeared neither realistic nor applicable to the working-class women. A working-class mother of two living in an apartment expressed the sequencing of family time in her life: "[I hoped] to have a family, to be a family, and maybe, eventually, [to have] a house." Similarly, Ramona, who was 22 when she became a mother, perceived no purpose in deferring childbearing. For her, like many working-class women, waiting for financial stability would mean never having a child:

> [In deciding when to have children] you can't say you wanted to get financially stable, because that never happens, and you'd never have children if you waited for that. It just seemed as good a time as any [to have children]. (Ramona: Bookkeeping Clerk)

For working-class women, the absence of middle-class life planning or postponement of childbearing should *not* be taken to indicate an "inability to defer gratification" or a subculturally based emphasis on immediacy rather than on a future orientation. As Rubin's (1976) study of white working-class families shows, the blame-the-victim bias in "culture-of-poverty" explanations of working-class behavior fails to appreciate that some people have neither the material resources to plan effectively nor realistic options for which to plan:

> For in order to plan for the future, people must believe it possible to control their fate—a belief that can only be held if it is nourished in experience. That seldom happens in working-class life. . . . It should be clear by now that the lack of planning to which I refer is not due, as some social scientists insist, to some debilitating inability of the working class to delay gratification. . . . Rather, in the context of their lives and daily struggles, looking either backwards or forwards makes little sense; planning for the future seems incongruous. (Rubin, 1976, pp. 38–39)

Not all working-class women have children when they are young. Twenty-five percent of the sample were 25 or older when their first child was born (Table 4.5). Sally, for example, was 26 when she became a mother. Unusual among the working-class women interviewed, Sally talked about readiness for children in terms of career and financial security. Sally had once thought she would not have children. By the time she became pregnant she had options and resources many working-class women did not:

I was guaranteed my same position, and my same job, and that
made a big impact as well, because I didn't want to give up my
career after having worked for over 10 years just because I had a
child. So that made a big difference. I was able to have a child and
come back to my same job. (Sally: Bell Service Assistant)

Sally's strategic thinking reflected not merely her years at work
but also the work involvement produced by experiencing advancement and a good benefits package. As Gerson (1985) emphasizes, a
woman's family and work commitments are shaped, not simply by
whether she works or not, but by the relative rewards and options
available to her at work and at home.[3] Sally had a "good job."

In this section we have seen how time conceptions surrrounding
childbearing were differentiated by social class. One must be careful not
to interpret the temporal sequencing and meaning of life events in
working-class women's lives by reference to middle-class patterns.
Rather, one must interpret these working-class women's actions in the
context of their lives, as women see them. At the same time, however,
women's subjective perceptions have objective consequences. For
working-class women, having children in their teens may not cause
poverty or disadvantage, but as Furstenberg (1992) points out, doing so
decreases the odds of avoiding either.[4] Early childbearing, I suggest, is
one of the ways in which structural gender, race, and class inequalities
are transformed into young women's private troubles.

"I DON'T WANT TO BE AN AUNT NO MORE":
FAMILY, FRIENDS, AND FELLOWS
IN WORKING-CLASS WOMEN'S
TRANSITION TO MOTHERHOOD

Many of the working-class women presented themselves as having
"always wanted" children (see Table 4.1). In many ways their accounts
suggested they were waiting to claim the identity of mother. We saw in
the previous chapter how the middle-class women frequently worked
to arrange the circumstances in which they became mothers. Many of
the young working-class women were more likely to claim motherhood first and deal with the circumstances of their claim later—often
by emphasizing the strength of their maternal motivation.

For many working-class women there appeared to have been a
pattern to the timing of motherhood. As Phoenix (1991a, p. 93) argues,

women's perceptions of the appropriate time for motherhood are shaped by their own social network rather than by national averages or social scientific views on the benefits of deferment. Repeatedly, what seemed like a right time for motherhood coincided with the traditional concomitants of pregnancy. That is, the working-class women were more likely than the middle-class women to talk about friends or family having children and their own recent or impending marriages as being associated with becoming pregnant. Seventy-five percent of the working-class women made reference to such events in accounts of their pregnancies; few middle-class women did.

Karen, a mother of three who had her first child when she was 19, explained:

> We were trying for one. . . . I did want one—the majority of my friends had one or two. And also just because I just got married too, eh? (Karen: Dry Cleaner's Shipping Clerk)

Concerned to emphasize her *own* desire for a child, rather than suggesting she was conforming to convention, Ramona observed: "It wasn't [just] like it was the thing to do." But then she added:

> You know, all our other friends had kids, and you could see how happy they were with their children, and you felt like you were missing out on something. Or you'd go to the hospital to visit your friend who just had a newborn: "A cute little baby."[5] (Ramona: Bookkeeping Clerk)

Marg's account shows how marriage and babies were closely associated for the working-class women. However, Marg's commitment to motherhood preceded her commitment to marriage: It was taken for granted. She was waiting to have *the baby*. In her mind, the baby already existed:

> Well, I guess we'd been together for a couple of years. We seemed more like, you know, the married type, and I just thought, like, it was a good time to have a baby. Get married first, but then have the baby. (Marg: Accounting Clerk)

Age consciousness and the fact that others close to her had become mothers—even those younger and thus presumably less deserving of motherhood—added an urgency to Marg's motherhood motivation.

> You know, you're 25 . . . and it's like, "I don't want to be 30 when I'm having my first baby," you know. . . . Especially when you have brothers and sisters [who have children] . . . and my sister is younger than me, and *she* had a baby, and my best friend had a baby. . . . [I said to myself] "I don't want to be an aunt no more." (Marg: Accounting Clerk)

It is interesting to note that Marg used her younger sister's maternity to support her own claim. The fact that her sister had become an unwed mother, and remained an alone mother, did not make her sister's motherhood status a less valid object of comparison for Marg. Whereas marriage legitimated working-class women's claims to motherhood, its absence did not necessarily devalue it. Thus when Mary, single and 17, became pregnant, seeing friends who had children helped her define her situation in conventional terms:

> Actually seeing [my unmarried friend] with [her daughter] Kate, I was more excited about having a baby. If she wasn't there, if she didn't have Kate, I don't think I would have been so excited to have [my son] Michael. . . . I have another friend who had her son when she was 17. She lived with me [for a while after] her father kicked her out of the house. . . . We talked about . . . things. . . . It's important to have support when you're having a baby. (Mary: Hotel Housekeeper)

Jackie, on the other hand, *did* see her pregnancy as a problem—her friends were *not* yet having children. Twenty years old and married, she was one of the few working-class women who felt that motherhood had come too soon. Jackie felt her reference group would see her behavior as questionable:

> [When I learned I was pregnant] I was scared and I was apprehensive. I didn't know what to do. I was actually embarrassed to tell people, because I had been married [only] a couple of months. And [I thought] people would sort of look at me and go, "You're only 20, you've only been married a couple of months, and you are having a baby already!" . . . [None] of . . . my friends have . . .

children. I'm the first to get married and the first to have a child.
(Jackie: Secretary)

Sally, too, was also unusual among the working-class women: She
had considered voluntary childlessness. Like many middle-class
women, she felt that her attitude toward children had changed over
the course of adult years. Unlike them, she attributed this change to
factors *external* rather than internal, to herself: Her friends were
becoming pregnant and having children:

> Just my outlook changed [when I was 25]. I had never wanted
> kids before. I just didn't want kids. . . . I think it was just from
> getting older, and a lot of my friends were getting pregnant and
> having children, and seeing the interaction there, and I think it
> changed my outlook. . . . And then I changed [so] that I wanted
> kids. And once I decided [I wanted kids], I got pregnant right
> away and I started having them. (Sally: Bell Service Assistant)

Sally had had little social support for a childless identity. She felt
pressure to have children:

> I thought I was different to a lot of people that I talked to. . . .
> [Tom's family were pressurizing me] to have kids, at the beginning
> of the marriage, [but] not so much after we had been married so
> long. I felt like, because I didn't want kids, a lot of people didn't
> seem to understand that. . . . [My husband] and I had only talked
> about that I didn't want kids right away. And I had told him that
> I didn't want kids, [but] I don't think he really accepted it or
> believed it. . . . He probably just thought that I was just saying
> that and that I would change my mind. (Sally: Bell Service
> Assistant)

The connection between men and motherhood was far more
immediate for working-class than for middle-class women. The
presence of men in the lives of the working-class women led to
pregnancy in ways that the presence of men in middle-class women's
lives did not. Whereas the absence of the "right relationship" was a
barrier to middle-class women's maternity, its presence did not
automatically lead to pregnancy. "Joint readiness" often had to be
achieved first. Among working-class women, on the other hand,
marriage, or its equivalent, was clearly associated with having children,

but the absence of the right relationship neither prevented nor devalued motherhood. Although only one working-class woman said she deliberately became pregnant outside a relationship, for many, a heterosexual relationship seemed to provide the occasion for claiming a gender identity that came to exist independently of the relationship—the identity of mother. Unlike the middle-class women, for the working-class women being a woman in itself seemed to represent acceptable grounds for becoming a mother.

"I LIKED THE IDEA OF BEING A MOTHER"

For the majority of working-class women in the sample (79%), motherhood was an identity and a role they had "always wanted" to claim for themselves. The issues surrounding having children appeared to be ones of *when* they would or could claim the desired identity of mother. Whereas time conceptions and not wanting to make a permanent commitment to childlessness eventually encouraged some of the middle-class women to opt for pregnancy, the working-class women's conceptions of a *positive* identity of "self as mother" appeared to be central to their reproductive behavior.

Working-class women in this sample "liked the idea of being a mother," and such positive self-conceptions facilitated biological conceptions. "I've just always wanted to have a child," was a typical response from Sue as an explanation for her planned pregnancy. She said, "I just couldn't wait to have one." Similarly, Mara had also "always wanted a child." At age 19, while living with her partner and planning their wedding, she accidentally became pregnant:

> I've always, *always*, wanted a child. I mean, I said to my mother, "Mom, I'm going to have a baby—just not right now, since I'm just sixteen." I've *always* wanted a child. . . . (Mara: Clerical Worker)

Mara's account of her pregnancy shows how positive conceptions of having children were implicated in accidental pregnancies. Thinking about wanting a child seemed associated with having one:

> I was thinking about [wanting a child] when I got pregnant. We were arranging the wedding when I found out I was

pregnant, but we were already talking about having a baby. . . .
I went to the doctor's one day, for something else. And
[afterward], as a joke, I said to Carl [my fiance]—I didn't say
anything. I just had a grin on my face. . . . and he says, "You're
pregnant." And I said, "No. What would you do if I was?" [He
said], "I'd marry you tomorrow. I want one so badly, and you
want one, too." And a week later I found out I was pregnant.
[But] we had already decided to get married. (Mara: Clerical
Worker)

To say that working-class women responded positively to the idea
of being a mother does not imply that they had clear or detailed
conceptions of motherhood. As a mother of two, whose first pregnancy "just happened," explained:

I always, I mean, you always wanted [children]. . . . I mean, you
just see a little, tiny baby; it's so cute and cuddly. You're not thinking
about the future. (Helen: Waitress/Cashier)

Similarly, Mary explained that when she became pregnant the
idea of becoming a mother was positive but also unreal for her. She
was 19 and single at the time:

It didn't really sink in until I was 8 months pregnant. . . . I didn't
realize it until I heard the heartbeat of [my son]. . . . Because, it's
like it's there, but you don't really *know* it's there—like it's really
hard to believe . . . that there's a baby inside you. I just didn't
realize it. It's like when I go on vacation. I don't realize I'm there
until I'm actually there. (Mary: Hotel Housekeeper)

Gradually the identity of mother began to claim her:

And then when I was about 8 months pregnant, I started to show.
. . . I actually had no plans [for after the baby was born, but] I
went out and bought a crib . . . when I was 8 months pregnant.
(Mary: Hotel Housekeeper)

To many of these young women, having a child expressed their
maturity and responsibility—both of which were highly valued. Sue,
a mother of three, recalled:

> I had just gotten married. I was working for the bank then, and
> I was out of school for about a year and starting to grow up. I
> was always mature anyhow. I always sort of took the responsi-
> bility. . . . I was getting a little bit more independent. . . .
> Instead of living at home I was now boss of my own home,
> [that] type of thing. I remember feeling more independent and
> responsible than I had been. . . . (Sue: Legal Secretary)

Sue felt that now she had a right to claim motherhood:

> I always liked kids and I wanted, as you say, "a baby of your own."
> . . . I was always brought up to believe that you didn't have sex
> before you got married and you didn't have children before you
> got married. I always wanted kids, and I thought "I'm married
> now—I can have a baby." (Sue: Legal Secretary)

For Sue and the other working-class women, having a child was a way
of claiming an adult identity—as a responsible person.

CLAIMING ADULT IDENTITIES:
MOTHERHOOD AS EXPRESSIVE BEHAVIOR

The accounts of those women who became pregnant as teenagers
indicated that the younger women were particularly attracted to
positive images of motherhood. Rita, an unskilled manual factory
worker, now married to a new partner, was 18 when she planned her
pregnancy and conceived by an earlier boyfriend. She, too, had "liked
the idea of being a mother." She planned to live with her boyfriend.
Like Sue's association of motherhood and maturity, implicit in Rita's
account is an image of motherhood as a challenge—a female rite of
passage that would test her qualities and measure her personal worth:
"Would I be able to handle it?" she wondered:

> Well, me and the father planned [the baby], but we didn't plan
> him [the father] leaving. We had planned to live together and have
> a baby. . . . I was wondering how I would be as a mother—
> whether I'd be able to handle it, whether I'd be patient enough.
> . . . "Can I actually be a *mother?*" . . . I just thought it sounded
> nice. I liked the whole idea of being a mother. (Rita: Unskilled
> Factory Worker)

June, too, described how her positive conceptions of becoming a mother dominated her interpretation of her situation when, at 19 and single, she unintentionally became pregnant. Though her pregnancy was unplanned, she recalled that at that time, she was thinking about "wanting a family." Her recollections also show how positive conceptions of motherhood shaped her responses to the unplanned biological conception:

> [I was] just wanting a baby. I've always wanted a baby. [When I found out I was pregnant] I was really happy. I was having a *baby*. I was bringing something into the world that *I wanted to*. I always wanted a child and I got it. (June: Daycare Assistant)

The young unwed working-class mothers in the study presented particularly strong motherhood motivations. Perhaps this was because their maternal careers were "deviant," perhaps not. What was clear, however, were the ways in which an adult identity of being responsible and the desire for love and connectedness were interconnected in these young, working-class women's responses to the idea of motherhood. Val's planned pregnancy as a single 19-year-old shows how she connected being grown up—"figuring out who she was"—and being "ready to take care of somebody." Getting love was one of the rewards:

> I was the motherly type. I always mothered my friends. [I started thinking about actually having a child] at 16; that's when I began to figure out who I was and what I was capable of doing. [I decided to get pregnant at 19.] I wanted something that was *mine*. I wanted somebody to love and to love me back. I wanted a reason for being alive. I didn't want to wait any more. . . . I'd been putting it off since I was 16. . . . [By 19] I had a steady job. . . . I had grown up a lot. I felt I was ready for something—I felt I was ready to take care of somebody and start a family for myself. (Val: Apprentice Mechanic)

Having a baby was a means of establishing a new adult way of being in the world for Val. Her account also shows how young working-class unwed mothers do not share concerned others' conception of them as victims or immature persons. In contrast to the characterization of young unwed mothers by many social work or public health professionals, the young mothers in this study empha-

sized both a feeling of responsibility toward their children and their
own characters as responsible persons (see Chapter 6). Val, like many
others, saw herself making adult decisions and realizing her values.
Among many of these young working-class women, becoming a
mother is better understood as expressive, rather than instrumental,
action. Motherhood is *expressive of an identity*, a claim to being a
responsible, loving, caring, grown-up person.[6] As we have seen, the
middle-class women indicated that they felt they had to achieve
maturity *before* having a child, but the working-class women's accounts
suggest that many saw themselves as achieving maturity *through* having
a child. The positive character of the identity of mother helps explain
how unplanned pregnancies among both single and married women
were met with the mixed emotions of being scared and thrilled, as
they so often were. Scared because circumstances were not right
(financial problems, housing problems, being unmarried), and thrilled
because access to a desired identity had been gained. Kathy, for
example, was single and had thought she would be in her mid-20s
before she had a child, but she was "thrilled to death" when, just after
turning 19, she discovered she was accidentally pregnant:

> I was thrilled to death when I found out. . . . I hadn't planned it,
> but when I found out. . . . I was scared to death for lack of
> knowledge. [I was] excited; it was a challenge. . . . I wasn't afraid
> so much of doing something wrong; just of the unknown. . . .
> The first time I had to dress him I had to remember he wasn't a
> doll from my childhood. . . . He used to scare me. I didn't know
> anything about children, [but] I had wanted a child. I wanted a
> boy. (Kathy: Accounting Clerk)

MOTHERHOOD: CONVENTIONAL
OR UNCONVENTIONAL IDENTITIES?

Although early feminist critiques made visible the gender inequalities
sustained by the social organization and romanticization of motherhood, they often obscured the positive dimensions of many women's
experience of children and family (Boulton, 1983; Rothman, 1989, p.
155; Sandelowski, 1990). Thus, though feminism supports choice, the
choice of motherhood by adolescent (or disadvantaged) women is
often seen as suspect—as conformity to social pressures (Nathanson,
1991, p. 221). Similarly, because of the high costs in personal develop-

ment apparently associated with early childbearing, Nathanson continues, it has been difficult for middle-class people to understand how motherhood is viewed so positively by many economically disadvantaged women.

For these women, however, motherhood may offer a means of (temporary) liberation from dreary work (Griffin, 1989) and remains one of the most personally valued aspects of the feminine role (Nicolson, 1993). For Phoenix (1991b), teenage mothers' desire for motherhood is not so much a desire to give birth as a desire for the privileges unavailable to those who do not have children.

Paradoxically, a defining feature of dominant images of both motherhood and female identity, the desire and capacity to care, presents both a resource and a source of oppression in young women's lives. Young girls not only learn to value caring for others but are *policed* to care and bear the costs of caring, especially for boyfriends (Miller, 1976; Reitsma-Street, 1991, p. 116; Sidel, 1990, p. 148). Reitsma-Street's (1991) study of adolescent women suggests that the expectation that young girls should acquire, care about, and keep boyfriends makes them vulnerable to pregnancies and to neglecting their own interests and well-being. Yet, as we will see in Chapter 7, motherhood also freed the young women in this study from some of the expectations of heterosexual caring.

Young working-class women are not simply traditional in their outlooks and gender identities. On the contrary, as Griffin (1989) shows, feminism has impinged on the lives and consciousness of many young women, who neither identify themselves as feminist nor express any overt allegiance to women as a political category. Many working-class women in this study held nontraditional views; for example, on the issue of working mothers, the division of domestic labor, and often on marriage (see Chapter 8). Pateman (1989) emphasizes the resourcefulness of young, single working-class mothers as social actors carving out meaningful lives in the context of difficult and changing economic circumstances. With limited employment opportunities of their own and the collapse of the social basis of the male breadwinner role, motherhood offers disadvantaged young women a socially (though not economically) secure and acknowledged identity (Pateman, 1989, p. 199). What is not clear, however, is the extent to which economically disadvantaged young women's unorthodoxy represents a challenge to patriarchal heterosexuality or to which it is simply an adjustment to their own and young men's economic circumstances. Although the price is high, Pateman (1989,

p. 199) reasons, motherhood gives young women the "appearance of self-determination": It is not an uncritical retreat into femininity.

HOW CONVENTIONAL IDENTITIES PRODUCE
UNCONVENTIONAL CAREERS

I have argued that, among the working-class women in this study, positive conceptions of motherhood were implicated in the conception of children. These positive images of motherhood, although shared by the majority of working-class women in the sample,[7] were most strongly expressed by those who were young when they conceived and who later became alone mothers. It could be argued that such mothers represented a "deviant" category and should be studied separately. However, in their motherhood motives, unwed mothers were not deviant but had exaggeratedly typical traditional motherhood images. It is perhaps more accurate to see unwed mothers' unorthodoxy as a *consequence*, rather than a cause, of their behavior. Becoming a parent does not constitute deviant behavior. Most adults become parents. But the consequences of becoming a parent if one is *unwed* set some parents apart from others, and men apart from women.

Deviance is not simply a matter of breaking the rules. Eichler (1983) points out that men can break the rules of parenting with little consequence. Giving birth to a child outside of marriage, she argues, has "a truly life-altering impact on the woman concerned, but only a minimal impact on the father with respect to altering his life chances" (Eichler, 1983, p. 209). For example, a U.S. study of 140 men who were collectively responsible for 176 extramarital pregnancies showed that, although these men recognized their behavior to be rule breaking, they did not perceive themselves as deviant, nor were they institutionally defined as being a problem (cited in Eichler, 1983, p. 208)—as alone mothers who go on welfare are often categorized. Thus the consequences of behavior and the subsequent labeling of identity as deviant or normal are differentially experienced by male and female unmarried parents. Furthermore, the consequences of deviant behavior are often falsely seen as flowing from the deviant act, when, in fact, the consequences originate elsewhere. For example, many of the negative features of alone parenthood for women and their children are produced, not by being alone parents, but by the combination of *poverty* and lack of social support systems for women who parent in this way.[8]

Finally, women's apparent "deviance" is partly a product of changing demographics (see Chapter 2). The young women in this study were not unusual for having given birth in their teens; historically, women have often been expected to become mothers early in life. In Laslett's (1971) preindustrial England, for example, it was the poor who often deferred childbearing, whereas aristocratic women gave birth in their teenage years. What was unusual about the women in this study is that they became teenage mothers in a period when fertility rates were falling, the average age at which women first give birth was rising, and there was a growing separation between marriage and childbearing.[9] Fertility has fallen dramatically in Canada in the past 35 years; however, the decline has been in *marital* fertility. Although women are less likely to give birth in their teens than they were 35 years ago, those that do are *more likely* to be unmarried and far more likely than in the past to keep their children rather than give them up for adoption. More precisely, white women are now more likely to keep their children. Solinger (1992) documents the racial patterns in social practices around adoption in the United States. Until the 1970s, she explains, white unwed teen mothers were expected, even coerced, into placing their infants for adoption—a policy aimed at restoring the social worth of mothers and babies. However, it was presumed that black unwed mothers (or their families) would keep their babies; social policy was aimed at preventing them from having more (Solinger, 1992, p. 204).

Of the 46% of working-class mothers in this study who conceived in their teens, whether they were living with permanent partners at the time or not, 82% were to become alone parents at some point in their maternal careers, and 62% spent part of their lives as mothers on welfare.

"WELFARE MOTHERS"?

The connections between alone motherhood and welfare (or the welfare state) are complex. Unwed motherhood is often popularly represented as a consequence of social welfare policies. While few sociologists support such interpretations, analysts of welfare states themselves often overlook the different ways in which men and women have been incorporated into the welfare state (Pateman, 1989).

Conservative political interests in the United States, according to Nathanson (1991, p. 156), have reframed the concern over adolescent pregnancy as a problem of (black) teenagers on welfare. This reframing, she explains, was the single most powerful force in shaping public policy toward "sexually unorthodox" women, including unwed mothers, in the 1980s. Yet impetus for the current moral panic over unwed mothers, Nathanson (1991) points out, coincided with a significant rise in *white* unmarried women's birthrates, not black women's rates. State welfare services, Nathanson (1991, p. 67) argues, came to carry the blame for leading unmarried women to have children—this at the same time that welfare service resources were being presented as in danger of being drained by unwed mothers' demands. Such a formulation of the problem expressed racist, class, and, as we will see, patriarchal interests. In this construction, young unwed mothers and the welfare system itself were no longer seen as legitimate recipients of society's support. Thus the moral panic about unwed mothers could be couched in terms of the "concern" to cut public spending and taxation.

Empirically, few adolescents engage in sex in order to become parents (Furstenberg, 1992, p. 240) and thereby claim welfare or housing subsidies (Phoenix, 1991a, 1991b).[10] Some theorists argue that high unemployment makes it impossible for many young men to support families. Unwed women's claims on welfare due to male unemployment can be represented as a failure of the welfare state (to generate full employment). But such an analysis misses the masculinist character of the welfare state itself in privileging the public sphere over the private sphere and male wages and employment over female wages and employment, and in representing many social services to women and their children as a *benefit* (a handout to the needy) rather than an entitlement. Unlike the labor of the worker, women's "private" reproductive and childrearing labor in modern welfare states does *not* entitle them to public recognition or state support. Their work is not recognized as a valuable social contribution. Yet the "fiscal crisis" of the welfare state, Pateman (1989, p. 192) notes, would be far more acute if women ceased to provide such private welfare through their family and caring labor. It is only through negating the social worth of childbearing and childrearing that economically disadvantaged "welfare mothers" can be called dependent on the state.

Contemporary moral panics over welfare mothers fuse class and race tensions in the social struggles over the control of women's sexuality and reproduction (Griffin, 1992; Nathanson, 1991; Phoenix, 1991b). For Griffin (1992, p. 492), these moral panics capture the racialized, class-specific, and gendered nature of heterosexuality in the professionally policed transition of American girls to adulthood. Thus President Reagan's family policies in the United States, Pateman (1989, p. 189) emphasizes, were as much about shoring up patriarchy as they were about restabilizing capitalism. Indeed, patriarchy can be distinguished from other forms of male-dominated societies in that it constructs paternity as *the* fundamental human relationship (Rothman, 1989). Children are primarily *men's* children—produced through women's bodies. Albeit itself patriarchal in character, the Canadian welfare state did offer the economically disadvantaged women in this study the possibility of an (impoverished) degree of independence from individual men. Yet for welfare mothers, writes Pateman (1989, p. 200), "The power and capriciousness of husbands is being replaced by the arbitrariness, bureaucracy and power of the state, the very state which has [hitherto] upheld patriarchal power." Not surprisingly, therefore, welfare issues and the State have been central to both feminist politics and family values countermovements.

THE IDEAL SELF AND IDENTITY SALIENCE: HOW UNPLANNED CONCEPTIONS BECOME WANTED CHILDREN

I have shown how positive conceptions of motherhood, which were widely shared among working-class mothers, were implicated in how these women became mothers—whether they described their pregnancies as planned or not and whether they were wed nor not.

Motherhood seemed to be involved in both the working- and the middle-class women's ideal self or identity prominence hierarchy (McCall and Simmons, 1978) in different ways. The middle-class women, as we have seen, chose motherhood when they were "ready" and the circumstances were "right." The working-class women, on the other hand, placed far fewer restrictions on the appropriate time for motherhood; they appeared ready to accept it when it came. Even unplanned conceptions among unwed teenaged women could be interpreted as welcomed pregnancies.[11] How are we to understand this?

The answer appears to lie partly in the concepts of womanhood and motherhood that women hold. Luker's (1984) study of motherhood and the politics of abortion shows how women's responses to unplanned pregnancies are shaped by their self-concepts and present-day commitments. Some women, she observes, see motherhood and reproduction as the most salient dimension of a woman's personal and social identity; others do not. The former group are more likely to be opposed to abortion than the latter. Those who see women's reproductive capacity as the core of female identity feel that their valued concepts of motherhood and womanhood are violated when women's mothering role is made subordinate to other roles or ambitions. For such women, Luker argues, a woman is primarily defined by the fact that she can become a mother. For women who hold such self-concepts, a pregnancy may be unanticipated but can only be ambivalently defined as unwanted. As Luker explains:

> [For those who see] women's reproductive roles . . . as having social primacy . . . the act of conception therefore creates a pregnant woman rather than a woman who is pregnant; it creates a woman whose life, in cases where roles or values clash, is defined by the fact that she is—or may become—pregnant. (Luker, 1984, p. 200)

For such women, defining a pregnancy or the resulting child as unwanted would mean rejecting the essence of female identity. Thus commitment to the primacy of motherhood in a woman's life can transform an unanticipated pregnancy into a wanted child.

To understand the ways, in this study, in which motherhood was differentially implicated in working- and middle-class women's self-concepts, it is necessary to distinguish between the notions of *identity prominence* and *identity salience*. Whereas "prominence" refers to the personal importance or psychological centrality of an identity to an individual, *salience* refers to the probability of its behavioral enactment. Thus even if motherhood was as central to the ideal selves of the middle-class women as it was to the working-class women—and the data suggest that before they became mothers it was not—the *salience* of motherhood in women's identities was different. Motherhood was more salient in the working-class than in the middle-class women's identities. That is, there were far more circumstances in which the identity of *mother* was likely to be claimed. The middle-class women limited their claims to motherhood to quite restrictive social contexts of readiness; the working-class women did not.

There was another way in which motherhood acquired a greater identity salience among the working- than the middle-class women. Sidel (1990, p. 126) argues that many young American women take risks where sex is concerned, but those with hopes for future careers, often on the insistence of friends and family, minimize the long-term consequences of such risk taking. But for those young working-class women in this study who wanted to avoid motherhood, there appeared to have been fewer avenues for its evasion. Not all working-class women have positive responses to pregnancies. Presumably many of those who do not will terminate their pregnancies. For others, like Renee and Tina in this study, becoming pregnant presented them with an undesirable, but *unavoidable,* self-transformation. Abortion seemed, or was, unavailable to them.

Renee was 17 and living with her common-law husband when she became pregnant. She felt her life was "ruined":

> [I] *never* wanted to have a child. Both [were] accidents; [The] first one and this one. It's called public awareness, or whatever. Nobody told me nothing. . . . I was living with Frank, common-law, at his mother's house. His parents, they are from a Catholic background too. When I got pregnant, the first thing that came in my head was abortion. I didn't know anything about it . . . [but] of course, if you become pregnant at that age, it's, you know, how do you get rid of it. . . . I thought, "Oh my God, my life is ruined." . . . I had everything set [for the abortion] through my family doctor. (Renee: Truck Driver)

However, Renee's escape from an involuntary maternity was blocked by her mother:

> My mum almost flipped the table over on me. . . . I said to her, "Mum, I'm pregnant." She took that very calm and she said, "I figured that was coming sooner or later." But then I replied, "But don't worry, I'm going to have an abortion." And that's when my Mum said, "No, you're not. You've got yourself into this. You're keeping it and you're having it." Everybody, you know, wanted me to keep it, so that, more or less, made you feel better too. (Renee: Truck Driver)

Thus for Renee, "everybody" wanting her "to keep it" and to continue her pregnancy encouraged her to reinterpret her own

responses and to "more or less . . . feel better" about becoming a
mother. Renee subsequently became strongly anti-abortion and defined herself as deeply committed to her children.

Unlike Renee, who was living with her boyfriend when she
became pregnant, Tina was 15, single, and going to school when she,
too, found her transition to maternity out of her control. She hid her
new identity. In time, however, this new identity of mother prevented
Tina's engagement of other adult identities:

> I always wanted a child. I thought it would be when I was [about]
> 20. . . . [When I learned I was pregnant] I was shocked. I kept
> thinking, "This can't happen to me." It was my first time and,
> ah—I never told anyone [that I was pregnant] 'till I was seven
> months. I kept wishing I could have a miscarriage—but never
> thought of abortion. . . . [I had planned] to finish school and
> become a nurse, like. It was so difficult going back to school with
> the baby. It got to me after a while so I quit. (Tina: Hospital
> Dietary Aide)

When Tina was asked whether were she to do things over, would she
choose to have a child, she replied:

> Yes, I would. I just can't imagine, like, I'd like to have been older.
> But I don't regret having him, you know. It's just I've always loved
> children, and it's just everything about it; the first time they call
> you Mommy. I just love being a mother. (Tina: Hospital Dietary
> Aide)

Tina became deeply invested in motherhood, but without adequate
social support, this commitment made her unavailable for investment
in education and career. Tina did not become a nurse.

TRADITIONAL CONCEPTS
AND UNANTICIPATED OUTCOMES

For most of the working-class women in this study, becoming a
mother was associated with the conventional biographical concomitants of parenthood—marriage or common-law relationship, friends
and family having babies, and so forth. However, about half the
working-class sample had also been alone mothers at some point in

their maternal careers. Typically, few women set out to be alone parents
but acquire the status through unanticipated life experiences. Table
4.6 locates the experience of being an alone mother in terms of the
broader experience of the Canadian population and the individual
maternal careers of the working-class women in the study.

Working-class women in this study acquired the status of alone
parent either when they first became mothers or after they had been
joint parents for some time. The age at which the women became
mothers affected the likelihood of becoming alone mothers (Table
4.7).

The ever-alone mothers did not appear to differ from the other
working-class women except that they were younger when they
became mothers and were more likely to say their first pregnancies
were unplanned. As Furstenberg (1992, p. 240) argues, adolescent
unwed motherhood does not result from a single decision but is often
the unanticipated outcome of a sequence of events: "having sex, not
using contraception successfully, becoming pregnant, and not obtain-
ing an abortion."

Unplanned pregnancies, however, were not necessarily seen as
problems; many of these women initially felt they were pursuing
normal maternal careers. Neither do unplanned pregnancies neces-

TABLE 4.6. Profile of Ever-Alone Working-Class Mothers

Percent of all mothers aged 40–49 in the Canadian population (in 1984) who had ever been alone mothers[a]	25%
Percent of working-class sample who were ever-alone mothers	54%
Percent of working-class sample who are currently alone mothers	39%
Percent of working-class women whose pregnancy was planned	46%
Percent of currently alone mothers whose pregnancy was planned	9%
Percent of currently alone mothers who began their maternal careers as alone mothers	54%
Percent of ever-alone working-class mothers who began their careers with partners	47%

Note. N = 15.
[a]Moore (1989).

TABLE 4.7. Working-Class Women's Age at Birth of First Child and Becoming an Alone Mother

Percent who gave birth by age 20 and became ever-alone mothers	85%
Percent who gave birth at age 21–24 and became ever-alone mothers	33%
Percent who gave birth at 25+ and became ever-alone mothers	22%

Note. N = 15.

sarily mean unwanted children. Kimberley, who was living common-law when she became pregnant at age 16, distinguished between her *then* accidental pregnancy and her *now* wanted child:

> It was an accident, really—*now* it's not an accident. I don't regret having him anyways. . . . At that time it wasn't upsetting at all. At that time it really didn't change anything except I knew we had to move. (Kimberley: Sheet Metal Worker)

At that time Kimberley did not know she was embarking on a career of being an alone mother and welfare recipient.

> [Later it changed things.] It changed the way the baby's father didn't spend a lot of time with him or I after. Plus I was having problems deciding whether or not to go to work, and plus I didn't have anyone to baby-sit. At the time [I found out I was pregnant] I was *pleased*. I didn't think anything about my life ahead at that time. (Kimberly: Sheet Metal Worker)

A once-married, now alone, mother of two explains how the terms "planned" and "unplanned" refer to complex realities—traditional concepts can have nontraditional outcomes:

> [My first pregnancy was] sort of [planned], but not—I don't know what to say, sort of. . . . There was no birth control, so obviously both people knew. So like, if it happened. . . .
> Maybe I thought [having a child] . . . was the way to make absolutely sure I'll have him [my husband at the time], which was maybe one of the dumbest things I ever thought in my life. You know, like really, it wasn't a trap, but it was kind of something that

was *his* and, you knew that no matter [what happened], you'd have it, sort of. . . . Like, I never in 5 million years dreamed he would do what he did either [by leaving]. . . . He did what he had to do, I guess. (Helen: Waitress/Cashier)

Twenty-nine percent of the working-class sample, and 54% of those currently alone, began their maternal careers as unwed or alone mothers. Typically they did not plan to become unwed mothers: Several had initially expected a future in which they would be living with the baby's father. Almost half (46%) of the currently alone mothers had once lived as joint parents, and about a quarter (23%) of the mothers currently with partners had once been alone mothers. A majority of the working-class women (54%) were currently, or had been, alone parents. Thus the terms "deviant," "unconventional," and "illegitimate" appear singularly arbitrary when applied to alone mothers.[12] These working-class women moved in and out of the statuses of being alone or joint parents, but the identity of mother was *enduring*.

ALTERNATIVE MATERNAL CAREERS AMONG YOUNG WORKING-CLASS WOMEN

Rubin (1976) argues that accidental pregnancies among young working-class women are often not truly accidental. The emotional pain of growing up in families scarred by poverty, she contends, creates particularly urgent needs to escape parental control, to assert adult identity, and to find safety and nurturance. These needs, she concludes, lead young working-class men and women to be participants in an unconscious drama of becoming accidentally pregnant and marrying (Rubin, 1976, p. 64). For Sidel (1990, p. 147), young working-class women's needs for intimacy and relationship in a social context of structural gender inequality make them vulnerable to unplanned pregnancies.

Middle-class young women, on the other hand, can find valued adult identities and self-esteem in the roles and relationships of advanced education or professional training (Rubin, 1976, p. 41; Sidel, 1990, p. 150).

What distinguished the young working-class women in this study from those Rubin interviewed was not their high rate of pregnancies when they were unwed but the fact that pregnancy did not lead to marriage[13] and that young, unwed, white working-class women no longer give their children up for adoption.[14]

Like Rubin's (1976) study, Freeman's study of abortion (cited in Russo, 1979) also links unplanned pregnancies to young women's orientation to the world, albeit in a different way. Most young women in her sample of those seeking abortions, she argues, were faced with unwanted pregnancies because they had not seen themselves as instrumental in planning their own lives:

> Pregnancy happened to them. . . . Their experiences had trained them to be receptive, to value themselves in terms of other's responses more than through their own contribution. They had no history of feeling what they did made any difference, that their own actions and decisions had any value to themselves and others. (cited in Russo, 1979, p. 13)

Unlike the clients of Freeman's abortion clinic, however, women in this study *did* come to define the consequences of their actions (their pregnancies) as *being of value* to them. Yet, like the women in Freeman's and Rubin's studies, they did not experience the world as being under their control. However, the young women's "problem" was not simply one of psychological orientation but one of social inequality in the organization of heterosexuality and responsibility for children. Solinger (1992) shows how social accounts of pregnancies of unwed mothers often discounted gender inequality and coercive heterosexuality in young women's lives in favor of psychological explanations. That is, they look inside young women rather than outside to social relations to make sense of unwed pregnancies.

Unequal gender arrangements mean that women, but not men, usually carry responsibily for children. Like several unwed mothers, Rita planned to live with her child's father:

> We planned to move in together, and then we decided to have a child as well, and I got pregnant very, very, fast. . . . There wasn't any main reasons [for me wanting a child]. At the time, her father was saying he wanted a child. I sort of liked the idea—I didn't think much [about] it before then. It was like O.K. It just happened I was pregnant two weeks later. . . . We didn't plan on him leaving [me]. (Rita: Unskilled Factory Worker)

Social commentators' representations of the problem-laden character of unwed motherhood was not shared by the women in this
study. Central to their accounts was the strength of their commitment
to a motherhood identity. They offset the unorthodox context of their
becoming mothers with the strength of their motivation for motherhood. Like the Chicana unwed mothers in Horowitz's (1987) study,
the working-class women in this study expressed strong maternal
motivations and traditionally feminine accounts of behavior. For
example, they talked about wanting a baby; about their desire to give
and receive love; and about their desire for permanent commitment.
As Mary told herself when she accidentally became pregnant at 19,
"You will always know you're loved."

The implications of unwed adolescent motherhood remain (variably) problematic for social analysts. Although unmarried motherhood has no inherent meaning, once identified as an exceptional
event, it calls for an accounting. Adolescent pregnancies and unwed
motherhood have had various historical constructions, shifting between sin and fallen innocence in the moral panics of 19th-century
America (Nathanson, 1991; Valverde, 1991) to a wide variety of
representations as group or individual pathologies, psychological or
cultural deficiencies, lack of education or contraceptive technologies,
and even sexual rebellion in more recent decades.

The ideology of domesticity and religious benevolence of some
19th-century U.S. homes for unwed mothers provided culturally
redemptive scripts for "fallen women" based on images of male lust
and female powerlessness (R. Kunzel, cited in Broder, 1994, p. 26).
However, the heightened concern with the "amoral" sexual behavior
of white middle-class youth in the 1960s, Nathanson (1991) explains,
coincided with the emerging definition of sexuality and conception
as mental or physical health rather than as moral issues. Medicalization,
as Nathanson points out, does not necessarily do away with moral
questions; it often merely relocates them: "The sexual 'morality' of
adolescent women was redefined to depend on their contraceptive
practices rather than their sexual conformity" (Nathanson, 1991, p.
71). Thus interventions subsequently focused on establishing a sense
of "responsibility," Nathanson explains.

Societal response to sexual deviance often depends on whether
the transgressor is believed to have been responsible or to have been
a victim of forces, external or internal—beyond her control (Nathanson, 1991, p. 211). For example, Rains's (1971) study contrasted the
identity of "good girl in trouble" constructed for unwed mothers in

a traditional maternity and infant placement agency with that of a
more psychiatrically oriented maternity home. The latter agency
viewed adolescent pregnancies as having identifiable psychological
causes for which the individual young woman should accept responsibility. The psychiatrically oriented agency encouraged the development of a (temporary) motherhood identity and mother–infant
bonding among young unwed women who were placing their
children for adoption as part of their taking responsibility for their
actions. The traditional agency, in contrast, discouraged the emergence
of maternal identities and minimized any contact between a mother
and her child: Their clients were not unwed mothers; they were "good
girls in trouble."[15]

The strong motherhood motives presented by the young alone
working-class mothers in this study provided not simply accounts
of how they became mothers. They also provided these women
with a mechanism whereby past actions could be interpreted in the
light of commitments to new identities. The salience of motherhood in these women's identities functioned to neutralize the
potentially degrading context in which they originally claimed
motherhood.[16] Motherhood, as we will see in the next chapters,
has "redemptive" qualities.

ALONE YOUNG MOTHERS:
A THREAT TO PUBLIC ORDER?

But why has there been such public concern about adolescent unwed
motherhood, especially in the United States? According to Nathanson
(1991, p. 214), the transition from childhood to womanhood has long
been considered dangerous both to girls themselves and to society.
Since the 19th century, Nathanson explains, the sexually unorthodox
young woman has been seen not only as individually deviant, but as
symbolic of social disorder. Adolescent nonmarital pregnancy and
motherhood violate hierarchies of age, gender, and family structure.
In patriarchal systems of gender stratification, Nathanson (1991, p.
208) argues, sexual autonomy is the prerogative, not simply of adults,
but of adult *males*: Women are expected to exchange their sexuality
and reproductive capacity for a man's protection and economic
support.[17] In practice, the patriarchal discourse of the male breadwinner disguised the exploitative conditions under which many black and

white working-class women labored to support their families (Jones, 1993; Kessler-Harris, 1993).

The structural conditions surrounding the organization of women's reproductive capacities have changed in recent decades. Whereas once a sexually unorthodox young woman was seen to risk her economic prospects by jeopardizing her marriage chances, today's young women are presented as jeopardizing successful careers by early childbearing.[18] Unlike those of young men, women's futures are portrayed as determined by their sexual behavior as adolescents (Nathanson, 1991, p. 208).

From a traditional (hetero)patriarchal standpoint, writes Griffin (1992, p. 491), almost any nonmarital pregnancy is a problem, but some are less acceptable than others. Women, Phoenix (1991b) and Rowland (1987) argue, are divided into worthy and unworthy mothers, defined as fit or unfit (or irresponsible) by the modern gatekeepers of appropriate motherhood—for example, medical, public health, child services, and social work professionals. Women's capacity to mother is evaluated without adequate appreciation of the material circumstances in which they live; thus the outcomes for children of disadvantaged young mothers are attributed to mothers' age or individual characteristics rather than to social conditions (Phoenix, 1991b).

Indeed, the construction of alone motherhood (or female-headed households) as a social problem and its identification with young women who are black or from marginal groups allow those "other" social problems of poverty, inadequate housing, and unemployment to be ascribed to the sexual behavior and individual attributes of the marginal individuals themselves (Nathanson, 1991, p. 224). Although, as Phoenix (1991a, p. 87) argues, moral panics about unwed mothers are less common in the United Kingdom than the United States; in the former, too, one finds the widespread but unfounded belief that disadvantaged adolescent women become pregnant in order to get welfare or subsidized housing. This belief further establishes their image as unfit mothers and as the undeserving poor (Phoenix, 1991b).

The moral panics surrounding adolescent pregnancies in the United States are codes for public concerns about unorthodox female sexuality, unwed motherhood, race relations, and a host of perceived related social problems such as school dropouts, welfare, and poverty (Phoenix, 1991b; Griffin, 1992; Nathanson, 1991). Although it is not usually made explicit, the debates are also centrally about women's sexual and reproductive autonomy but are framed in the context of race and class inequalities (Nathanson, 1991). Moral panics, Nathanson explains, are responses to crises of moral boundaries—the blurring of boundaries between deviance and respectability. Significantly, Nathanson (1991, p. 218) points out, the recent emergence of adolescent pregnancy as a public problem in the United States "coincided with a shift in public perception of the social location of heterosexual deviance from black to white young women," just as the earlier moral panic over prostitution coincided with public concern about *white* slavery. By reframing sexually unorthodox women's challenge to the gender order as one of unwed black teenaged mothers on welfare, the challenge presented to U.S. society as a whole is reduced to a problem of its black minority (Nathanson, 1991).[19]

SUMMARY

It is commonplace to suggest that becoming a mother has to do with becoming an adult. The relationship between adulthood and motherhood in this study, however, was complex and shaped by social class. On the one hand, when middle-class women talked about having their first child, they put forward claims to maternal identities as *achieved*, as social accomplishments. A certain kind of maturity, they held, had to be achieved *before* they were "ready" to have a child.

On the other hand, many working-class women saw themselves as achieving maturity *through* having a child. But maturity as what kind of person? For young working-class women, becoming a mother was more expressive than instrumental action. Claiming motherhood was expressive of an identity, of an ideal self as a loving, caring sort of person. In the act of having a child, these young women could realize or claim at least some of the positive cultural meanings of being an adult woman, accomplished, *not* through marriage, heterosexual attractiveness, or personal achievement, but through that *other* set of "feminine" cultural resources—being responsible for a child. Responsibility for a child was a way of establishing that one was "grown-up."

As we have seen, however, middle-class women had to be grown-up *before* they had children. But, again, grown-up as what kind of person? Borrowing from conventional masculine models of adulthood and applying them to motherhood, middle-class women *achieved* readiness to have a child: They became the sorts of persons who could properly have children.

Rather than considering having a child as a precondition to

female maturity, as is conventionally argued, it can be seen as a way of engaging and manipulating alternative cultural identities of adulthood. But if engaging the *identity* of mother (and, by implication, avoiding the cultural meanings of being a woman who did not or could not have children) was central to having children, the everyday relationship with children themselves later became central to being a mother (see Chapters 7 and 8).

Images of adult identity have political, not simply personal, significance. The dominant U.S. cultural metaphors of the self, Bellah and colleagues (1985) argue, emphasize the autonomy, achievement, and self-reliance of "the individual" and thus support a culture of (social) separation. Individuation and achievement become central to establishing adult identity. Such images of the individual, it is argued (Bellah et al., 1985; Pateman, 1989), express and legitimate the political culture of liberal individualism. The concept of career, for example, presents life as a linear, personal project: Adults are expected to make something of themselves. However, this conception of the adult individual, Pateman (1989) points out, carries the historical class and gender priorities of liberal democracies and is empirically unachievable by many women and minority persons. Generally only the middle-class women in this study had the material and cultural resources to engage and claim the identity of adulthood based on personal achievement, which (ironically) they did as a *precondition* to claiming motherhood.

Pregnancy and motherhood, argues Rothman (1989, pp. 60–63), embody a challenge to liberal democracy and the political culture of separation and individualism: Becoming a mother is the *physical embodiment of connectedness*. Motherhood offers an adult identity through connectedness and responsibility for a child. But such adult identities of connectedness are little valued within the rhetorics of modern liberal individualism, thus leaving many professional observers to wonder why so many young women make such "bad choices."

However, if motherhood has the potential to symbolize alternative bonds between human beings as Rothman (1989) stresses, in practice motherhood under patriarchal capitalism can lead to the commodification of children and the devaluation of women's reproductive and caring labor. It can also mystify inequality *among* women. The rhetoric of choice in the context of the class and gender inequality of contemporary capitalism attaches individuals to the social consequences of "their choices." Collapsing the potential meanings of motherhood into the discourse of personal choice allows inequality in the conditions in which women have children to be seen as legitimate. Inequality in a world of private choice does not threaten the political order because the inequality is seen as the outcome of individual choice, not the outcome of unequal social relationships. Certainly women should have the choice to mother or not, but when motherhood is constructed merely as an expression of personal preference, the poverty in which some women raise children is seen as their private problem rather than a societal responsibility (see Chapter 6). Such a representation of motherhood disguises the contribution of women's mothering to the collective well-being and thus denies social responsibility to provide support for it.

Ironically, although becoming pregnant may represent a gendered challenge to the dominant political construction of individual and contractual social bonds, in practice becoming a mother may exacerbate existing inequalities between women. I argue that the different circumstances by which the women in this study became pregnant and came to have children had to do not simply with the transformations of personal identities but with the reproduction of inequality through the production of babies.

5

Motherhood as Moral[1] Transformation: Middle-Class Women

In the previous chapters we looked at the transition to pregnancy and motherhood among working- and middle-class women. In this and the following chapter we look at how these women developed self-conceptions as mothers. This chapter focuses on middle-class women; the next chapter, on working-class women.

Both the working- and the middle-class women experienced themselves as new persons by becoming mothers. We will see how the experience of change they described went beyond the new role learning process typical of secondary socialization in adult life. Women's socialization into motherhood corresponded more closely to what Berger and Luckman (1966) have called "resocialization." Resocialization experiences—for example, religious conversions—require of their participants not merely a change of behavior but a change of *heart*. Like primary socialization, resocialization is highly emotionally laden and is typically achieved through interaction with significant others.

I will show how, for the majority of women in this study, motherhood was different from what they had expected. However, the "surprises" of motherhood varied by social class (see Table 5.1). We will see in this chapter how middle-class women found themselves unprepared for both the work associated with children and their own emotional responses to their children. Indeed, many middle-class women described themselves as overwhelmed or surprised by their feelings of connectedness and love.

Drawing on the sociology of emotions, I argue that the women's feelings can be seen as guides to the nature of the social bonds between these women and their children, in particular to the ways in which being a mother is constitutive of self and gender identity. Indeed, building on Simmel's (1984) analysis of love, I suggest that central to understanding the women's bond with their children is the uniqueness of the nature of the relationship between self and other. I will also argue that becoming a mother did not simply express gender identity but allowed the women to *achieve* a feminine identity as a loving, caring, responsible person.

My analysis of the role of love and emotion in the development of the maternal identities of the women in this study offers a sociocultural interpretation of their bonds with children rather than a psychosexual explanation based on concepts of feminine personality. As argued in Chapter 1, the meanings and practices of motherhood are socially and historically shaped and are complexly related to the broader social order and organization of gender, class, and race relations. The meaning of motherhood among the women in this study is further explored by looking at their responses to images of nonmotherhood. Both middle- and working-class women indicated that the image of remaining childless signified not merely the absence of children in their lives but also feelings of personal loss or incompleteness.

Finally, I will suggest that love and motherhood effected a "moral" transformation in these women's self-conceptions. I will show that maternal love carried many of the mythological themes and functions we usually associate with romantic love, and that it provided a major symbolic resource by which identity and the meaning of the women's lives were structured.

Although the pervasive influence of gender arrangements in society meant there were clear parallels in the middle- and working-class women's experiences, there were also differences—sometimes stark, sometimes subtle.

The purpose of Chapters 5 and 6 is *not* to exhaust what could usefully be said about maternal love or its ideological representations; rather it is to show the role that love and motherhood played in the participants' identities. The aim of Chapters 5 and 6 should also be distinguished from other studies of women's initial responses to motherhood, which have focused on the sense of crisis and shock that characterizes many women's experience in the early weeks and months after giving birth (Oakley, 1979). The women in this study had already been mothers for at least 6 months, most for 2 or more years (see Appendix 1).

It would be almost impossible for me to write these chapters about love and female identity without being influenced by the lively debate within feminism that emerged in response to the work of Carol Gilligan (1982). Gilligan's work represents an important challenge not just to liberal feminist analysis but to social psychology in general.[2] As indicated by the response to her work, Gilligan's theory has an intuitive fit with the way many women see themselves, especially in contrast to the way they see men.[3]

Gilligan calls attention to what she sees as the different ways men and women have of constituting the self and morality. Women's moral thinking, she argues, is governed by an ethic of care and responsibility to others; men's is governed by principles of justice and rights. Women, Gilligan adds, tend to define themselves through relationships with others, but men typically achieve identity through separation. For many women, therefore, Gilligan's work explains women's apparently greater capacity for intimate personal relationships and concern for others.

Gilligan's emphasis on the importance of connectedness with, and responsibility for, others in women's ways of thinking and talking about the world were echoed and reechoed by the mothers in this study. This observation persistently challenged me to be more critically reflective about the explanatory power of my own theoretical approach. In this and the next chapter, therefore, some of the ideas from this approach to feminist social psychology are discussed in the context of analyzing the experiences of the women in this study.

This chapter begins by looking at how middle-class women's experiences of motherhood compared with what they had expected.

"THIS MOTHERHOOD THING IS A TOTALLY OVERWHELMING EXPERIENCE": MIDDLE-CLASS WOMEN'S EXPECTATIONS AND EXPERIENCE OF MOTHERHOOD

Although half the middle-class mothers in this study had "always wanted" to be mothers and many others had come to claim a strong

TABLE 5.1. Middle-Class Women's Experience Contrasted with
Expectations of Motherhood

Motherhood different from what was expected	90%
Surprised by how much they could care or by their emotional responses to their children	65%
Surprised at the work involved	65%

Note. N = 31.

commitment to motherhood by the time they gave birth, the majority of these middle-class women were unprepared for the experience of being a mother. They described themselves as having been overwhelmed, shocked, surprised, and amazed.

When asked how their experiences of motherhood compared with their expectations, most of the middle-class women (90%) said it was different, and the majority (68%) said it was *very* different from what they had expected (Table 5.1). Only two middle-class mothers felt their expectations were realistic or accurate.[4]

Two major categories of unanticipated experience emerged from women's descriptions of how motherhood was different from their expectations: women were amazed at their own emotional responses to their children (65%) and also at the work involved in being a mother (65%) (Table 5.1).

These middle-class women had greatly underestimated the amount of work and the demands involved in having children. A mother of two preschoolers describes her sense of shock at the reality of mothering:

> I don't know what I thought it was going to be [like], I'm so deeply engrossed in the reality of diapers and the baths, screams, shrieks . . . flying of food and hair pulling . . . just the constant stuff that goes on with them every minute when they are around and not sleeping. . . . I think the biggest thing was I had no idea of how much work was involved. I had *absolutely no idea*. It's an incredible amount of work. . : . I found the work load absolutely incredible. (Fran: Lawyer)

Kim, a librarian and mother of a 1-year-old and a 2½-year-old, describes her responses to the wholly unexpected transformation of her life:

One can never envisage what it's like to work full time and have two children of this age. . . . You never really know how hectic life is until you actually find yourself on this treadmill. . . . The books, literature, everything you ever thought, never prepares you nor gives you any semblance of what it's like. . . . I don't want to sound overly negative, but it's not [what I expected]. (Kim: Librarian)

Perhaps more than anything, it was the lack of sleep that stood out in several mothers' minds:

I have a [2-year-old] child who sleeps far less than I ever thought was humanly possible for a child to sleep. That was the biggest shock of all. (Mary Lynn: Policy Analyst)

For the majority of the middle-class women, motherhood held other surprises; not only were these women unprepared for the demands and work, they were also unprepared for the emotional experience of being a mother. Women were surprised by their own feelings. Their responses to their children often came as a revelation to them. Marilyn, the mother of a 2½-year-old boy, explained that she had never known she could feel the way she came to feel as a mother:

It's nothing like I expected at all. It is completely different. I hadn't realized how hard it was . . . how much *hard work* was involved in it. . . . I also hadn't expected the way that my son would fill up my life. . . . I didn't know that I could feel that way. (Marilyn: Literacy Coordinator)

Rachael, a mother of two preschoolers, was unprepared for the work, but she was more unprepared for the emotional experience:

I had probably heard about it, but it never sunk in, how physically and mentally demanding children are. On the other hand, I never—I would never have known the kind of joy they could bring and . . . the love I was capable of having for my children. Every time they go through a new stage, I'm amazed. I find the whole thing a miracle. (Rachael: High School Teacher)

Several women who were professionals or experts on children and child development found that even their specialized training had

not prepared them for their own children. Nina, a childhood education professional, described her surprise as one "who supposedly is an
expert on children":

It's much more demanding, it's much more emotionally absorbing.
. . . I really was not prepared for the emotional impact on myself
of having a child—it was *profound*. I mean just *profound*. . . . The
whole experience was very overwhelming. . . . (Nina: Director,
Nonprofit Organization)

Jean had shared parenting with a previous partner and his
daughter for 5 years and was prepared for the work, but she was
unprepared for the feelings:

The actual reality of having a child in my life wasn't that much
of a surprise. I think the only thing that was a surprise was the
intensity of the emotional side. Not that I didn't expect to care
about him, but there is a different level of emotional involvement
than I anticipated. (Jean: Archivist)

The women had expected to love their children—yet surprisingly they experienced the intensity of their feelings as both unanticipated and unfamiliar (Table 5.1):

I didn't expect I'd love my child as much as I did—immediately.
I remember watching other parents and thinking, "Oh, how do
they put up with this and how do they put up with that?" But
then, when I had my own, it was like *"instant falling in love."* I was
totally absorbed. (Rebecca: Counselor)

It was perhaps Wendy, a policy analyst, who had her first child at
36 years, who most clearly captured the emotional gap between
expectations and experience that the majority of middle-class women
in this study described:

It's so far a very positive experience. I hadn't expected it would
be quite so overwhelming. I've become all mushy about it. I'm
all mushy about motherhood [which I didn't expect] . . . I
expected it would tie me down, and it does—but I don't resent
it. I expected I would and I don't. . . . This motherhood thing is
a totally overwhelming experience. (Wendy: Research Advisor)

We must not assume, however, that all mothers instantly (or even ever) fall in love with their children. On the contrary, Oakley (1979, 1980a) found that up to two-thirds of the British mothers she interviewed shortly after the birth of their children expressed negative feelings and ambivalence in their relationship with their new babies.[5] "Falling in love" and becoming a mother are better understood as processes of (mutual) socialization, rather than instant responses.

"I NEVER KNEW I COULD CARE SO MUCH": MOTHERHOOD AS FALLING IN LOVE

The middle-class women in this study described themselves as having been surprised by their feelings and overwhelmed by their emotions when they became mothers—as totally absorbed by their children; as though they had fallen in love.

Until recently, feelings and emotions have been largely neglected in sociology partly because of the "tacit assumption that emotion, because it seems unbidden and uncontrollable, is not governed by social rules" (Hochschild, 1979, p. 551) and partly because our society places a high value on rational behavior. One consequence has been that much of our emotional experience and expressions have been ignored or trivialized.[6] Given that, culturally, feelings are women's office (Goffman, 1987), a large part of women's world has been neglected. Maternal love, for example, has been typically ascribed a presocial, biological, or ideological function.[7] At the same time, much of what could be described as (culturally) female ways of thinking and knowing have been interpreted (and misinterpreted) as being essentially emotionally expressive and thus of lesser interest or value (Belenky et al., 1986; Gilligan, 1982). However, in this study I could not dismiss the women's expressions of their connectedness with their children as being simply emotionally expressive and thus of lesser sociological interest, especially since their descriptions of their feelings were central to their accounts of motherhood. But how was their talk about feelings to be interpreted?

A key contribution of the current interest in the sociology of emotions is to remind us that sociological explanation has been overly cognitive and behavioral and to demonstrate that feelings, as well as actions and ideas, are socially organized (Hochschild, 1979).[8]

To say that feelings are socially organized is not to suggest they are not real.[9] It does mean that to understand fully people's expressions of emotion, we must analyze them in their social context. The focus thus shifts from debating whether or not some emotions—be they maternal love, grief, or aggression—are universal, to a recognition that *all* human beings experience emotion-provoking situations. It is the variations in these situations and the responses to them that are sociologically interesting (Mills and Kleinman, 1988).

Like behavior and ideas, feelings are also governed by rules: we come to feel in ways that are appropriate to the situation or identities we claim (Hochschild, 1983). Situations usually carry proper behavioral and emotional definitions of themselves—as occasions for grief, joy, or love, for example.

There also appear to be different rules governing how emotions are interpreted and handled among different groups in society. Kohn (1977) and Bernstein (1971) show how class differences in childrearing practices reproduce class-differentiated emotion management practices. Goffman (1987), Gilligan (1982) and Hochschild (1979, 1983) point to the different expectations about feelings and their expression that govern the behavior of men and women. Indeed, women's (cultural) specialization in emotionality and their (perceived) greater vulnerability to feelings is popularly taken as proof of their feminine nature (Hochschild, 1979, p. 567).

To argue that social rules govern emotions is not to say that the feelings of love and being overwhelmed by emotions expressed by middle-class women in this study were not genuinely experienced or were mere acts of conformity to social expectations. On the contrary, as Mills and Kleinman (1988) point out, descriptions of being swept away and falling in love are not merely rhetorics of legitimations; people do feel intensely; they are overwhelmed by emotion. However, when and how people experience themselves as overwhelmed by emotion is typically socially patterned.

People are more likely to feel overwhelmed by their emotions during periods of intense personal or social change. People are more likely to fall in love when they feel vulnerable, for example.[10] The disruption and transformation of their daily lives that the middle-class mothers reported represent just such periods of intense personal change that are likely to occasion the experience of intense emotions.

Indeed, as anthropologists so clearly point out, societies organize both the social location and the times in our lives for intense and overwhelming feelings; funerals, weddings, religious rituals—all encourage strong emotional responses and frequently require their expression. Social rituals and institutions function to define and limit what is legitimate human behavior and what are legitimate human feelings and appropriate expressions of those feelings. People may experience themselves as overwhelmed by their feelings. But these feelings are socially patterned. Indeed, according to Mills and Kleinman (1988), many forms of spontaneous action are best understood "as part of the life course, or as a structured rite of passage" (p. 1014).

Motherhood, I will argue, can be understood as just such a structured time for intense emotion: an emotionally structured rite of passage in the transformation of female identity.

First, however, we must look more closely at the nature and meaning of love as an emotion.

LOVE: A GUIDE TO MEANING AND THE SELF

The middle-class women in this study felt surprised and often overwhelmed by their emotional responses to their children. How should we understand these responses? Hochschild (1983, p. x) argues that the key to understanding emotions lies in their signal function— to signal or communicate to us information about the world. In particular: "Emotions function as a messenger from the self, an agent that gives us an instant report on the connection between what we are seeing and what we had expected to see, and tells us what we feel ready to do about it." Feelings, in short, are a clue or guide to the self-relevance of things; they indicate what meaning an event or person has for us. For example, anxiety, as Freud pointed out, signals internal or external psychological danger to the self. Similarly, embarrassment signals that an individual's claim to identity has been discredited in the eyes of an other *and* that the individual cares that the other should so view her discredited identity (Hochschild, 1983, p. 215). Sadness, love, and admiration all tell of a self vis-à-vis a situation. And as with all guides to meaning, these emotions are subject to interpretation.

The names we give our emotions, according to Hochschild, refer to the way we apprehend a situation—the aspect of it we focus on—and what our prior expectations about it were:

> In sadness, I am focusing on what I love, like or want and also on the fact that it is not available to me. I do *not* focus on what has

caused the loss or absence . . . [but] I do focus on my relationship to the loved object. . . .

We call it *love* when we focus on the desirable qualities of a person or thing and on our closeness to him, her or it. We call it *admiration* when we focus on the desirable qualities of the person in light of some attention to social distance. (Hochschild, 1983, pp. 225–226)

Women's emotional responses, therefore, signal the self-relevance of children in their lives. In calling their feeling love, women are focusing attention on their connectedness with the objects of their love—their children—and on the perceived valued nature of children.[11] Children, as Zelizer (1985) points out, have acquired the symbolic character of culturally sacred objects in American society.

We must ask, then, what was the self-relevance of children for the women in this study, and what was the nature of the connectedness or bond they felt toward their children?

"I WOULD FEEL EMPTY WITHOUT CHILDREN—LIKE SOMETHING IMPORTANT WAS MISSING"

One way to learn about the nature of connectedness is to explore its absence. The women in this study were asked how they thought they would feel if they had never had children. Their responses reveal the centrality of attachment in their experiences of self. The idea of being without children was not experienced simply as an absence but as a *loss*.

The majority of middle-class women in the sample (81%) said they would feel empty or incomplete or that something important was missing if they had never had a child. About a third of the middle-class women also felt they would be depressed or sad as nonmothers, and a further 13% thought they would be lonely as nonmothers. Almost a fifth of the middle-class women felt they would have suffered a sense of failure or decreased self-worth if they had remained childless (Table 5.2).

The concept of something important being missing must be distinguished from the notion of missing out. The former concept refers to a sense of incompleteness—a loss. To say something is missing is to say that something that should be there is absent or lost; something is not whole, not full; things are not as they should be. The reference is to

TABLE 5.2. Middle-Class Women's Responses to the Image of Never
Having Had a Child

Would feel empty/incomplete/something missing	81%
Would feel sad, depressed, or lonely	47%
Would feel less self-worth/sense of failure	22%

Note. N = 31.

a moral rather than a utilitarian order. The concept of missing out, on
the other hand, may refer simply to lost opportunity. As we shall see
shortly, many of the women also felt that without children they would
be "missing out" on an important experience of personal growth or
pleasure gained through having children. The feelings of incompleteness,
loss, and emptiness evoked by images of themselves as childless, however,
were expressive of the sense in which children were constitutive of self
among women in this study. The absence of children meant the violation
of the integrity of self, not simply missed opportunity.

Margaret expresses the way in which, for her, children were
linked to feeling complete.

I'd feel a void [if I had never had a child]. I'd be one of those
people who look at kids and cry because I couldn't have one.
. . . I never felt complete until I had a child—and I can't even
explain what I mean by complete. (Margaret: Flight Attendant)

Tess's reflections are an example of how children were both
constitutive and *integrative* of the self in many of the women's self-
conceptions. Even their imagined absence was experienced as a loss:

[If I hadn't ever had a child, I would feel] a great loss—as if an
important part of me were missing. . . . I would see myself as
unfulfilled. . . . I see all of the things I have done in my life . . .
have been leading up to the point where I would have a child
. . . they were supposed to lead up to something. . . . Having a
child was such a fundamental thing . . . [an important part] of
who I see myself being. (Tess: Senior Policy Advisor)

For Tess, a child provided at once a coherence to her sense of her self
and to her life. For Marie, the image of herself as a nonmother, as a
woman who had never had a child, aroused feelings of loss and grief:

I am sure I would have to work through the loss of not having a child. . . . I would see it as a loss—as a grief issue. . . . I never imagined myself without [a child]. (Marie: Education Consultant)

Lofland (1982) shows how loss and grief can be understood as the other side of social attachment and connectedness. In our experiences of grief, she argues, what is *lost* are the threads of connectedness that bind the self to others. The experience of loss, therefore, can tell us a great deal about the nature of the social bonds that tie people; how self and other are linked. And social and cultural variations in *how* social bonds are organized help explain the observed cultural variations in how grief and, by implication, other emotional linkages such as love are experienced.

The threads of connectedness that Lofland analyzes to explain the experience and variations in patterns of grief also reveal the nature of grief's counterpoints—attachment or love. We are attached to others as role partners, for example, and the loss of significant or irreplaceable partners or of *potential* partners will be expressed in feelings of grief. If the other is lost or never found, so is the opportunity for playing that role. One cannot be a spouse without a partner, a mother without a child, and so on.

However, the experience of loss that the women in this study described in response to the prospect of childlessness went beyond the notion of absence of role partner. It spoke to a disruption in the phenomenological experience of self. In explaining how grief reflects such an experience of loss of self, Lofland writes:

> In the loss of a single other, part or all of self is lost as well. . . .
> [This interpretation reflects] a long tradition in social psychology which understands the self and its components importantly as the ongoing creation of the significant others who surround the actor. From within that tradition, reports of self loss are not viewed merely as descriptions through analogy but as literal depictions. That aspect of self (or those multiple aspects) that was significantly and uniquely generated and/or sustained in interaction with the other is, quite literally, lost when the other is lost. (Lofland, 1982, p. 226)

Or, in the case of the women in this study, the self experiences not simply loss but a sense of *incompleteness* when another who is central to an individual's self-conception has never been found. Thus psychol-

ogical integrity is threatened by absence as well as by loss: by the failure
to find the *particular other* who allows the realization of valued
self-conceptions.

Indeed, for Simmel (1984) it is precisely the irreplaceability of
the other to the self that lies at the heart of the phenomenon we call
love. According to Simmel, the key to understanding love lies in the
uniqueness of the relationship involved—a relationship in which
neither the integrity of the "I" or the "Thou" is lost. Love, he argues,
is not simply a response to the qualities or attributes of the other, for
these can be found in perhaps even greater perfection among others.
Mothers, as we know, do not love only babies who are cute or pretty.

But for many of the middle-class women, children were constitutive not just of a relational self but also of a "transcendent self." The
notion of relational self refers to the self culturally defined primarily
through connectedness with others, rather than through separation
and individuation (Lyons, 1983; Sampson, 1988). Women are often
socially defined in terms of their relationships; men, by their (supposedly) individual accomplishments. From a symbolic interactionist
perspective, of course, all identities and selves are relations, but they
are not always culturally represented as such.

The notion of transcendent self refers to the experience of self
not simply in terms of situated or biographical identities (see Appendix 3) but as located in the individual's sense of relationship to the
universe, sacred forces, or some generalized other that functions to
make overall sense of experience. Almost 40% of the women in the
sample felt that without children the meaning of life would have
become problematic for them:

[Without children] I would feel I had a kind of hollow, empty
life of just working and piling up money and material things.
. . . I think of the women I know who don't have kids, and I just
think, at the end of their lives what will they have to show for
their lives? Great wardrobe, nice cars. . . . (Janette: Manager)

The semireligious function of children in relation to such transcendent issues as death and the purpose of life are captured by Jenny's
reflections on remaining childless:

It's like knowing death, to never have a child—to experience your
own death as you are living. It's not so much that *I'm* going on
with her, it's just that *everybody is going on.* That life goes on. And

that's important for some strange reason. I don't know why, but it is. . . . That's probably it, you know, knowledge of your own death. (Jenny: Executive Secretary)

Nina shows how, for her, children fuse the sacred and the secular. That is, children integrated middle-class moral concerns regarding personal growth and development with universal and transcendent questions:

This is going to sound terribly philosophical. . . . In some respects I see life as being a quest for self-actualization and all of that. And I don't think anything does it like having a child. Now, I didn't actually know it [would do that] before having a child . . . [but] it's really broadened my perspective on life and the universe and my place in all of it, and who I am and what I am doing here. (Nina: Director, Nonprofit Organization)

The responses of the middle-class women to images of themselves as childless women provide important insights into the nature of women's connectedness with their children. Their feelings of connectedness reflected the extent to which children were constitutive of self in women's lives. Images of childlessness evoked in women a sense of loss, and for many women it made the very meanings of their lives problematic.

LOVE: THE EXPRESSION OR THE ACHIEVEMENT OF FEMALE IDENTITY?

So far in this chapter, women's accounts of motherhood might be seen to support many of the popularly held notions about women's inherent maternal natures. However, I will offer a more sociological explanation of women's connectedness to children in terms of the meanings children have in women's lives and in women's self-concepts. I have argued that children were experienced as constitutive of self among mothers in this study. We have seen that more than four-fifths of the middle-class participants said they would feel empty or incomplete or that something important was missing if they had remained childless; also that a similar number indicated they would see themselves differently if they had not had children. What then is this self in which being a mother is so central a part? And how does it arise?

To answer these questions, I begin with the concept of gender identity that I use to refer to the identities that women claim and that others attribute to them because of their biological sex. The relationship between motherhood and gender identity among the women in this study, however, was far more complex than it first appeared.

The development of gender identity can be understood as a central aspect of the development of self (Cahill, 1987, pp. 89–94). Sociology traditionally sees gender as learned, diffuse role behavior acquired through sex-specific socialization experiences, rather than a reflection of innate differences between male and female.

For Goffman (1987, p. 51), sex classification and gender identification are exemplary instances, if not the prototypes, of all social classification. Gender identification, like other forms of social identification, defines the meanings or nature of social objects and also defines how actions should be directed toward them (and ourselves). Both gender and sexuality, I argued in Chapter 1, must be understood as historically and culturally relative. Since the 19th century, Weeks (1981) argues, sex has provided the basis for the social and moral definitions of the person. A culturally dominant, essentialist understanding of sexuality means that gender identification has become profoundly constitutive of self concept (Weeks, 1981, p. 2). Such an understanding thus now informs one's deepest ideas and feelings about one's own and others' essential natures. It can, for example, mask the empirical social determinism of race and class. Goffman explains:

> Every society seems to develop its own conception of what is "essential" to, and characteristic of, the two sex classes. . . . Here are the ideals of masculinity and femininity, understandings about ultimate human nature which provide grounds (at least in Western society) for identifying the whole of the person, and provides also a source of accounts that can be drawn on in a million ways to excuse, justify, explain, or disapprove the behavior of an individual or the arrangement under which he lives, these accounts being given both by the individual who is accounted for and by such others as have found reason to account for him. (Goffman, 1987, p. 53)

Thus gender identification informs how we think about ourselves and provides a socially available gendered vocabulary of motives by which to make sense of our own and others' behavior. Gender, therefore, is not simply a set of behaviors or a role. It is a perspective: a way of acting, thinking, and feeling in the world.

Central to this perspective are the ways in which women claim love, and have love and emotionality attributed to them, to account for their behavior. The identification of women with love and emotional sensitivity is a relatively recent cultural product (Cancian, 1987; Smith-Rosenberg, 1975). As a consequence, according to Cancian (1987), there is a feminized and overly *expressive* concept of love in American culture that ignores typically male and practical ways of loving and leaves women with a problematic model of self-development.

I want to argue that in claiming the centrality of love and emotion in their experience of motherhood, the middle-class women in this study were not merely *expressing* a female identity; they were *accomplishing* it. Rather than seeing maternal feelings as a reflection of women's "female personality," we need to understand how becoming a mother allowed women to claim or produce a "woman-like" identity. By exploring the nature of the identities women claimed as mothers, we can understand how children became constitutive of self and a source of value to the self.

MATERNAL IDENTITY AS CHARACTER

The participants in this study occupied a social position of mother. As incumbents of this position, these women, like occupants of any social position, negotiate their identities and establish claims to being "certain sorts of people" who ought to be acted toward in certain ways. A person's identity is not established simply by the social position she or he occupies but also by the character she or he establishes in that role. "Character" refers to claims made about the kind of person oneself or another person is. Rosenberg (1979, p.16), for example, points out that although individuals may present themselves to others in terms of a status or role identity, they are *more* likely to think of themselves in terms of abstract personal qualities that testify to the type of persons they "really" are. Thus roles may be filled by people who are very different kinds of persons, and the character persons claim in those roles affects the identities they establish. A woman's character is centrally implicated in both the social and the personal identities she can claim as a mother.

Having children allowed middle-class women in this study to claim the *character* of mother by providing them with access to feelings and personal qualities that are characteristically feminine but that hitherto in some sense had apparently been inaccessible or unavailable to them (see Table 5.3). These middle-class women were surprised at their feelings. Motherhood evoked emotions and qualities that the women experienced as new or unfamiliar. "I wasn't expecting the intensity of feeling and how it affects the way in which you look [at things]," explained Cindy (Coordinator of Language Studies). "I never knew I could care so much," recalled another mother. Marilyn (Literacy Coordinator) put it like this: "I hadn't expected the way my son would fill up my life; I didn't know that I could feel that way." For Rachael (High School Teacher), "[Without children] I would never have known . . . the love I was capable of having." The reaction of Nina (Director: Nonprofit Organization) was similar: "I really was not prepared for the emotional impact on myself. . . . The whole experience was very overwhelming." Although feelings of attachment and emotional expressiveness are conventionally seen as "quintessentially feminine," it was becoming a mother that allowed these women to experience those "feminine" feelings—the female character of being a loving and caring person:

[The best thing about having a child is the] emotional discovery. It's sort of like falling in love, only it's different. Unless you've done it you don't have that central experience in your life. It's very intense. (Penny: Managing Editor)

Motherhood, in this sense, did not express women's maternal nature; it allowed them to claim that nature:

Somehow, I didn't expect that much. Even the day before he was born, I really didn't expect [that much]. . . . The shift is so [significant]. . . . For the longest time you *aren't* [a mother] and when you *are*, you are in a different state altogether. I hadn't expected so much maternity on my part. (Wendy: Research Advisor)

Character assessment, as we know, plays an important role in social identification. The display of emotion can greatly influence character assessment (Heise, 1989). Displays of emotion, for example, can influence the identities attributed to people; for example, the visible presence or absence of remorse influences the way that "deviants" are treated. Similarly, emotions register an impression of one's identity not just to an external audience but, equally important, to *oneself*. In claiming and attributing identities, as Heise (1989) notes, the issue of "real" identity may hinge not on behavior but on *feelings*:

> The question [of identity] is not merely what kind of person would engage in such conduct, but rather who would engage in such conduct and feel the way this person feels. Reassessment of the person's [or our own] character must take account of the emotion displayed. . . . (Heise, 1989, p. 14)

For the middle-class women in this study, I suggest, giving birth is no longer the defining test of identity, but achieving (what is culturally seen as) an essentially female character of a caring, loving person is. And motherhood, as we shall see shortly, was seen as central to realizing just such a character transformation. But the identity these middle-class women claimed through motherhood was not simply one of gender, but a *gendered* identity, or self. That is, through motherhood these middle-class women achieved not just a female adult identity but a *feminized* adult sense of self. Anna, an alone parent of a 2-year-old, explains how the character, feelings, and identity she acquired through becoming a mother were interwoven in the new sense of herself not just as mother and woman but as *human*.

> [Without children] I think I would probably be emotionless— "emotionless" is a strong word. I don't mean hard. I mean superficial, not very deep. I'd see myself more as a sister or daughter. And those roles would be very important to me. And [as a] friend. Friends would be extremely [important]. [I see myself as a] friend still, but it's changed. I'd see myself as a career person [if I were without a child]. (Anna: Community College Teaching Master)

Note how Anna contrasted the relative "superficiality" of her experience of role identities as sister or friend with the deeper sense of self she felt she gained through motherhood—her sense of self as a *human being*. Even gender identities relate back to that more *fundamental* self, which, ironically, her gender allowed her to access. Anna continued:

[Now] I want to get my career on track for financial security, but I think [without a child] I would have viewed myself as an administrator/teacher instead of—now I view myself as a *human*. I have to say *human* because woman means one thing if I view myself as a woman and mother means another thing. I feel very *human* and within that those roles are woman and mother and that's the vulnerability that's come about. (Anna: Community College Teaching Master)

The experience of self-transformation, we will see shortly, was one of the dominant, if not *the* dominant, experience of motherhood for these middle-class women.

In this section I have argued that motherhood did not merely allow women to express gender identity; it also allowed them to achieve a *gendered* sense of "real self." The roles of love and children in the achievement of a gendered self among the women in this study become clearer when we consider what women say about how they were transformed through having children.

MOTHERHOOD AND THE TRANSFORMATION
OF SELVES AMONG MIDDLE-CLASS WOMEN

For the majority of the middle-class women in this sample; becoming a mother led to a sense of profound personal change. Ninety percent felt themselves changed by the experience of motherhood; 68% felt they were changed a lot; and 22% felt somewhat changed. Women experienced themselves as having changed in both external and internal ways—in the practical details of everyday life and in the ways they experienced themselves in the world (Table 5.3).

When women were asked to describe how they felt themselves to have been changed, three major grounded categories of change emerged: personal growth and development; transcendent change (changed relationship with the universe, the rest of humanity or some generalized other); and practical changes in life-style and the use of their time. Although the last category of change is the most obvious and the one most commonly referred to in general conversation and popular culture, it was the first two categories that were the focus of women's self reflections.

Eighty-one percent of the middle-class women experienced themselves as transformed through a process of growth and development that motherhood effected in their lives. Forty-two percent experienced a sense of transcendent change; that is, they felt their relationship to the world, to life, or to humanity had been transformed. Twenty-six percent referred to practical transformations in their lives when describing how they had been changed by motherhood (Table 5.3).

The most frequently mentioned forms of personal growth and development that the middle-class women felt motherhood had produced in their lives were learning about one's self; awareness of one's values; and a transformation in one's personal qualities, such as becoming more patient, less selfish, and more mature and confident. Loretta described how motherhood changed her:

> [Becoming a mother has] . . . made me more realistic; it's made me more giving; it's made me more tolerant; and it's made me busier. It's made me more tired. (Loretta: Elementary School Teacher)

It would be easy to dismiss these accounts of personal change experienced by women because they invoke qualities we typically attribute to mothers in society. We expect mothers to be giving, tolerant, and tired. However, to the women in this study, their sense of having been changed was neither superficial nor taken for granted; they were frequently surprised by the depth of self-change they experienced. Fran, a lawyer and mother of two, explains:

> I've grown up a lot [by having children]. I have gotten rid of a lot of problems—a lot of problems I didn't know about. . . . So it's been very helpful for my personal growth. That was sort of the unexpected benefit with each child. . . . It can be quite surprising how you can change *yourself* as a person—the growth you experience as a person. (Fran: Lawyer)

TABLE 5.3. Ways in Which Middle-Class Women Felt Motherhood Had Changed Them

Changed through personal growth and development	81%
Experienced transcendent change	42%
Changed in practical ways	26%

Note. N = 31.

Interestingly, the middle-class women talked about their experiences of motherhood in ways we usually associate with romantic love. Sociology and anthropology have long recognized that a culture's ideological and religious images provide the symbolic resources that structure and give meaning to individual lives. These symbolic resources are typically central to the resolution of predictable life crises such as birth, the achievement of adulthood, or death.

Swidler argues that in Western cultures the mythology of romantic love has provided just such a symbolic resource in the achievement of adulthood. Like all myths,[12] the love myth's power comes from its ability to fuse contradictory elements: in particular, the tension between social commitment and individual identity—between self and society—that is characteristic of modern adulthood.

> In Western culture love has played a central symbolic role in integrating the issues of individual identity, moral choice, and social commitment. Courtly tradition made love a moral matter, ennobling and disciplining the self; bourgeois culture made love a central symbol of the individual quest for identity, integrity and fulfillment. (Swidler, 1980, p. 125)

By the 19th century, according to Swidler, love had come to provide a key cultural motif for middle-class women's lives. The association of love and marriage in bourgeois society meant that love represented not simply the expression of the "true self" and personal identity for women; it *also* represented the achievement of social identity and social position. Falling in love and getting married organized a female status passage; it "concentrated into one critical event all the questions about livelihood, [social] mobility and achievement that were becoming so critical for the middle class" (Swidler, 1980, p. 123). Thus the quest for identity and self-fulfillment was incorporated in the quest for social position. The association of emotion with femininity was institutionalized in the class structure of bourgeois society and in the subjectivities and priorities of its members.

The culture of love and emotional expressiveness among 19th-century American women, as Smith-Rothenberg (1975) points out, was reinforced by the rigid gender segregation of that period and also by the increasing value placed on children and the transformed medical and social definitions of good mothering.

Listening to women in this study speak of the bonds they felt with their children, and seeing how these women came to define themselves through their relationships with others, it would be easy indeed to conclude that women do indeed have a "distinctly female personality" characterized by an ethic of care, responsibility, and intimacy (Gilligan, 1982; Chodorow, 1978). Instead, however, by understanding the social and historical context of women's cultural specialization in love and caring for others we can offer a socially reflective perspective on women's emotional bonding.[13] To further explore the relationship between female identity and maternal love in its cultural context we must first look at how changing images of self, of love, and of identity were reflected in these women's thinking about motherhood.

LOVE AND THE SYMBOLIC STRUCTURING
OF MODERN ADULT IDENTITY
AMONG MIDDLE-CLASS WOMEN

Critics of contemporary American society argue that "expressive individualism" and "narcissism" are replacing the notion of commitment in modern conceptions of love and social responsibility (Bellah et al., 1985; Lasch, 1979; Ehrenreich, 1983). Some have pointed to the women's movement as reinforcing or extending this trend (Berger and Berger, 1983; Lasch, 1979).

Although love and marriage no longer socially determine the achievement of adult identity for middle-class women as they did in the past, one cannot conclude that the love myth has lost its symbolic role in the structuring of personal identity and the meaningfulness of women's lives. Indeed, among the middle-class mothers in this study, maternal love performed many of the functions attributed to romantic love and structured a female identity in which commitment to children rather than to a man was central.

Repeatedly, what Swidler (1980) identifies as the key themes of the romantic love myth emerged in the women's accounts of the self transformations they experienced with motherhood. These themes express love's symbolic power: Love transforms and reveals character; love allows us to find our true selves (and just reward); love is a moral test in which we discover our own true worth; love allows one to know and be known—and thereby to know one's self; love can overcome individual isolation and call out the "true self"; and love

changes people and marks significant turning points in the development of self.[14]

> In loving and being loved, people give themselves over, at least for
> brief periods, to intensely moving experiences through which
> they achieve new awareness of self and other. Love can make
> possible periods of crystallization or reformulation of the self and
> the self's relationship to the world. Beliefs about love permeate
> people's hopes for themselves, their evaluations of experience, and
> their sense of achievement in the world. (Swidler, 1980, p. 121)

Middle-class women felt themselves profoundly changed by
motherhood (Table 5.3). Their stories reaffirmed the core elements
of love mythology: Motherhood occasioned both a transformation of
self and a rediscovery of what already existed in the self, albeit deeply
buried. For these women, the self-transformation of motherhood was
at once both integrating and liberating: The new and the old were
born and reborn. For Patricia, like many women, change was experienced as self-realization, both in the sense of achieving self-knowledge
and in the liberation and development of the self's potential:

> [Becoming a mother changed me a lot. It meant] maturing. I've
> had to look at myself honestly and openly. I've had to define my
> own values. I've had to reexamine my own values. It gives you a
> real good look in your own face. It led to confidence—confi-
> dence to go back to school. It liberated me. (Patricia: Community
> College Teaching Master)

For Penny, motherhood meant more self-recognition than self-
transformation. Coming to know one's self can bring pain:

> [Becoming a mother changed me a lot.] It made me worse and
> better—[no,] it certainly hasn't made me worse. It has made me
> more realistic about my faults, though. I mean, I've discovered all
> these nasty things [about me]. I mean, I'm impatient and I'm
> selfish and things like that. But in discovering those things you
> become less so, you know, you become more grounded. . . .
> (Penny: Managing Editor)

Like Penny, Joanne saw motherhood as a form of moral testing:

Certainly, I learned a lot about myself. It focused my life. . . . I think that the abilities that I had became highlighted. . . . My weaknesses became obvious, too. I think you are tested on every level when you become a mother. So you discover the good and the bad [about yourself.] (Joanne: Elementary Teacher)

The theme of motherhood as moral testing—exposing the good and bad, the strengths and weaknesses—was a recurring one and provided a context for women's self-evaluation. Beth explained how motherhood has changed her:

It has changed the structure of my life in terms of how I spend my time. It's taught me a great deal. . . . It has given me a lot of self-knowledge. I am more aware of my flaws—aware of [my] limitations. . . . It's also given me an appreciation for some of my strengths. I've much more patience than I realized. (Beth: Management Board Officer)

Beth also shows how motherhood transformed her broader sense of being in the world:

I've become much more pessimistic about the world, much more concerned about that, much more anxious. I can't think more than a couple of years into the future—it's too scary . . . because I've a stake in the future. . . . Theoretically we all have . . . but it's a very dramatic immediate thing when you have children. (Beth: Management Board Officer)

Most middle-class mothers in the study felt that motherhood had transformed their personal sense of themselves; many also felt it had transformed their transcendent selves, their relationship with the universe or humanity. Tannis, who had been an alone parent for several years and who is now remarried, explained how having a child affected both the way she felt about herself and her place in the world:

I think I have become more responsible and more stable. I think it has matured me a great deal. It has given me more focus for my life. In some ways I do feel more important as a mother. I mentioned [how having a child makes me feel I have] a stake in the future. I do feel I have some importance. (Tannis: Counselor)

Middle-class women also talked about their feelings of having a different commitment to the world, a different stake in the future, and a different relationship with humanity, all of which came with motherhood (Table 5.3). Margaret explained how the connection with a child that motherhood brought transformed her experience of connectedness with the world:

> How has it changed me? It's so hard to look from the outside in. I guess I'm more community concerned—in a global sense: not just self-oriented. I really look at children as the bead of life. And I have a more global perspective, and I feel closer to humanity. Having gone through childbirth and just raising a child is such a universal thing to do. It's really opened my mind . . . about a lot of issues. I've learned to love people more, because we were all children once. (Margaret: Flight Attendant)

Thus women's sense of connectedness to their own child can produce an identification with humanity. For other women, it was their sense of connectedness with a specific section of humanity that was transformed—their identification with other women:

> I think I'm aware of my limitations, of how women are limited. I guess I have a lot more sort of sympathy for women as a whole, for understanding what it's like to be a woman in this society. (Tess: Senior Policy Advisor)

We have seen, therefore, how these women experienced themselves as deeply changed by the experiences of becoming mothers and that in their apparently private experiences of themselves, women expressed the mythological themes of their culture.

THE "GOOD" MOTHER: COMMITMENT WITHOUT ENGULFMENT

For many of the middle-class women in this study motherhood also brought a "moral" transformation. I use the term "moral" because the changes described relate to a (perceived) typically female value system or ethic of care and responsibility (Gilligan, 1982; Lyons, 1983). Middle-class women typically felt they had undergone a particular form of moral development into less selfish and more responsible or caring persons. Marilyn, for example, contrasted herself as mother and nonmother by reflecting that "I think I would be a totally different person than I am now. I think I would be a more selfish person." Similarly, Tannis contrasted her present self with her previous nonmaternal identity and with nonparents:

> [Having a child] has been really good for me. . . . I think I would feel a little empty and rootless [without a child]. I talk to friends who don't have children, and they seem to have so much time, but they seem to fill it sometimes with things . . . that don't [matter], things I don't value particularly. . . . I see myself as a more responsible person [than if I hadn't had a child]. (Tannis: Counselor)

As Swidler (1980) points out, love does not simply symbolize the struggle for adult identity in the dominant American cultural tradition; it also embodies a struggle for moral perfection.

> [My child] provides the opportunity to be giving . . . My former life was much more taking. The opportunity to be giving rather than taking is a marvelous feeling. (Wendy: Research Advisor)

Repeatedly, women saw themselves as having achieved the characteristically feminine moral attributes of giving and caring through motherhood. As Carolyn (Secretary) put it, "In some ways I'd feel I never had to give anything up [if I hadn't had children]."

For Laura, this moral transformation of self isn't simply an act of will:

> I see myself as more responsible, more unselfish. . . . Children force you to be less selfish because they tend to be very selfish. . . . I mean, you have no choice. So, you *have* to be less selfish and you *have* to be more responsible. (Laura: Accountant)

Similarly, Sandra explained that she would have seen herself as being "much more self-centered without a child." Like Sandra, Loretta also experienced a moral shift in the relationship between self and others through becoming a mother:

I think having a child . . . certainly [makes you] less self-centered. . . . Before I had kids . . . I was much more . . . egocentric . . . looking much more at the immediate, you know, just having a good time and having a fairly good social life. (Loretta: Elementary School Teacher)

Thus many of the middle-class mothers came to see themselves as less self-centered persons through motherhood; however, these middle-class women did *not* present motherhood as a form of self-sacrifice.

In the middle-class women's descriptions of "good" and "bad" (or poor) mothers, the emphasis is on process rather than on product. That is, women saw the criterion of "good" motherhood as lying within the nature of the mother–child relationship, rather than as the outcome of that relationship or the behavior of the child. Good mothers, they explained, love and care; they are sensitive, responsive, and empathetic to their children and their needs. Good mothers were expected to interact appropriately; to *show* love, nurturance, and patience:

[A good mother is] someone who takes time to listen to the child and to understand from their point of view, [who] doesn't get short and shout at them too much. (Jean: Archivist)

Penny explains:

What seems to be hard on kids and hard on mums are a lot of expectations, a lot of, you know, "the way a kid should behave" or "the way a mother should behave." I think we are our own worst enemies. And the mothers who seem very good at it [mothering] are the ones who relax and enjoy their kids. (Penny: Managing Editor)

Good mothers are expected to enjoy their children. The current changes in the amount of time women are available to their children can affect how women see mothering:

I think it's good to *enjoy* all the time I do spend with Jennie. I have a very limited amount of time with her, but there isn't very much time when I'm not really *glad* to be with her or interested with her. I think [the role of a good mother] is mainly stimulating the child. And if I'm happy and satisfied, I pass that on to Jennie. (Janette: Manager)

While emphasizing the connectedness of mother and child, middle-class women also employed "strategies of separation" that limited the total absorbtion of self and the mother role. Almost 40% of the mothers felt that to be a good mother, a woman should have developed a strong sense of herself, have self-confidence, or have realistic and manageable expectations about herself as a mother:

> [A good mother involves] having a good sense of herself. . .being able to integrate the child in aspects of her life . . . being able to integrate the two so that the mother wasn't totally given over to one or the other. . . . I feel it's harmful for a mother to be totally engrossed in the child to the exclusion of everything else. On the other hand, a woman who tries to have her life remain totally unchanged by having children, . . . I think that has a bad effect on the children. (Marilyn: Literacy Coordinator)

Women pragmatically adjusted the ideals of the mother role:

> [A good mother is] a person who has some self-knowledge so that they can know their own limits . . . and don't [feel] that they have to be a supermom all the time. [They accept] that they are going to yell at their kids and get pissed off. . . they have to accept the negatives and acknowledge that they are not going to be able to do everything. (Sandra: Civil Servant)

These women struggled to have role commitment without role engulfment. The issue was not simply one of role conflict; it was also one of role redefinition in a context of abstract and ill-defined expectations. Mother love was no longer equated with self-sacrifice or self-denial, and by defining good mothering as a matter of the right feelings, women could continue to claim the uniqueness of the mother–child relationship:

> [A good mother] is happy in the choices she's made. She is willing to put her child's needs ahead of hers quite often, maybe not all the time. . . . A good mother's love is not conditional. (Loretta: Elementary School Teacher)

The middle-class women's definition of good childrearing also functioned to limit role engulfment. If mothers were not to be totally absorbed by their children, neither were children to be totally created by their mothers. The majority of the middle-class mothers (55%) said that respecting a child's separateness or psychological autonomy was an important part of being a good mother. As Cindy put it, "[A good mother] is able to accept her child and [does] not try to mold that child into something that is alien to him or her." For most of the middle-class women, the ideal of mothering was that their children should develop their own potential and not be the mere product of their parents. It was a mother's task to provide the "right environment":

[A good mother] is really just able to unconditionally love and accept their child for who they are and where they are and what they are all about, and not try to mold them into something to meet their expectations. I think it's someone who can be there but in the right context. (Nina: Director, Nonprofit Organization)

Women in this sample interpreted the ideals of motherhood in ways that were consistent with their lives. Where there is little consensus on the rules of motherhood, women may use their feelings as guides. Ultimately, these women emphasized, good mothers are those who have and show the *right feelings* toward their children.

The strong emphasis on emotions and caring in the middle-class women's definition of good motherhood allows these women to continue to claim the uniqueness of the motherhood experience. At the same time it allows them to affirm the desirability of having others share in traditional motherly activities of childcare and early childhood education. By using *emotions* as the central element in motherhood women's unique claim to their children is less threatened by behavioral changes in the maternal role.

SUMMARY

In this chapter, I have argued that, for the middle-class women in this study, motherhood performed many of the symbolic functions that love in the romantic love myths played in structuring experiences of adult identity transformation. Like romantic love, motherhood played a symbolic role in integrating issues of individual identity, moral choice, and social commitment in these women's lives. The themes of moral transformation in the middle-class women's accounts of becoming mothers speak to love's symbolic power to both transform and reveal character. Building on Hochschild's (1983) analysis of emotion, I conceptualized maternal love as expressive of the relevance of children to the women's experience of "real self." Love, as Hochschild (1983) reminds us, focuses on the perceived value of the other (the child) and the closeness of the self to that valued other. For Simmel (1984), love points not merely to closeness to the valued other but to the latter's irreplaceability to the self.

Middle-class women talked about the connectedness and relationship they felt with their children; I have argued in this chapter that children should be understood as constitutive of these women's phenomenological sense of real self. In this sense, motherhood was experienced as an "essence-making" process. Indeed, it appeared that it was having children that allowed women to claim or realize this phenomenological sense of real self in ways that reaffirmed certain cultural ideals of womanhood. That is, becoming a mother *produced*, rather than simply *expressed*, gender.

As we have seen, becoming a mother for these middle-class women was not only a matter of giving birth to a child; it was also experienced in terms of a moral transformation of self. Many experiences in adult life leave individuals feeling profoundly changed, but few are so publicly and privately recognized as so consequential for identity as is becoming a mother. And few, I suggest, carry the cultural resources needed to effect such a symbolic transformation of the self. However, the association between motherhood, morality, and self-transformation raises more questions than answers. What is it about motherhood that has the cultural power to so symbolize moral transformation in a woman's life? And what are the cultural meanings of children, such that they seem to be so central to the production of gender through motherhood? In what ways do children function as cultural resources in reconstituting, as "morally enhanced" persons, women who become mothers? And how, if at all, is the production of gender and moral character through the cultural resources of motherhood and children connected to the reproduction of classed and raced gender identities? Specific cultural meanings of children and motherhood, I argue in the next chapter, entwine gender identities with broader social processes.

On the one hand I have argued that the concept of gender-role socialization is inadequate in understanding the process of becoming a mother. Motherhood, I have emphasized, produced gender: It did not merely express it. I pointed to the surprise women felt at their feelings for their children, the ways in which they felt they were unprepared for what children would mean in their lives, and the profound ways in which they felt themselves changed. On the other hand, I argue here, socialization and culture *are* central to becoming a mother. That is, these women implicitly "knew" the cultural associations of caring, morality, and character in women's lives. Using Swidler's (1980) notion of culture in action (see Chapter 1), I suggest that the ways in which gender is tied to caring and the symbolic possibilities of love constitute elements of cultural repertoires that can be differently engaged by women and men—and differently engaged by different women. Clearly such associations are *not* universal. At the same time, cultural motifs engage or play upon the possibilities of selfhood. The moral links between children and women's characters are such that it feels right to love one's child, and to mothers who do not feel such love, its absence is deeply disturbing—it feels wrong. The social and psychological implications of seeing one's self as, or being perceived as, an unloving or bad mother are profound. Dominant representations of women's character, as I will suggest in later chapters, so tie women to caring, and in particular to caring for their own children, that it becomes unthinkable for a woman not to act in a responsible way toward her child—to be an irresponsible mother. (There may, of course, be profoundly different interpretations of what "responsibility" means.) This is not to suggest that men do not, or cannot, care for their children: Indeed, they do. But for middle-class men, I suggest, character is still culturally more tied to achievement. Thus, although for the middle-class women in this study, achievement was often a precondition to becoming a mother, children continue to carry profound implications for women's characters and the production of gender. It is in this sense that motherhood can be experienced as moral transformation. This point becomes clearer when we look at the working-class women's experience of becoming mothers.

6

Motherhood as Moral Reform: Working-Class Women

We saw in Chapter 5 how middle-class women experienced themselves as having been changed through motherhood. I argued that becoming a mother was experienced as a form of resocialization in which women's sense of connectedness with their children became constitutive of new experiences of self. In this chapter we look primarily at working-class women's experience. Although the working-class women in this study were far less likely than the middle-class women to say that motherhood was different from what they had expected, they, too, described themselves as transformed by motherhood. However, their descriptions of moral transformation were dominated by themes of "moral reform" rather than by themes of personal growth or self-actualization.

I use the term "moral reform" for several reasons. The changes the working-class women described can be considered moral, in Goffman's (1963) use of the term, as indicating that which pertains to the self. The term "moral reform" is also used here not simply because the working-class women frequently described themselves as having become better persons through motherhood; it is used also because the changes in self they described fit what Gilligan (1982) describes as a typically female value system or ethic of care and responsibility. For these working-class women, motherhood meant "settling down."

Finally, I suggest that motherhood has long had "redemptive" qualities in culturally Christian narratives of female biography, and that such guiding metaphors helped create and sustain an experience of self as a unitary and coherent subject: Life is experienced as organized around an enduring, meaningful, and changing self. But such guiding metaphors, I argue, also hold implicit political meanings.

This chapter looks at how working-class women talked about their feelings of connectedness with their children. Like the middle-class women, their responses to images of themselves as non-mothers pointed to the centrality of mothers' connectedness with their children in their phenomenological experiences of real self (see Chapter 5).

Finally, the chapter looks at similarities and differences in how the working- and middle-class women talked about their ideals of mothering. Class differences in how women talked about their definitions of good and bad mothers are interpreted not simply as class-based ideological differences; they also reflect differences in the material contexts in which these women mother.

This chapter begins by looking at how the working-class women's experience of motherhood compared with what they had expected.

WORKING-CLASS WOMEN'S EXPECTATIONS AND EXPERIENCE OF MOTHERHOOD

We saw earlier that the majority (90%) of the middle-class women in the sample found motherhood to be different from what they had expected (Table 6.1). Working-class women, on the other hand, were *less* likely to have been surprised by motherhood. Almost half of them (46%) said that being a mother was similar to what they had expected, whereas only 6% of the middle-class women had that reaction.

Eighteen percent of the working-class women suggested that prior experience with children had prepared them for motherhood. Yet this form of preparation was discounted as inadequate by those middle-class women who mentioned having previous experience with children.[1]

To my surprise, alone working-class mothers were *not* more likely than mothers with partners to say that their expectations were violated by the realities of motherhood. Almost half (45%) of the former felt

TABLE 6.1. Experience Contrasted with Expectations of Motherhood

	Middle-class women	Working-class women
Motherhood different from what was expected	90%	54%
Surprised by how much they could care or by emotional responses to their children	65%	14%
Surprised at the work involved	65%	32%

Note. N = 31 for middle-class women, 28 for working-class women.

that motherhood was as they had expected it to be. Val, an alone mother, explained that she knew what being a mother would be like: being a mother meant being loved.

> No. [Being a mother is as I expected.] The way I felt when I said I wanted someone to love as much as they love me, and getting that feeling, the amount of work it takes, the challenges, the cares. All of that, for some reason I knew that, and it's everything I expected. There is nothing different and new that I never thought of before I had her. (Val: Apprentice Mechanic)

But for just over half of all the working-class mothers (54%), being a mother *was* different from what they expected. Of these, two-thirds found motherhood unexpectedly demanding, especially in terms of work and time. Although the women who said they had been unprepared for the work of mothering were a minority among the total working-class sample (32%, compared with 65% of the middle-class mothers), their sense of not having realized how much would be required of them was nonetheless very strong. Sally, a mother of two, put it like this:

> Yes, definitely [it's different from what I had expected]. I hadn't really been around babies. I didn't really understand about all the work and the time and the energy. . . . And you can't really tell people how much energy and time [it takes]. People go, "Yes, yes, I know." But unless you really have to do it yourself, and day after day, I don't think you can really . . . know how much it entails. It *really, really* takes a lot of energy. (Sally: Bell Service Assistant)

Although Sally had a partner, she experienced the workload as if she were alone:

> And in my case, you know, I'm the only one here—I'm the one who picks the kids up and drops them off. . . . You know, *I'm it*. I didn't really realize how much [work it was]. (Sally: Bell Service Assistant)

Forty percent of those who were surprised by their experience also found motherhood more rewarding than expected, either emotionally or practically. Again, although only a minority of the working-class mothers (25%) said their experience was better than they had anticipated, it was the *contrast* with expectations that stood out in these women's minds, not the "taken for granted."

> It's better than I ever could have imagined. I didn't think anything could be as wonderful as this. It's the best thing that ever happened to me in my life. [And] I was afraid of babies, too. I was afraid of handling them. (Barb: Clerical Worker)

Whereas most of the middle-class women were unprepared for their own emotional responses to their children, only 14% of the working-class women said they were surprised by their feelings. This does not imply that the working-class women were somehow less caring than the middle-class women; they may simply have had more realistic expectations about both the costs and the rewards of having children.

Similarly, the class differences in how women described being overwhelmed or surprised by their feelings may reflect more general class differences in the way people talk about emotions (Komarovsky, 1962; Rubin, 1976), in their emotional management practices, and in their emotional self-reflectivity (Hochschild, 1979, 1983). Or the class differences may reflect different assumptions about having control over one's life such that the unanticipated is not experienced as surprising.

Although just over half of the working-class women found motherhood to be different from what they had expected, few expressed the sense of shock or amazement that so characterized the middle-class women's accounts. To understand the class differences in women's responses to motherhood, it is necessary to look at the images of self and motherhood that working-class women articulated, and also at the practical circumstances in which they mothered.

"I HAVE RESPONSIBILITIES NOW":
TRANSFORMATIONS OF SELF
AMONG WORKING-CLASS MOTHERS

Like their middle-class counterparts, the working-class women in this sample (82%) experienced themselves as having been changed through motherhood (Table 6.2). Fifty-four percent said they had changed a lot; 28% said they had changed somewhat.

Whereas the middle-class women described their transformations of self in moral terms, in terms of personal growth and development, of transcendent change, and, to a lesser extent, in terms of practical changes in life-style, the working-class mothers described a subtly but importantly different experience of change.

At first I thought working- and middle-class women were describing similar experiences of the personal growth and development they associated with becoming a mother. Like their middle-class counterparts, the working-class mothers made frequent references to "maturity" and "responsibility" to describe their experiences of self-transformation. However, when I looked more closely at the data, it became clear that middle- and working-class women's conceptions of maturity and responsibility referred to different experiential realities. Middle-class women spoke in terms of psychological self-discovery, self-actualization, increasing self-confidence, and becoming less self-centered as results of motherhood. For working-class mothers, the self-transformation experienced through motherhood was described through the imagery of acceptance of limitations, lack of choice, self-denial, and moral reform. They talked of concrete

TABLE 6.2. Experiencing the Self as Changed through Motherhood

	Middle-class women	Working-class women
Felt themselves changed through motherhood	90%	82%
Felt motherhood changed them a lot	68%	54%
Felt motherhood changed them somewhat	22%	28%

Note. N = 31 for middle-class women, 28 for working-class women.

restrictions and self-abnegation: Motherhood meant "settling down" (Table 6.3).

Working-class mothers felt that having children had forced them to "become responsible" and "settle down." Over three-quarters (79%) described the changes they experienced with motherhood in this way. Only 11% mentioned the themes of self-actualization and personal development referred to by the middle-class women.

Both working- and middle-class mothers talked about achieving maturity, or "growing up," through the experience of motherhood. However, for the working-class women, "growing up" meant confronting the restrictions of working-class life: a life with few choices and resources, a "harder" life. As Jackie observed:

> [Becoming a mother means I have] more responsibility—you have to take a harder outlook on life. You have to look at things more realistically, in terms of facts as opposed to dreams. (Jackie: Secretary)

Like both working- and middle-class women in the study, Renee felt she had become more "responsible" through having children. Without a child, Renee explained, her *life* would have been easier, but *she* would have been "worse": She would have been less mature and responsible:

> [Without children] I think it would make a difference—it would be the responsibility part, because, you know, you *have* someone that's counting on you to come home and feed them. I think it would be worse, maybe it would be worse if I didn't have a child, like for responsibility-wise, for [my] maturity, or whatever. . . . [Without a child] you wouldn't have to worry . . . and I probably wouldn't get as frustrated. (Renee: Truck Driver)

TABLE 6.3. Ways in Which Working-Class Women Felt Motherhood Changed Them

"Settled down" and became "responsible"	79%
Self-actualization	11%
Experience of transcendent change and changed connectedness to the future	17%

Note. N = 28.

The reality of "responsibility" for Renee was not simply a psychological process of personal development. Eight months pregnant with her second child and working as a contract laborer driving a municipal garbage truck, Renee's routine involved getting up at 4:45 A.M. Having a child made a traditionally working-class male occupation particularly difficult. Until recently Renee had been an alone mother. However, in her new relationship, she got few of the domestic privileges often provided to those who hold "men's jobs." She was still a woman.

> Yeah, I get frustrated or irritated. Like, I'll yell at [my partner] Bob, or something. Like it seems it's always woman's work, right? I'm the one that gets up in the morning. I have to get up at 4:45 A.M. I have my shower and get ready. Then I cook on the stove, get her lunch all ready, get her up. . . . And then I come home and you've got to cook, clean, bathe her. Some days are worse than others. (Renee: Truck Driver)

As mothers, the working-class women confronted the realities of class society in new ways; life became harder and more restrictive, but in other ways it acquired more positive meanings. Working-class women repeatedly recalled their prematernal selves as carefree. And they tended to interpret the restrictions and difficulties currently in their lives as the outcome of their *own* private decisions and commitments to children. They did not usually ascribe them to class-based inequalities in their society, though some did attribute them to unequal gender arrangements.[2] Hardships were described as "responsibilities," about which these mothers expressed neither surprise nor outrage: It seemed to be the price of having children.

Karen was 24 and the mother of three preschool children when I interviewed her. She was earning minimum wage as an unskilled manual worker at a dry-cleaning store. Her partner worked part-time and sometimes "babysat" the youngest child, but Karen said she did the other domestic work. She described becoming a mother as "settling down" and becoming "more responsible":

> They [the children] changed me. I feel more dependent now. When I didn't have them I was carefree. But now I can't be like that. . . . I have responsibilities. They settled me down. (Karen: Dry Cleaner's Shipping Clerk)

Karen's words discount the notion that by speaking of the cost of having children she might imply that she didn't love them. For her, the joys and hardships of life as a mother appeared inextricably intertwined. The joys may have made the hardships more acceptable but did not make them less real:

> Now that I have mine, I love them for all the world. They change your life, they make your life joyful. Then sometimes they don't. I'm not going to lie and make it sound like everything is rosy. Sometimes they stop you from doing things with your life that you want to do, right? (Karen: Dry Cleaner's Shipping Clerk)

The working-class women in this study felt that becoming a mother shifted their experience of self in relation to others. Judy, for example, described her self-transformation as a process of learning that "[now] I have to put other people before me." Similarly, Rita's response to being a mother was to shift the balance between self and other in her primary relationships:

> [Now that I'm a mother] I don't think of *myself.* Before, probably, I thought of myself more than I thought of everybody else. Now I stop and think of other people before I think of *me.* (Rita: Unskilled Factory Worker)

Many of the middle-class women, as I showed earlier, described the new relationship between self and other that came with motherhood as a process of becoming "less self-centered," but one that was neither self-sacrificing nor self-denying. They redefined themselves through connectedness with their children, but in a way that limited the engulfment of self in that relationship.

The working-class mothers were more likely to describe the new relationships of motherhood as "putting others first." For Marg, motherhood shifted her perspective and her priorities: Family, she said, came first.

> [Since I've become a mother] little things don't matter as much, like materialistic things don't matter as much. I guess I am just concentrating on my *family* and making them happy. (Marg: Accounting Clerk)

It is sometimes pointed out that a strong commitment to family among working-class or poor people reflects in part an economic survival strategy for dealing with material deprivation and uncontrollable life circumstances (Bridenthal, 1982; Sacks, 1984; Stack, 1974). Working-class women's focus on family also offers a psychological coping mechanism (Pollert, 1981). By "just concentrating" on their families, working-class mothers like Marg could shift their attention from the reality of what Marg described as "materialistic things that don't matter as much" and over which she had little control to a personal world shaped by commitment to her children.

In listening to these women speak, at first it seemed to me that they held traditional conceptions of motherhood that emphasized self-sacrifice and self-denial. Gradually, however, I came to understand that these women were using the language of a traditional ideology of motherhood to symbolize the process of self-change they experienced in adapting to lives that were more concretely difficult but at the same time deeply meaningful. To these women, motherhood, I argue, did not mean the sacrifice of self. Rather it meant the "death" of an earlier sense of self and the emergence of a new self through a process of moral reform. In this context, the notion of self-sacrifice for one's child is rhetorical in that the self has been transformed in ways in which self and other are integrated. Thus when women spoke of self-sacrifice, it was the sacrifice of other selves rather than the self as mother to which they were referring.[3]

MOTHERHOOD AS MORAL REFORM

In Chapter 5 I showed that middle-class women talked about motherhood in ways we usually associate with romantic love. Similarly, motherhood provided the symbolic resources or guiding metaphors for the expression of a transformed sense of self among working-class women. Their accounts carried many of the mythological themes identified in Swidler's (1980) analysis of romantic love: Love was a moral test, love transformed and revealed character, and love changed people and marked a significant turning point in the development of the self.[4] Participants' constant references to having responsibility communicated implicit images of mature commitment, personal competence, and moral worth—a taking on of important social obligations, of making a social contribution. For both middle-class and working-class women, motherhood carried the symbolic power to reconstitute them as morally enhanced persons. For the working-class women, it carried redemptive powers.

The motif of redemptive motherhood was widely shared among the working-class women but was strongest among alone working-class mothers. Eighty-two percent of them expressed such an imagery. Mary, a young alone mother of a 6-month-old, explained that becoming a mother meant she gave up her old ways of frequenting "bars" and of "dancing"; motherhood did not merely require her to take on responsibility, but it enabled her to do so.

> [Since I've become a mother] I've been able to take on more responsibility. . . . Before I used to go dancing, bars. . . . I had nothing to worry about except myself . . . and you don't really have much responsibility except for yourself. (Mary: Hotel Housekeeper)

That Mary felt a greater responsibility for her *child's life* and his impact on the world than she did for her own raises questions about how Mary had previously conceived of herself or her own worth. But it points also to the cultural significance of children as symbolic keys to the future in modern society:

> But when you have a baby you sit there and look. Well, now you have a *life* to look after. And also, you know, it's going to change the world because it's one more human being. . . . To do this is a lot of responsibility. (Mary: Hotel Housekeeper)

Changed self-conceptions dictated new codes of behavior. June, a daycare assistant, said her new identity as "a mom" led her actively to change and control her behavior—to forgo going out and having fun. At the same time she found she occasionally had to remind herself that she had become a new person and should therefore act differently. The funny, crazy person she had been was gone, she said, and was replaced by a mother:

> Sometimes I get frustrated and tired of it. . . . I just want to go out and have fun, leave [my son] John at home with a sitter. But I'm a *Mom.* I have a child that I've got to support. [I used to be] funny and crazy. . . . yeah, I was like that before. I was funny. I was

crazy. I was nuts, but *now* . . . I think I've matured more since I've
been a mother. (June: Daycare Assistant)

Although having children entailed costs and difficulties, working-class women, and alone mothers in particular, felt they were better
persons for it. Kathy, a young alone mother, explained how having a
child represented not simply moral reform but personal redemption:
Becoming a mother saved her.

> I don't want to think about [my life without a child]. I'm glad I
> do have one. I think my life would be in a *mess* right now. I was
> too wild when I was single, and crazy, and I probably wasn't going
> to advance too much. . . . I used to go out and party too much.
> . . . Now when my apartment is in a mess I think I have to clean
> it mostly for Pete, whereas before . . . I wouldn't even see it or
> care. . . . Now I am a hundred percent different. Not in my views
> and values, but my attitudes in some ways and also my actions. I
> work for him now and I put more effort into it. I've gained, and
> so has he. (Kathy: Accounting Clerk)

Thus the working-class mothers saw their changed lives in terms
of their own new moral characters as mothers.

Many alone mothers held a self-identity not just as mother but
also as an alone mother. Although aware that such an identity was
unorthodox, several of the women attempted to engage this unorthodoxy to construct (at least for themselves and me) an enhanced
maternal identity: an identity that provided the motivational basis for
greater efforts in terms of work, providing for their children, and
"being responsible."

> I look at things differently [now]. Being a single mother I try
> harder with things, to prove that I can do it without Brian's father
> around. It has made me grow up a lot and take on responsibilities
> more. . . . Before, I was so carefree. (Diane: Clerical Assistant)

No doubt these mothers' engagements of the moral meanings of
motherhood were partly inspired by the widespread view that alone
motherhood represents not the expression of female responsibility but
rather that of immaturity and irresponsibility. These alone mothers
emphasized that they were mature and responsible.

In practice, the class and gender structures within which these young alone working-class mothers lived made the realization of their aspirations to be responsible mothers and to better their own and their children's lives very difficult. Motherhood effected a transformation in self-conceptions, perspective, and motivation that objective structures of society were likely to frustrate. Yet although the responsibilities of alone motherhood placed heavy restrictions on these young working-class mothers, several of the women mentioned that they drew strength from their special maternal identity and the intensity of their relationship with their children. In some ways children were both the occasion of and the compensation for the "hardness" of life.

> Especially now that I'm separated [from my child's father], it doesn't matter how hard everything else gets, and all that. She's the only one that doesn't—you know what I mean. I would never give her up for anything. . . . I would give up anything—just as long as I had Tara, I wouldn't care about anything else. (Mara: Clerical Worker)

In Mara's account, her child helped her not to resent the hard terms of her life and at the same time provided her with an enhanced identity as a mother—as someone for whom her child meant the world. Mara implied that it was only through her child that she could come to feel good about herself:

> Tara makes me feel good about *me*—before her I was not feeling good about me, you know what I mean. I can't think how to say it. [Without her] I'd be sort of independent. I'd be doing things a lot faster than I am now—as far as school and all that goes. I'd be working a lot harder at those goals. But they are back seat to her now. (Mara: Clerical Worker)

What was it about being a young woman that meant that to become a mother offered the opportunity to feel like a better person, to feel good about herself? Had she previously felt of little value? What seems clear is that their children helped the working-class women make sense of their lives by making them feel like changed and better persons.[5] Cultural motifs of motherhood provided guiding metaphors by which to integrate biography. Sally, a married mother of a 2- and a 4-year-old, articulated the connection between the meaning of life and the nature of individual identity that was implicit in many of the women's accounts of motherhood. The practical responsibilities of motherhood represented a form of moral testing for Sally:

[Without kids] I think I would feel like I wouldn't have as much responsibility—kinda like a weight lifted off your shoulders. I'd be able to buy things when I wanted and do things when I wanted. I think I would be more self-centered. I don't know if I'd feel like a real part of it, of the community, or not. I'd probably feel more like a machine than really contributing . . . like someone who is just here for a joy ride. . . not really making a contribution, just doing what they wanted. . . . [Children] help you be a better person. (Sally: Bell Service Assistant)

Working-class women in this study felt themselves changed by becoming mothers. Their stories of personal change were characterized by images of moral reform. This imagery, I suggest, is partly the symbolic representation of these women's coming to terms with the concrete restrictions of their life circumstances as working-class women with children. But it also expresses, I will argue, specific but often implicit meanings of motherhood that women engage both when they have children and, as I argued earlier, when they remain childless. Motherhood and children can implicate women's "essential" character.

COUNTER IDENTITIES:
IMAGES OF SELF AS NONMOTHER

The working-class women in this study had similar, though not identical, responses to images of themselves as nonmothers as had the middle-class women (Tables 5.2 and 6.4). Forty-three percent of the working-class mothers said they would feel empty or as if they were missing part of themselves; 43% felt they would be depressed, sad, or lonely; and 29% said they would feel like a failure or would have less self-worth as nonmothers. A total of 75% responded in one or more of those ways (Table 6.4). Fourteen percent also mentioned they would feel they were not complete women if they had never had children.

As with the middle-class women, so also for the working-class women the notion of something important being missing and the feeling of being in some sense incomplete or not whole must be

TABLE 6.4. Working-Class Women's Responses to the Image of Never Having Had a Child

Empty/incomplete/something missing	43%
Depressed, sad, or lonely	43%
Less self-worth/sense of failure	29%

Note. N = 28.

distinguished from the notion of simply "missing out" on an experience (see Chapter 5). An alone mother of a 3-year-old put it like this:

[If I had remained childless] I'd be heartbroken—empty. I don't think I'd feel *whole*, you know what I mean. . . . I don't think I would have any self-confidence or respect or . . . (Tina: Hospital Dietary Aide)

Pam, a married mother of two, reflected:

[If I had remained childless I would feel] like I was missing something in my life. An empty spot. I would probably feel like a big part of my life was missing. (Pam: Clerical Worker)

The feelings of incompleteness or emptiness evoked by the prospect of childlessness, as I showed earlier, relate to a disruption in the phenomenological experience of self. These feelings also indicate the value of a self that would never have been found without motherhood. Motherhood allowed Barb, a married mother of a 2-year-old, to find something she was really good at: being a good mother:

[If I had remained childless I would feel] lonely, unfulfilled. I'm not really a career person, so it's very important to be [a mother]. So I'd guess I'd be very unhappy, very unhappy. . . . I can honestly say, and I don't say I'm good at anything, but I'm a *good* mother. I'm a really *good* mother. And it's the only thing you'll hear me say that about. It's the only thing in my life I feel I'm *really good at*. Otherwise I'd be going through life thinking I was OK or rotten at all these things. Now at least I can say, "Yes, I'm really good at something." (Barb: Clerical Worker)

Twenty-nine percent of the working-class women felt they would have been missing out on some valuable or important experiences by not having had children:

> [If I hadn't had a child] I *would* have one. I would feel unhappy. I would feel lonely. . . . I think one of my main reasons for having a child and wanting more children was because I'm looking at my future. . . . I don't want to be lonely in my old age. I want to have a family. I want to have kids around [me]. (Rose: Secretary)

For Sue, a marrried mother of three children, not having children would have meant missing out on the experience of having a family. But, in contrast to many mothers, Sue would *not* have felt the integrity of her sense of self was threatened: Indeed, childlessness held attractions for her.

> [If I had remained childless] I would miss the family, the family development and closeness. But I think I would have adjusted. I would have led a totally different life. I would have been a totally different person. I would have been a little bit more self-centered. I would have pampered myself a lot. I would have dressed differently. I would have been able to afford a whole different life-style than I can now. . . . Now, I *have* to be responsible. (Sue: Legal Secretary)

For Sue, as for other working-class women, the notion of responsibility mediated the concreteness of restrictions and individual identity in ways that turned class and gendered social arrangements into issues of personal character. But *unlike* many of the other mothers, Sue was mother not only to a preschooler but also to older children (aged 7 and 13). As their children grow up, women's experiences of motherhood change in practical and symbolic ways. The cultural association of early childhood with innocence and the construction of women's role as guardians of the innocents, I argue shortly, helps imbue mothers' character with moral worth.

Although the women in this study repeatedly referred to their connectedness and commitment to their children, their feelings about motherhood were far from simple. Almost a third of the working-class mothers had ambivalent responses to images of their lives without children. Eleven percent said they felt they could adapt to being childless; 18% said they would feel free or relieved without children, although most of these mothers also said they would feel empty or lonely without children; but 7% were sure they would feel better in terms of greater self-worth and greater self-confidence if they had remained childless.

When both middle- and working-class women were asked, "If you were doing things over again, would you still choose to have a child?" the majority (83%), as might be expected, said yes. The others were unsure or thought they would not choose to have children again. However, working-class women were somewhat more likely than middle-class women to be ambivalent about choosing to have a child if they were doing things over. Ninety percent of the middle-class women, but only 75% of the working-class women were *unequivocal* about whether they would still choose to have children if they were to do things over again. *None* of the middle-class mothers, and 11% of the working-class mothers said they would *not* have children again. An alone working-class mother of a 5-year-old boy put it as follows:

No. I don't want to say no. But . . . if I was doing things over again, no. When I had [my son], that was an accident. I don't know how that came about. [Now] I'd want to work . . . just to get ahead, I guess. (Kimberley: Sheet Metal Worker]

Kimberley thought she would feel better without children. That is, she felt she would be more secure in a job and less anxious about money to buy groceries.

[Without a child] I'd probably feel a little—*a lot*. . . better because I know I'd have a job. I'd be saving my money and I wouldn't worry about groceries and how much [money] I'd have left over and everything like that. (Kimberley: Sheet Metal Worker)

An additional 14% of the working-class mothers said that perhaps they wouldn't have children if they were doing things over again or perhaps they would not have children under the same circumstances:

I'm not sorry I have Brian. But I wouldn't have done it. . . . I wouldn't have chosen to have a child . . . not under those circumstances. . . . I don't think even if I'd been married I'd have wanted to. . . . I just didn't want kids. I never wanted any. . . . If it hadn't been an accident, I don't think I'd have Brian—even now. (Diane: Clerical Assistant)

At first it appeared that the class differences in women's responses could be explained simply by marital or partner status. Alone mothers seemed more likely to be ambivalent toward the idea of repeating motherhood. Indeed, 45% of the alone working-class mothers were ambivalent or hesitant about choosing motherhood over again. However, the alone middle-class mothers showed no such ambivalence: All of them said they would have children again if they were to do things over. Thus feeling hesitant or ambivalent about "doing it over" was associated not simply with being an alone mother but with the circumstances of being an *alone working-class mother.* Although these mothers may have felt ambivalent about doing things over, they were not ambivalent in their feelings of commitment toward the children they now had.

Mothers in general, and ambivalent mothers in particular, found it hard to articulate their reservations about being a mother. By talking about the regrets they felt, these women risked symbolically denying both their children and the depth of their love for them.

The women who were clear that they would not have children if they were to do things over again were but a small minority of the working-class sample (11%) and only 5% of all the women in the study. These women had been alone mothers and, like most of the ambivalent mothers, had been welfare recipients for part of that time. The ambivalent mothers often explained that they would have liked to be better off financially or to have more education before they even had had to consider motherhood—if they were to do things over again. Like these ambivalent mothers, the women who clearly would not have had children again tried to separate their reservations from their present commitment. It was one thing to suggest that one might not choose to be a mother over again; it was quite another to suggest that one was a less than a loving mother. Kimberley, for example, who said she would not choose motherhood again, emphasized her current attachment to her son:

[Getting pregnant] was an accident really. Now it's not an accident. I don't regret having him anyways. . . . I don't regret having a child (Kimberley: Sheet Metal Worker)

Although Kimberley said she would feel better if she did not have a child, her identity as a mother was central to her account of her life. According to Kimberley, it was her child who motivated her to want a good job and "to get ahead." That is, having a child had led her to aspire to exactly those things that were made difficult to achieve because of the combination of her being an alone mother and her class position—further education and job advancement. Yet it was as though Kimberley previously had felt she could not claim for *herself* the things she had now come to want; she could only claim them now on behalf of her son:

[Having a child] changed me in that I know I want to do good for him by working and getting where I want. I want *him to know*, like, we are going to get ahead. . . . [And I want to get ahead] for me, too. I want him to know that I'm not going to be on welfare or things like that. . . . I just don't want him resenting anything, well, *resenting me* for anything later on in life. (Kimberley: Sheet Metal Worker)

Similarly, Kathy, also an alone mother, explained how becoming a mother changed her goals and provided a new source of motivation:

I probably wasn't going to advance too much [the way I was before I had a child]. Now I have a clearer mind on what I want to do—just keep on working and keep advancing. . . . I do things I really put aside before. I say I'm doing them for him. (Kathy: Accounting Clerk)

The alone working-class mothers' feelings of ambivalence about having children over again came not from any lack of love; rather, they arose partly from the concrete difficulties of being a mother without adequate material or economic resources. The ambivalence came from the ways in which their disadvantaged social circumstances frustrated their ideals of good mothering, leaving them anxious not just about their own futures but, more troubling, about the futures of their children.

In general, these mothers did not apply a utilitarian cost–benefit analysis to their experience of having children. For a minority, the price was vaguely sensed in retrospect and articulated only with great difficulty. For the majority, the price was never calculated at all. Marg, a married mother of a 6-month-old baby explains:

[If I didn't have a child] I guess I would . . . probably put all my
energy into work . . . so I wouldn't have to worry about money
when I get older. . . . But having a baby, I guess I think more of
loving more. . . . [It's] better than the materialistic sense. That's
one thing I've noticed since having the baby. I'm less materialistic
than I was before. (Marg: Accounting Clerk)

Because their attachment to their children was experienced as
moral rather than instrumental, both Kathy's and Marg's experience
of themselves and the nature of their connectedness with their
children would have felt violated by the imposition of a utilitarian
framework. The absence of such a framework, however, leaves much
of the objective cost of children to the women hidden from themselves and from public view. But it also suggests that we need to look
closer at the moral benefits of children, especially for alone working-
class mothers for whom, according to social commentators, the costs
of motherhood are high.

THE MORAL BENEFITS OF CHILDREN

We saw that both the working- and the middle-class women had
negative images of how they would have felt had they remained
childless. Although alone working-class mothers were more likely
than other mothers to be hesitant about saying they would have a
child again if they could do things over, they were also *more* likely than
mothers with partners to have strongly negative projections of their
lives *without* children. Eighty-two percent of the alone working-class
mothers typically presented images of themselves in which they
would be "feeling terrible"; "lonely"; "lost" and "depressed"; "going
crazy"; and feeling like a failure as a woman or having low self-worth
if they had remained permanently childless. Tina, an alone mother of
a 3-year-old who became a mother at 16, reflected on the prospect
of remaining childless:

I'd be heartbroken—empty. I don't think I'd feel whole, you
know what I mean? I wouldn't feel like I could be a *woman*.
. . . I don't think I would have any self-confidence or respect
or. . . . I don't think I would enjoy life as much. (Tina: Hospital
Dietary Aide)

For some women, the image of their own lives without children was shaped by the beliefs they held about the unhappiness of childless women. Helen, an alone mother who worked very long hours to support her two children, explains her feelings:

> [If I never had children I'd feel] probably lost, you know, *bad* that I didn't have the experience. . . . Probably I'd feel less, you know, you hear about all these people who don't have kids and they feel so [bad], you know. . . . [I'd feel] less as a person, a mother, I mean, a woman, whatever. It may be stupid, but. . . . (Helen: Waitress/Cashier)

Like many working-class women, Helen represented the social inequality she experienced as a consequence of being a mother, as rooted in the individual circumstances of her life as a woman, rather than as a consequence of the social structure.

> [If I didn't have children] probably I could have done differently in work, you know what I mean? I could have probably went to school and maybe be paid much higher than I am now [and] not being used so much as I am . . . because with kids [you need money right now]. (Helen: Waitress/Cashier)

The alone mothers' accounts stand in sharp contrast to ways in which they are often publicly or professionally represented. Many held a devalued view of their lives *before* they became mothers, and the majority found it hard to sustain positive alternative conceptions of themselves or their existence without children:

> [Without children] I would probably feel empty, probably terrible, probably gone crazy or something silly. . . . I know David has chained me down a lot . . . but I prefer to stay home, wake up early with him, get my full weekend in and feel good about it with him, than [to] wake up and say, "I don't want to get up . . . I've got a headache from drinking too much," or whatever. (Cora: Word Processor)

It is hard to know whether these young women's representations of their lives before motherhood were empirically accurate, or symbolic of the ways in which they felt morally changed, or whether they were expressive of resistance to dominant, pejorative images of young, unwed mothers. The alone working-class mothers, however, were well aware that having children restricted their choices, and many experienced frustration. But they did not express resentment toward their children for "tying them down"; they explained their restricted circumstances in terms of how their children made them feel better about themselves and their lives.

For example, although Val thought she would be more carefree without a child, she explained how her daughter provided her with a sense of self-worth and in some sense anchored her in the world. Without her daughter, she reflected, she didn't know who she would be or why she lived her life:

> [If I hadn't a child, I would see myself differently]. I would definitely have no self-worth. She is my life right now. And if I didn't have her I probably wouldn't be doing anything that I am now. She is my reason for living. That's exactly how I feel about it. . . .
>
> If I didn't have her, I don't know what I'd be doing now. I don't know what job I'd have, what friends I'd have. I think about that a lot and then I forget about it, because I can't *imagine* [not having her]. I probably wouldn't be as responsible; I'd be more carefree and not thinking about anyone else. (Val: Apprentice Mechanic)

Val's daughter allowed Val to value herself. Motherhood provided access to self-worth for the other women like Val who, in feeling good about their children could feel good about themselves, and who, in caring for their children, could care about themselves. A child provided at once a new way of thinking and feeling about oneself *and* a new self. In describing the best things about being a mother, Val comes close to saying that her child is herself:

> [The best things about having a child are] watching her grow up, watching her learn, being with her. She is mine. She is *all* me. She is my twin, something I am proud of. I can show her off. She makes me feel wanted and needed. Every time I think about her she makes me smile. I glow. I don't know how to put my feelings into words. (Val: Apprentice Mechanic)

Thus children allowed the alone working-class mothers in this study to escape from a life—and by implication, a self—they felt was of little value. It allowed them to achieve a sense of self that they respected and to try to claim legitimate access to the conventional rewards of our society, such as educational or occupational advancement, not on behalf of themselves, but *in the name of their children.* Middle-class women, in contrast, from the vantage point of conventional occupational success, claimed children on behalf of themselves.

In the next section we look at what working-class women said about their ideals of motherhood.

MATERNAL IDENTITIES: "GOOD" AND "BAD" MOTHERS

Middle-class mothers in this study, as we saw, presented images of good and bad mothers in ways that focused on process rather than on product. Their descriptions of good mothers emphasized the connectedness of the mother–child relationship while at the same time acknowledging the separate identity of each. Good mothers were those who loved, cared, empathized with, and were sensitive and responsive to their children and their children's needs.

Working-class women's descriptions of good and bad mothers also emphasized the nature of the relationship between mother and child but were more *behavioral* than those of the middle-class women and referred to different concrete experiences.

Four themes dominated working-class women's discussion of good and bad mothers: spending time with their children, good communication, correct interaction with their children, and the provision of adequate material care (Table 6.5).

Good mothers spend time with their children, and poor mothers do not, according to a majority of the working-class mothers (57%). They did not, however, specify how much time. Good mothers also communicate with, understand, or are sensitive and responsive to their children. Lisa reflected:

[Being a good mother] I think involves being able to communicate with her. OK, me and my mom were never close actually until I got married. . . . See, my mom is European, and she never talked about the pill, about boys, about sex, any of that. I probably will be the same way, but I want to be able to talk with [my daughter] about these things anyways. (Lisa: Data Entry Clerk)

TABLE 6.5. Themes Identified by Mothers in Their Descriptions
of Good Mothering

	Middle-class women	Working-class women
Understands/empathic/responsive/ communicates	68%	50%
Spends time with her children	18%	57%
Mentioned patience/not getting irritated	32%	46%
Respects the child's separateness	55%	14%
Raised issues of discipline	13%	21%
Doesn't abuse	7%	32%

Note. N = 31 for middle-class women, 28 for working-class women.

Good mothers also have patience and avoid becoming irritated or frustrated with their children, according to many of the working-class mothers. These mothers talked about patience in ways that were somewhat different from those of the middle-class mothers. The working-class mothers were more likely to introduce the topics of irritability, bad temper, and physical and emotional abuse of children as characteristics of bad mothers and as behavior to be avoided:

A good mother is someone who would respond to their child. Love is probably the primary factor. . . . [And] patience. You have to be very, very patient. . . . [A good mother] would try not to be too stressed out or fly off the handle. She'd try to count to 10. She'd try not to use physical discipline if it's unnecessary. . . . She would try to build up the child's self-esteem, and she would teach the child good moral values and a sense of responsibility. (Sally: Bell Service Assistant)

Given the variability of parenting, it is easier to be specific about what is *not* acceptable than about what constitutes the ideal:

Every mother is different. . . . Basically . . . as long as they're not *beating* the child, child abuse. . . . A mother that does things with their children, I guess. Just like I say, every mother is different. (Karen: Dry Cleaners' Shipping Clerk)

Almost a third of the working-class, but only 7% of the middle-class, women mentioned child abuse in talking about good and bad mothering. Finally, working-class (50%), but *not* middle-class, women mentioned providing adequate physical and material care and keeping children clean, healthy, and well dressed as part of being a good mother.

Oakley (1974) points out that vague and abstract ideals of motherhood tend to produce anxiety because it is difficult for a mother to know when she has reached an acceptable standard of performance; this is no doubt the case. At the same time, high ideals but vague behavioral prescriptions may allow the very varied everyday lives that parents and their children lead together to proceed, precisely *because* ideals can be variably interpreted in light of the prevailing circumstances. Every child is different, parents remind themselves. Problems arise, however, when behavioral expectations established in one set of circumstances are transported to other circumstances. Child welfare workers and their clients, for example, do not always share the same definitions of good mothering. For the working-class women in this study, providing for their children's material and physical needs both expressed and demonstrated that they were good and responsible mothers. No doubt because it was so taken for granted by them, and perhaps relatively easily accomplished, that keeping their children clean, healthy, and well dressed hardly merited mention in middle-class women's discussions of good mothering.

About a third of the working- and middle-class women said that a woman's selfishness or her unwillingness to adjust her own life for her child's would make her a bad mother, but only a small minority of either category said that a woman would have to put her child's needs or interests first to be a good mother. In general, both middle- and working-class women defined good mothering in ways that did not make the child's and mother's interests mutually antagonistic. Each group of women did this in different ways and perhaps with different degrees of success. Nancy, an alone working-class mother of two, said:

[A good mother] makes the effort to understand the kid. You can't always be there for them . . . [but] if you really listen to them, then you can sort of beat time. . . . Having a strong sense of identity [makes you a good mother]. . . . Underlying everything I am trying to accomplish, the kids are there. In some part I'm doing it for them. In a sense, everything I do is for them. It's not quite putting their needs before yours, but acting with them in mind. (Nancy: Secretary)

The majority of the middle-class women, as we have seen, emphasized the need to limit the mutual absorption of mother and child and stressed what they saw as the essential and desirable integrity of the separate individual, be it mother or child. However, only 14% of the working-class mothers mentioned this as an aspect of good or desirable maternal behavior. Yet both middle- and working-class women reduced the potential for conflicts of interest between mother and child by conceptualizing good mothering as good communication and empathetic interaction rather than self-sacrifice. They acted with their children in mind.

GOOD MOTHERING: IDEAS IN THEIR CONTEXT

Initially, differences in the working- and middle-class women's descriptions of good and bad mothers appeared interesting, but their significance was unclear. Questions about good and bad mothers were intended to capture ideological responses rather than objective differences between mothers' actual behavior. Most of the women responded with apparent reference to women in general rather than to their own behavior. However, it gradually became clear that there were patterns in the differences and that these patterns related to the different material circumstances in which these women mothered.

For many of the working-class mothers, the maternal ideals of spending time with, providing good material care for, and having good communication and good interaction with their children (not being stressed or irritated) were ideals that were often either mutually exclusive or difficult to realize. For example, Helen, an alone mother of two children, worked long shifts in her job as a waitress, which greatly restricted her time with her children:

I don't know [what makes a mother a good mother]. Maybe that's what my problem is too, like I feel *guilty a lot*—an hour in the morning and an hour at night and not being able to [afford things for the kids]. . . . Michael can't stay after school [to play hockey, because I can't afford the fee], or he can't go to Boy Scouts on Tuesday because Mommy is at work, and he has no way of getting there. . . . (Helen: Waitress/Cashier)

For Helen, the conflict between the goals of having time with her children and having enough money to support them appeared irreconcilable. In practice, Helen could achieve neither ideal. And the time she spent with her children increased her anxiety because some of it was spent disciplining them:

> I'm just hoping they're going to be OK. Like, there's nothing [I can do]. I can't change life—anything. So I just try to do the best with what [I have] . . . but you get the guilt—a lot. . . . [I have so little time] and when you spend some of that time [disciplining them] . . . you think, "Oh my God . . . how can I spend that time [like that]?" but you have to; otherwise they are going to run, run you. . . . I really don't know what to say. (Helen: Waitress/Cashier)

As we will see in the Chapter 7, the issue of disciplining children is one that seemed to raise more concerns for working-class than for middle-class women.

Like Helen, Kimberley found the conflict between supporting her son and spending time with him irreconcilable. As a semiskilled sheet metal worker, Kimberley worked shifts and overtime. She worried about her lack of time with her son. Traditionally, male blue-collar jobs like Kimberley's allowed men to be "good parents" by being good providers. However, the long, irregular hours and the physically tiring nature of the work made it hard to be a "good" mother, where good mothering required time and energy to care for children *as well as to be a good provider*. Kimberley could have taken less physically demanding work. However, working-class women's traditional jobs do not pay enough to allow an alone mother to provide the standards of material care that "good" mothering itself dictates. Kimberley, like many alone working-class mothers, would have been financially better off on welfare than in a traditionally female (and thus low-paying) occupation. She could achieve some of the ideals of being a good mother, but she *could not* achieve all of them:

> It's important to spend time with your child when you finish your job. A lot of times I just come home and I go to sleep. I'm so tired, I can't see him that long, eh? It all works out in the long run, you're getting paid good money, but you [can't spend much time with your child]. (Kimberley: Sheet Metal Worker)

Only a minority of the working-class women indicated they felt guilt or concern about the adequacy of their *own mothering* in response to questions about their idea of good and bad mothers. But the frequency with which they, rather than the middle-class women, raised the issues of time, material care, and irritation with children suggests these were issues that concerned them. How are these issues to be understood?

Working-class women may have talked about spending time with their children as a characteristic of good mothering *not* because they felt that they had failed in that respect but precisely because they felt they were *achieving* their ideals of good mothering. Staying home evenings and weekends could be presented as time given to, or as pleasure forgone on behalf of, their children. For Karen, a married mother of three preschool children and whose partner did little coparenting, a poor or bad mother is one who goes out evenings:

> Yes, some mothers are poor mothers. Some mothers, to them, the first thing is to put on [a] coat and go out and have a good time, even knowing that there's a child in the room. (Karen: Dry Cleaner's Shipping Clerk)

For Stephanie:

> I think there's people who shouldn't even have kids! They constantly go out, leaving their kids unattended, thinking of themselves first. (Stephanie: Clerical Worker)

Thus time "given to" children by not going out in the evenings provided tangible evidence of good mothering.

There is another explanation for why the issues of time, material care, irritation with children, or child abuse dominated working-class rather than middle-class women's discussions of the ideals of mothering. It is not that the problems they mentioned were peculiar to working-class experience. Rather, I suggest, it is because parental behavior among working-class women, and alone mothers in particular, is far more *visible*, or is made potentially visible by professional surveillance and public discourse. Mothers who are poor, young and unwed, or from certain minority groups, I argued earlier, are often constructed as social problems—as less than good mothers. Indeed, the public regulation of socially powerless women's maternity provides a coercive reminder to all women of the ideals of "true" motherhood—and of the consequences of transgression.

The working-class women in this study also lived less private lives as mothers than did the middle-class women. They were more likely to live in apartments than in single-family homes and were more likely to share childcare with relatives, neighbors, friends, or nonprofessional child minders. Other mothers and their children were more visible and audible to them. And it is often easier to see others' behavior than one's own. Working-class mothers had more behavioral impressions about other mothers' performance and referred far more frequently to concrete examples of the good or bad mothering they described than did middle-class women. Pam, for example, has strong views about some other parents in the building in which she lives:

> [Being a bad mother means] ignoring your children. . . . I've seen so many parents where the children are dirty; they are poorly fed; they are not hugged and kissed enough. And half the kids who live around . . . or in this building probably fall into this category. And those children are horrible, horrible, children. Filthy, dirty, disgusting mouths . . . but it's the parents' fault, they don't care what they say in front of their children. (Pam: Clerical Worker)

Pam's construction of noncaring parents allowed her to clearly distinguish herself as being a good mother. The contrast she drew between kissed children and those with filthy disgusting mouths also expresses the overwhelming responsibility parents, and mothers in particular, are believed to hold for preserving the innate goodness of children— the protective and transformative power of parental caring.

SUMMARY

In this chapter we saw that the working-class women in this study were less likely to have been surprised by motherhood than were the middle-class women, either by the work involved or by their emotional responses to their children. As with the middle-class women, motherhood provided the working-class women with the symbolic resources for the transformation of deeply felt senses of self. The characteristic motif of this process of self-transformation was that of moral reform, which working-class women articulated through the language of "responsibilities" and "settling down." Class differences in how women talked about their experiences of self-transformation, I argued, were partly shaped by the different material contexts in which they mothered. Typically, working-class women interpreted the restrictions and difficulties in their lives as consequences of their personal commitment to their children. By appearing as part of the price of motherhood, class and gender structural inequalities were thus less likely to be perceived or resented.

But what is it about motherhood that has the cultural power to symbolize moral transformation in a woman's life? I argued in Chapter 1 that the gendered subjectivities produced by becoming a mother also express the broader social relationships in which they arise. That is, the ways in which women experience themselves as mothers carry sociopolitical meanings as well as interpersonal or personal ones. I pointed to the historical transformations in family relationships and in the meanings of childhood as having been central to the rise of romanticized, domesticated, privatized mothering. I noted how the multiple symbolic links between motherhood and female morality established in the white bourgeois family became embedded in culturally privileged images of mothering such that these images also implicitly carried their shadow counterimages of immoral women (nonmothers) and bad or improper mothers (unwed, nonwhite, or improperly sexed women).

The importance of the cultural associations between motherhood and morality in the United States and Canada must be understood in the context of the historical, political, cultural, and economic importance of the colonization and settlement of these countries predominantly by peoples with Christian religious beliefs. For example, Valverde (1991) documents how moral issues in turn-of-the-century Canada served as sites for the expression of sociopolitical tensions such that culturally Christian discourses on motherhood and proper mothering had important ideological functions in managing divergent social interests concerning empire; nation-state building; and changing gender, class, and race relations.

Clarissa Atkinson (1991), however, shows that Christian constructions of motherhood and the associated links between female morality, motherhood, and gender politics have shifted radically over time. Early Christianity, for example, was antifamily, considering it a distraction incompatible with holiness in men and women. With Christianity's political ascendancy, asceticism, expressed by men and women through virginity and poverty, replaced martyrdom as a route to holiness. Family life and motherhood thus excluded women from a truly holy life. However, increasing devotion to the Virgin Mary and her sacred motherhood expressed transformed attitudes toward maternity and morality. Gradually the sufferings of motherhood were constructed as a specifically female route to holiness. Atkinson (1991) points, for example, to the great mother–saints of the late Middle Ages.

What is particularly significant for this study, however, are the complex ways in which specific links between motherhood and morality that were culturally established by the Protestant Reformation became vested in the emerging forms of private property relations, privatized nuclear family relations and secularized and privatized morality of that period. Historically a socially significant characteristic of Protestantism was the ways in which it shifted the sacred to the secular. And with it, Atkinson (1991) points out, marriage and parenthood became constructed as earthly vocations (for men and women): Family life took on new moral meaning. Even by the early 17th century, Atkinson (1991) observes, among many Protestant religions there was a widespread belief that *everyone* belonged in families. Bastardy laws became more stringent, and the criminalization of unorthodox female reproduction increased. The Protestant rejection of the independent power of the Virgin Mary symbolized new kinds of social restrictions on women's maternal power and their independent access to holiness or a moral life outside family. Indeed, the structure of the Protestant nuclear family made a woman dependent on *her husband* for access to God. To be a "good" woman was exclusively defined in terms of being a wife and mother.

Nineteenth-century America saw a softening and "feminization" of Protestantism (Valverde, 1991, p. 30), which allowed women to take greater responsibility for domestic morality and piety and later to extend these moral responsibilities to maternal activism in the public sphere. Culturally the association of family, morality, and motherhood was established as a powerful theme in U.S. and Canadian societies and, I argue, continues to provide a guiding metaphor by which many women in this study made sense of motherhood.

But this legacy of "privatizing" social issues as personal and moral, and of restricting women's caring to the privatized sphere of family-like issues, limits the political potential of women's cultural specialization in caring. That is, it limits the political potential of motherhood and the politics of (women's) "difference."

At the same time, one cannot fully understand the meanings of motherhood in U.S. and Canadian society without seeing how they are inextricably linked to the changing cultural meanings and social worth of children.[6] Representations of children as embodying innocence and virtue and as redeemers of adult failures became powerful cultural themes in 19th- and 20th-century American society (Best, 1990; Zelizer, 1985). Indeed, Best (1990) argues that contemporary concerns about social ills are often expressed in terms of concern about threats to children or to their innocence. The "sacrilization" of children (Zelizer, 1985) meant that mothers became represented as facilitators of this boundless potential and as protectors of priceless innocence. Mothers' social role as guardians of the innocent no doubt contributed to the moral character of motherhood.

The moral worth of mothers, however, may have gradually been replaced by the social worth of children in contemporary meanings of motherhood. Shifting moral meanings of motherhood are reflected in the changing treatment of mothers—particularly mothers who are marginal or deviant. Until World War II, for example, the older evangelical maternity homes in the United States retained their long-established practice of doing everything possible to encourage unwed white mothers to keep their babies (Nathanson, 1991). Their policy expressed a social faith in the redemptive powers of mother-hood and domesticity to rehabilitate the (white) unwed woman. The emerging professionally run maternity homes, on the other hand, encouraged and often even required unwed white mothers to place their babies for adoption—in the "best interests" of the child (Nathan-son, 1991; Solinger, 1992). At the same time, the lack of social services offered to unwed black mothers, as Solinger (1992) argues, may have been expressive of the belief that black unwed mothers were "inca-pable of redemption" or that their children were not worth "saving."

Motherhood, it seems, may have lost some of its public symbolic moral power, retaining primarily private, personal value and a social worth derived from association with valued children. The removal of idealized (white) womanhood from its moral pedestal in the sociocul-tural transformation of recent decades, Best (1990) argues, means that "children have become the last sacred category of innocents to require society's protection" (Best, 1990, p. 182)—though one might ask, which children? Indeed, Rothman (1989, p. 187) points to major reconstructions in contemporary images of motherhood: Mothers are no longer portrayed as self-sacrificing and all-loving but as untrust-worthy or potential enemies of their children.

References to moral transformation by mothers in this study, therefore, are not merely expressive of implicit cultural associations of motherhood, morality, and the sacredness of children; they are also expressive of the extent to which the social worth of motherhood and mothers is currently contested or devalued.

7

Women's Everyday Lives
as Mothers

In earlier chapters I emphasized that becoming a mother is not simply an expression of a gender identity acquired in childhood; it is also an experience that produces and reproduces in women a gendered sense of adult self. That is, it reproduces ways of acting, thinking, and feeling that are conventionally associated with being female. Howard Becker (1981) has coined the term "situational adjustment" to describe the process of adult socialization through which people come to take on the characteristics required by the situations in which they participate. The concept offers an understanding of the patterned ways in which the participants in the present study described their experiences of motherhood: not by appealing to deep-rooted feminine personality traits and needs but by pointing to the shared socializing experiences of similar circumstances in which women find themselves once they give birth to a child.

This and the next chapter focus on some of these shared circumstances: the responsibility for children's well-being, the work involved in caring for and about children, the juggling of family and paid work, and the gendered organization of caring as activity and emotion. This chapter also looks at the costs and rewards of mother-hood.

As I wrote the earlier chapters, I wondered whether I was overemphasizing the relational aspects of women's experience of becoming mothers in ways that disguised the work involved. Because it is so often seen as an extension of caring, as an expression of love, women's daily practical caring for others is frequently not recognized as real work. I reassured myself by thinking that I would deal with the practical realities of motherhood in later chapters. This chapter and the next do that. However, women's experience resisted any neat separation of emotional relationship and work, of identity and practice, that I might have attempted to impose.

In Chapters 5 and 6 I showed how the experience of motherhood as a mythological journey of self-transformation was widely shared among the mothers in this study, albeit characterized by class-specific motifs of self-change. The consistency in women's accounts of their personal "journeys," however, was in contrast to the outer, more worldly experience of the practical realities of motherhood that women described: Here the dominant pattern was that of contingency. Often obscured from women's view, however, are the ways in which the broader social relations of inequality structure the personal and practical experience of family life and caring for children (Hochschild, 1989; DeVault, 1991).

To learn about the day-to-day experience of being a mother, I asked participants questions about the daily realities of having children. For example, I asked about the costs and rewards, the work involved, the division of domestic labor, and daycare and social support networks. And repeatedly they turned to their feelings for answers to my practical questions, not because they had no other answers but because their feelings so frequently provided the context for interpreting experience. DeVault (1991) shows how social analysts and women themselves often lack adequate language and concepts for making visible the everyday activities of caring and the production of sociability through family work. There is, she points out, almost no way to talk about sociability work—the skills, activities, and effort that produce and sustain the possibility of a social world and the connections of group life that we call family. Conventional concepts of work, DeVault contends, do not easily fit mothers' experiences of domestic work. Equally significant, perhaps, are the ways in which the language of caring organizes and yet mystifies the implications of women's connectedness with children. Caring work can be both joyous and burdensome and is a way of establishing bonds with others. Moreover, the meanings of caring work expose the limitations of those theoretical approaches to understanding social life that assume the individual to be, or to properly be, radically separate and independent from others. Ironically, talk of caring can both mystify and make transparent the nature of the social relationships surrounding the organization of motherhood.

Sociological challenges to socially prevalent conceptions of the individual are not new. Symbolic interactionism has long emphasized that individual and society, self and other, must be understood as mutually generating and sustaining processes rather than as separate entities. Independently of the symbolic interactionist tradition, many feminists have called for social psychological perspectives that can respect and adequately explain women's apparently greater experiences of connectedness with others. Feminists have offered explanations from a variety of different perspectives. Gilligan (1982) and Lyons (1983), for example, point to the masculinist bias in how traditional psychological theory conceptualizes the self, identity, and self–other relationships. Traditional models of human development, they show, have emphasized the role of individual separation and the establishment of psychological autonomy in the achievement of adult identity and have often seen women's concern with attachments and relationships as forms of dependency and immaturity, albeit quintessentially feminine (Caplan, 1985; Gilligan, 1982; Rubin, 1984). By contrast, some feminist theorists assert the value of women's apparent tendency to define themselves in interpersonal relationships (Miller, 1976) and suggest that the *real* "problem" lies in historically constructed male models of thought that glorify individualism and disconnected autonomy and devalue social attachment (Gilligan, 1982; Ruddick, 1984b; Squier and Ruddick, 1983). Some point in particular to forms of "patriarchal thought" that denigrate motherhood and mother-like connections (O'Brien, 1981; Rothman, 1989).

Other feminists have turned to a psychoanalytical perspective to reevaluate "women's ways," the persistent nature of gender differences in social life and the apparently different ways of constructing self and self–other relationships.[1] Chodorow (1978), for example, argues that gendered experiences of self–other relationships are grounded in children's early development. A major psychic task for little boys, she suggests, is to realize that they are *different* from their mothers and, unlike little girls, cannot grow up to be like them. The socializing effect of this distinction from the mother, Chodorow holds, creates distinctly gendered experiences of identity: Boys are defined through separation and autonomy from others, girls through connection and personal relationships.[2] In these kinds of theoretical accounts, prob-

lems of identity and personal development for men are understood
to be experienced as problems of handling relationships in the context
of their core sense of separation and individuality; for women, the
problem is seen as that of establishing a separate identity while
maintaining relationships (Chodorow, 1978; Gilligan, 1982; Rubin,
1984). Indeed, Chodorow suggests it is this early identification by girls
with a mother who nurtures that produces in women a desire and a
capacity to mother, whereas separation produces men whose nurturing capacities and needs have been repressed.

Spelman (1988) points to Chodorow's (1978) neglect of the
full range of social relationships, including race and class relationships, in which the experience of self as a gendered self emerges.
To argue that women are relationally defined or experience themselves through connectedness obscures the empirical existence of
hierarchical relations among women in a society based on class and
race inequalities. Noncontextual analyses of women's experiences
of self and of caring miss the ways in which women's caring and
connectedness are socially and politically organized. Such analyses
tend to construct caring as a female personality trait rather than as
a feature of specific social relationships. Caring work is not merely
gendered; it is classed and racialized. Certain kinds of caring work
and personal service occupations are assigned to less privileged
members of society. Nurturance is bought and sold—often at
minimum wage. Rothman (1989) discusses the ways in which the
social organization of privileged white women's motherhood in
the United States is often predicated on racially, economically, and
emotionally exploitative social relationships. Mothers' emotional
bonds with their children, she observes, are culturally validated, but
those of employed caregivers are not.

The project of reevaluating and validating women's experience
of connectedness is also difficult in other ways. A cultural construction
of woman as "being for another," as caringly attached to others and
having no value in her own right, Grimshaw (1986, p. 139) points out,
has been endemic to Western social and political thought. Indeed,
women's attachments to others have been considered as rendering
them incapable of the universalistic, detached reason required of
genuine individuals in society and thus have excluded them from full
legal and political rights (Grimshaw, 1986). In many ways, caring
connections have been a liability.

And while it is truly important to value caring connections, it is
also important not to conclude that such phenomena are inherently

feminine, whether biologically or psychosexually grounded. If we fail to recognize the socially constructed nature of gender differences, we are in danger of accepting a "feminist essentialism" (Alcoff, 1988). Acceptance of such a perspective, according to Alcoff, raises the risk of constructing women not only as essentially different from men but also as morally superior. It presumes a false unity among women on the basis of some assumed (essential) common trait or experience and thereby marginalizes the lives of women who do not fit this image of being a woman. As Kerber and colleagues (1986) point out, because many women have historically been associated with more nurturant and less aggressive social roles than men, there is a tendency to see women as being better than men.

Thus, while the data from this study show that the participants found connectedness with their children both deeply rewarding and central to their transformed sense of self, it would be a mistake to think that only women are capable of nurturing relationships, that women are consistently more caring than men, and that all women do and should care. Research on men who take full responsibility for parenting (rather than simply helping out), for example, suggests that such men also develop many of the nurturing capacities usually associated with women (Pruett, 1987). Also, as Greeno and Maccoby (1986) have noted, although women consistently rate themselves, and are rated by others, as more empathic and caring than men, this behavior may not hold cross-situationally. Women may be more empathic in relation to friends and intimates, but the evidence suggests such empathy may not hold in relation to strangers (Greeno and Maccoby, 1986; Ruddick, 1984b). Citing the dangers of mistakenly assuming that nurturing capacities are restricted to women, particularly to biological mothers, Rothman (1989) has argued that we need to see care and nurturance as components of particular *relationships* rather than as characteristics of one gender. By conceptualizing motherhood as a *nurturing relationship* rather than as a status or genetic relationship, society can extend to men or to nonbiological parents the socially beneficial effects motherhood has in socializing individuals into nurturant, caring ways of relating to others:

> There are powerful reasons why men should mother, and it is not to save the children from their mothers. Men should mother, should provide intimate, daily, ongoing nurturing care to children, in the interests . . . of men themselves, and of achieving economic justice and a better world. (Rothman, 1989, p. 225)

Men can develop traditionally female characteristics through per-
forming traditionally feminine roles, Rothman continues:

> I think in mothering we hone our empathic abilities. . . . I think
> that the experience of mothering teaches people how to be more
> emotionally and intellectually nurturant, how to take care of each
> other. It is not the only way we learn that lesson, but it is hard to
> mother and not learn it. (Rothman, 1989, p. 226)

However, one needs to be reflective of the broader social organization
of caring before assuming its beneficial social consequences.

IDENTITY AND CARING

Conceptualizing identities as social processes allows us to understand
how many women come to vest a valued sense of self in particular
interpersonal relationships, and permits us to see this without interpreting this vesting as "dependency" or concluding that men and
women follow different developmental trajectories. We can recognize
that the characteristics of nurturance, caring, and responsibility associated with women are socially grounded and arise—when and if they
do—by virtue of social experience.

What also needs to be made clear, however, is the sociopolitical
significance of caring in the constitution of female identity, as well as
the dual implications for women it carries—of love and labor (Graham, 1983). "Caring for" and "caring about" are conflated in one
word in ways that construct caring work to be evidence of, and the
natural expression of, women's love. Thus women who resist the
implications of the conflation of meaning become vulnerable to
charges of not really caring and of suspecting themselves of being
selfish. Women's caring work in the family, DeVault (1991) points out,
may express their love for their children, but it also expresses the
hierarchical gender relations embedded in the social organization of
caring and domestic work.

Self-conceptions and self–other relationships are situationally
contingent. Men and women experience themselves and self–other
relationships in gendered ways because social situations tend to be
deeply gendered both in the structures that organize them and in the
expectations we bring to them (Goffman, 1987). We cannot assume
that women are innately more caring, nurturant, and peaceful and vest

their identities more in interpersonal relationships, and that men are more aggressive and personally autonomous, without recognizing that men and women are allocated to social positions that require or encourage just such characteristics. And we cannot understand the meanings of caring without recognizing the gendered power relations that exist in the lives of those to whom such social characteristics are ascribed.

But let us turn now to how the women in this study described their everyday lives as mothers.

"THE REWARDS . . . ARE HARDER TO ARTICULATE": MIDDLE-CLASS WOMEN AND THE BEST THINGS ABOUT HAVING A CHILD

For the middle-class mothers in the sample, the best things about having children were the pleasures or rewards they got from watching their children learn and grow (65%) and the special connectedness or relationship they felt with their children (65%). About half of the middle-class women (52%) also spoke of the fun or enjoyment they had being with their children (Table 7.1).

Penny's response captured the two most frequently talked-about rewards of motherhood: watching their children learn and grow and being connected. Although Penny used the analogy of "falling in love" to describe her bond with her son, it is important to stress that not all women equated their connectedness with children with feelings of love.

TABLE 7.1. Women's Perceptions of the Rewards of Motherhood

	Middle-class women	Working-class women
Watching their children learn and grow	65%	64%
Feelings of special connectedness or special relationship with their children	65%	54%
Fun or enjoyment being with their children	52%	43%
Rediscovering/reexperiencing the world through their children's eyes	35%	11%
Strengthening of other social bonds	23%	12%

Note. N = 31 for middle-class women, 28 for working-class women.

[For me, the best thing about having a child is] the emotional discovery—it's sort of like falling in love, only it's different. Unless you've done it, you don't have that central experience in your life. It's very intense. Aside from that it's [also] lots of fun. . . . I've had a lot of pleasure from things he's said and things he's done and [from] watching him grow. (Penny: Managing Editor)

For many of the participants, emotions were the coin of exchange in interaction with their children. Feelings were given and received. But as Loretta pointed out, feelings are hard to measure or put into words:

[Before I had a child] I couldn't realize the attachment or the rewards that come from having your own child. . . . The changes in [your] life-style . . . are very visible, [but] the rewards are not that clear. They are there, but harder to articulate. They are harder to see. They are more *felt* than visualized. (Loretta: Elementary School Teacher)

The rewards of motherhood were often lived in daily experience and emerged as feelings of attachment. Children were described as offering a very special kind of love:

[The best things about having a child are] just the daily rewards; watching them grow and learn. You share so much with them. . . . Just having someone who loves you, unconditionally, 24 hours a day, 365 days a year [that's the best]. (Margaret: Flight Attendant)

Thus the rewards of having young children were frequently immediate, physically tangible, emotionally special, and seen as inherent in the relationship:

It's so hard to articulate; the hugs, you know, you share. . . . And children also are really wonderful, because they love their mothers unconditionally. . . . And that's the amazing thing. Just like you unconditionally love that child, even though I was never, you know, like, baby crazy, you know. (Alice: Graphic Designer)

Many of the women felt there was a *special* bond between self and other in the mother–child relationship, one not to be found in other relationships, and this was one of the best things about being a mother. For Joanne, this special bond with another transformed the phenomenological experience of being an isolated self in the world into a feeling of permanent *belonging*. Her new attachment to the world was independent of the specific other that had brought about that attachment but was inherent in the nature of the relationship itself; that of mother and child:

> [The best things about having a child are that] it's like having a permanent friend, in a way. It's like a security against loneliness that I really was surprised to discover. For some people it would be a dependency. But for me it means I have a place in the world. . . . It focuses my life very well, which I think I needed: [which] I think everyone needs. Well, it has focused me in a way that nothing else has. (Joanne: Elementary School Teacher)

Joanne felt her connectedness was *not* contingent on her son's personality:

> You know, I happen to really like him a lot. I suppose I could have had a child I didn't really like a whole lot. . . . It does make a difference, the fact that he is so much fun and so pleasant and so easy. But even if he were troublesome, I think I would really enjoy just having that responsibility and having that focus. (Joanne: Elementary School Teacher)

In discussing women's connectedness with their children in this study, I am *not* talking about the endocrinologically based mother–infant attraction posited by bonding theory.[3] The concept I use here is grounded in women's reports of the ways in which they experienced themselves and their relationships with their children. Thus grounded in participants own representations, the concept carries no assumptions concerning the biological basis of mother–child connectedness; neither does it assume that feelings of connectedness emerge spontaneously, immediately, or even *at all*, following the birth of a child.[4]

Rebecca, an alone mother, explained how the mother–child attachment she found so rewarding was both a feeling of social belonging and a form of phenomenological self-extension in time and space:

> The best things about having a child are the love you get and give. It's corny stuff like having a family, caring about each other,

doing things together. [It's] that sense of continuity. Immortality, is that the word? Like I know he is going to be here and he'll have kids. I like that. I like seeing him with my parents. I like seeing him with my father, they get along really well. A lot of times I look at him as an extension of myself, in a lot of ways. (Rebecca: Counselor)

Rather than subscribing to the idea that biology produces specific social relationships, I want to point to the ways in which social relationships shape our understandings of biology. Natural or bodily processes often provide social symbolic resources through which cultural meanings are expressed (Douglas, 1970). Indeed, Frazer's *The Golden Bough* (1890/1987) gives multiple examples of how ritualized mimicry of gestation and birth were used in nonindustrial societies to express and establish unique *social* bonds between mothers and their adopted children, even when the adoptees were mature adults. The relationship between natural reproductive processes and social psychological experiences of connectedness has been extended beyond the symbolic in Mary O'Brien's (1981) analysis of the politics of reproduction. She argues that *men's* alienation from the reproductive process and from the ways in which motherhood allows women to (symbolically) experience continuity in time and space has generated the impetus for the social construction of enduring patriarchal social and political institutions. Such institutions, she suggests, represent a masculinist attempt to overcome men's fundamental alienation.

Most women in this study, however, used the language of emotions and social relationships rather than that of biology to express their connectedness with their children. But the parallels between the biological mother–child relationship and the social psychological connectedness of self and other that the women described were quite striking. The ways in which interpretations of biological relationships can symbolically express and heighten social relationships occurred to me during a very moving interview with an alone mother who herself had been adopted as a child and who had therefore experienced a disjuncture between biological relationship and the social psychological attachment this relationship can signify.

Della wept as she explained why having a child was so important to her:

Looking at my history, one of the things that's important to me . . . I just always thought it was very important to continue my line, you know. Without having a child myself, I wouldn't be able to do that. There is no heritage of the Della line, you know what I mean. So that's always been very important to me. I have a brother somewhere, a natural brother, but I don't know him. And although I never knew them very well, my [natural] parents were always important to me. And the sense of *family* was always very important to me, and without having a child of *my own*—even if it was an adopted child, it wouldn't be a child of *my own*—having experienced birth of them and that whole. . . . It wouldn't be the same. (Della: Childcare Social Worker)

Having children provided many of the participants with a valued sense of enduring connectedness, but other rewards of having children were clearly recognized as being temporary:

I love the way he makes me look at the world all over again—with fresh eyes. . . . And I love the hugs and the kisses that are so unquestioned at this stage. I know it's going to change soon enough, but I really love that. (Mary Lynn: Policy Analyst)

About a third of the middle-class women talked about how, through their children, they briefly reentered a child's universe of sensual experience and recaptured a child-like joy for life:

[One of the best things about having children is that] I think it makes me live and enjoy the moment. . . . I think children make you stop and you rediscover the world again, not just through their eyes but through your [own] eyes as a child. And also they have such enthusiasm for *living* that it brings back the joy and the optimism. (Rachael: High School Teacher)

Children can revitalize adult life:

I think the laughter [is one of the best things about having a child]. I think I have laughed more in the last year and a half than I've laughed in my life, or in my adult life. . . . And it slowed me down. It really slowed me down and made me observant. I think you stop and smell the flowers. You notice details that you probably missed for years and would have gone on the rest of your life not observing. (Anna: Community College Teaching Master)

A third (33%) of the middle-class women who were living with partners also talked about the strengthening of existing social bonds as one of the best things about having children. For some (15%) it was the stronger bond they experienced with their partners.[5] For others, children turned a couple into a family:

> [The best things are] I like what it's done to us, I mean to our family unit. I mean I would never have called us a family before. There is really something quite pleasurable about it all. (Marie: Education Consultant)

"IT'S THE WAY SHE MAKES ME FEEL": WORKING-CLASS WOMEN AND THE BEST THINGS ABOUT HAVING A CHILD

The working-class women in this study generally agreed with the middle-class women that the best things about having children were teaching them or watching them learn and grow (64%) and the connectedness they felt with their children (54%). Participants' responses are summarized in Table 7.1. However, there were some subtle differences in how each group talked about the rewards of having children. Some of the working-class women (more commonly those with partners), for example, explained that helping their children learn and grow gave them a feeling of having an impact or influence on life that they found very rewarding. For some, it meant the chance to give their children a better life than they had themselves:

> [The best things about children?] I don't know where to start. . . . I don't know how to answer. I guess by loving and teaching them . . . you have a little bit of control . . . of maybe making them better than what you are. It makes me feel good to be able to produce a baby. I really feel really proud of myself, you know. I am just really so happy. She makes me happy. (Marg: Accounting Clerk)

And for Lisa, teaching her daughter meant not repeating the mistakes of her own life:

> [The best things are] when she's taking a nap [laugh]. Somebody where you can teach them the things *you* know. I don't want her making the same mistakes I made. . . . And yesterday we were

laughing. Some of the things she does, it's just hilarious. . . . It's just fun watching them. (Lisa: Data Entry Clerk)

Working-class women's descriptions of the social support they got from connectedness with their children were often more immediate than the sort of "existential" grounding in the world the middle-class women talked about:

[The best things are that] Jessica means everything to me. She sticks up for you, you know. Kids, they stick up for you no matter what you do or what you say. Well, you get to watch them grow up. You teach them what you know, what you've learned. It's nice to see them grow up. (Renee: Truck Driver)

On the whole, working-class women were somewhat less likely than middle-class women to mention the pleasure or fun of daily interaction with their children (43% vs. 52%), and only 11% of the former mentioned that sense of rediscovering the world through their children's eyes that the middle-class women (35%) talked about.

More than other women, alone mothers, especially alone working-class mothers, singled out love and connectedness as the central rewards of having children. They pointed, for example, to the fusing of self and other in motherhood and to the indestructible nature of their bonds with their children:

[The best things are] watching them, you know what I mean? Knowing that they are part of you, watching them learn, watching them grow—everything. I mean, knowing that they are yours. Nothing can change it. You're their mom, you know what I mean. A *mom*, a *mom*, you know. (Helen: Waitress/Cashier)

Mara, an alone mother of a 3-year-old, also felt that the best things about having a child were the unique feelings she had for her daughter. They represented the central and irreplaceable relationship of her life, she stressed, not simply because she no longer loved her ex-husband; rather, because women love children *differently* and *more* than they could ever love a man. She began explaining her feelings as follows:

It's the way she makes me feel. . . . She makes me feel so happy and so needed and . . . I love watching everything she does. I love listening to her, watching every achievement. . . . I just feel so proud. (Mara: Clerical Worker)

Mara felt that in having a child she had discovered the true meaning of love. She pointed to the social support she had received for her view that the other expected major object of a woman's love, a husband, could never rival her love for her child. Although she no longer had the former, his absence was relatively unimportant compared with what she did have: her child. Conventionally, marriage supposedly binds men, women, and children "naturally" together, fusing heterosexuality and maternity in apparently complementary ways. Yet for women like Mara, a child limited the claims of conventional heterosexuality on her capacity for love and attachment and provided her with the opportunity to use conventional cultural resources of maternal love as support for resistance and self-assertion:

And this friend of mine. . . . Her and I always talk about it. Doesn't matter how much you love your husband or anybody, your child you love more. She said she loved Ken [her husband] with all her heart, but when she had Anne, her first [child], she realized she didn't love him as much as she could actually love somebody. Like she would always love Anne more. She wouldn't care, it wouldn't bother her . . . if Ken walked out the door. It would hurt her and everything, but as long as she had her kids, that's it. And it's the same with me. Didn't matter if everybody walked out of my life, as long as I had *her*. (Mara: Clerical Worker)

The giving and receiving of love has traditionally been seen as a distinctly feminine characteristic. I suggested earlier that their children seemed to provide the young working-class women in this study access to sources of self-esteem and positive feelings about themselves from which they may have been excluded by the class and gendered structures of their society. However, I am *not* arguing that their maternal commitment in general arose because the women felt defective or lacked self-esteem before they had children. Rather, I suggest, becoming a mother transformed these women in ways they valued, and it allowed them to feel they had realized, at least in their private worlds, traditional female values of love, care, and connectedness with others—connectedness with culturally and personally valued others: children. So becoming a mother was experienced as rewarding by a woman not simply because she now occupied a positive social role (indeed, it is questionable how positive a social role motherhood is publicly recognized to be). Rather, with motherhood, a woman became a positively valued self within a culturally "female value system." Children allowed these women to claim to be the sort of selves they personally valued. The women's discussions of mother-hood, I suggest, have much to do with how they felt about themselves, about the identities they claimed, and about their ideal social relation-ships—expressed in terms of their feelings for their children. Anna, an alone middle-class mother, explains how becoming a mother forced her to become softer and more vulnerable and stopped her from becoming the "tough" person she might have been:

> I've had to readjust my value system—what's important to me. . . . Having a child is so wonderful. I was becoming a very tight, rigid, single person with fixed opinions. And he has *forced* me to be flexible, or [to] return to that. He has made me so much softer than I was. . . . And more open . . . and vulnerable, but I would prefer that to becoming the *tough* person I had been becoming. There is so much love in my life right now. I had him for love, and I just have so much affection in my life. So much warmth and affection. (Anna: Community College Teaching Master)

For the alone working-class mothers, achieving a valued self within a value system that "puts children first" was perhaps the major source of self-value available:

> If that question asked, "What is the most important things in your life?" working would never be, not even close. I would give up anything—just as long as I had [her]. I wouldn't care about anything else. . . . It's the way she makes me feel. She makes me feel so happy and so needed. . . . I love watching everything she does . . . every achievement. . . . I just feel so proud. (Rose: Secretary)

However, even if these women realized traditional female ideals in the private sphere of intimate relations—and statistical data on child abuse, for example, suggest this is far from always the case[6]—mothers do not necessarily effect a transformation or feminization of the broader social world around them. To the contrary, the women in this study often found themselves mediating and absorbing structural contradictions between the different systems within which they operated. They personally mediated, for example, the conflict between caring for others and the social organization of paid work in society. Mothers felt that caring for others, and their families in particular, was important and valuable. But as this work is often neither socially visible nor publicly valued, managing the intersection of family life and paid work is particularly difficult. The political, organizational, and ideological contradictions between these spheres, as DeVault (1991) points out, are reduced to a *private* problem of organizing and scheduling—a personal problem of balancing. And motherhood had obliged some of the middle-class women to *withdraw* from pursuing "female values" in other areas of their lives—whether in female friendships, volunteer work or feminist activities, in order to care for their children:

> [Becoming a mother changed me] in terms of my activities, yeah. I used to do a lot of work for feminist causes, and I don't do that anymore. . . . [If I didn't have a child] it would be totally different workwise, political activities. I would be very involved in different issues. (Marie: Education Consultant)

As Beth put it:

> [Having children] has changed the structure of my life in terms of how I spend my time. . . . Having children has gotten in the way of friendships. (Beth: Management Board Officer)

In many ways the privatization of caring in family households risks subverting its political potential and renders invisible the political challenge that many feminists see as being implicit in caring and in "womanly ways."

THE WORST THINGS ABOUT HAVING CHILDREN: MIDDLE-CLASS WOMEN

La Rossa and La Rossa (1981) explain that being a parent acquires its distinctive, even paradoxical, character not from the nature of the rewards and costs involved but because the costs and rewards, the highs and lows, are so *extreme*.

Part of the paradoxical character of motherhood is surely reflected in varied accounts, popular and scholarly, of its effects on women's identities. Women's connectedness with their children is depicted as both destructive and positive. Boulton (1983), for example, points to the monopolization and loss of personal identity but also to the sense of meaning and purpose in life that children brought to the middle-class, full-time mothers she studied. Lopata (1971) talked of identity crisis. Oakley (1980b) likens the postnatal depression many women experience to a period of mourning for old identities. And Suleiman (1988) describes the experience of being torn between seemingly irreconcilable allegiances that many women writers experience: commitment to their children and commitment to their creative selves.

The mothers in this study also experienced their connectedness with their children as both rewarding and costly. However, their accounts are not so much of a loss of personal identity, of maternal ambivalence and a struggle between self and child. They spoke instead of how motherhood had changed them and their lives and the way in which their maternal and nonmaternal identities sometimes come into conflict.

As participants relfected on the disadvantages of having children, their focus often shifted between their inner experience and the outer, practical realities of motherhood (Table 7.2).

The worst things about having children, according to middle-class women, had to do with the work and practical demands of caring for their children (52%) and problems of time (52%). Twenty-nine percent of the middle-class women spoke explicitly about sleep deprivation, echoing the women in Hochschild's (1989, p. 9) study

TABLE 7.2. Women's Perceptions of the Disadvantages of Motherhood

	Middle-class women	Working-class women
No "worst things"/difficulty in articulating any disadvantages of motherhood	3%	25%
The work or practical demands involved	52%	29%
Problems of time/time pressures	52%	18%
Feelings of responsibility/concerns about one's parenting behavior	45%	46%
Changed pattern of life/constant need for planning and scheduling	35%	43%

Note. N = 31 for middle-class women, 28 for working-class women.

who "talked about sleep the way a hungry person talks about food."
Some of the women in the present study talked about constantly
feeling rushed; and, for about a quarter of the middle-class women,
the sense of "not having any time for myself" was among the worst
things about having children:

> The worst things? One of the big ones, I guess, is the time
> commitment. I feel like [my partner and I,] we've absolutely *no
> time* to do anything . . . together, which is probably a little bit
> arguing [against my point] because we tend not to go out too
> much together without the children. Because we both work . . .
> we feel that we want to be with the children when we have a
> free moment. And the other thing is just *time for yourself.* Even
> little trivial things . . . [like] you have a shower in the morning
> and you race out of that. Once in a while [you would like time]
> to file your nails—you just don't have any time for yourself. (Jill:
> Marketing Manager)

About a third of the middle-class women (35%) spoke of the
changed pattern of their lives as being unwelcome; freedom and
spontaneity had been replaced by a *constant* need for planning,
scheduling, and organizing. And about a third of those with partners
(30%) felt that their marital relationships had suffered—often, they
said, because they hadn't had enough "time for each other."

Research findings support these mothers' accounts. Mothers
in full-time employment do indeed have greater demands on their
time than do other sections of the population. Michelson's (1985)
study of Toronto families showed that women who were employed
full-time worked (paid and unpaid) about an hour more than their
partners on each workday. Hochschild (1989) estimates that employed U.S. women work 15 hours (paid and unpaid) more than
their male partners each week; they also get less sleep.[7] She calls
such unpaid family work "the second shift." Many of the costs of
this work, Hochschild notes, are not recognized, even by those
involved.

Time constraints, on the other hand, are often recognized. Time,
La Rossa and La Rossa (1981) explain, is a scarce resource for parents,
and conflict about time is central to a couple's transition to parenthood. But conflict over time acquires this central role, they argue,
partly because of cultural expectations that children be provided with
constant coverage care, while the responsibility for this care is not

socially shared. Thus parents find themselves in a zero-sum game-like situation *with each other.*

If feelings of connectedness were among the best things about having children, their flip side, feelings of responsibility, were often among the worst. "It can be very frightening," explained Marilyn, "to be so important to someone . . . such a big part of their world." Forty-five percent of the middle-class women talked about the potential for loss, anxiety, or pain that came with feeling so close and responsible for another[8]:

[The worst things are] sleep deprivation, the time commitment . . . the responsibility that I feel for her, the love. I mean this phenomenal love. What happens if something ever happens to her? I mean—I'm catastrophizing—[but] the risk, the fear. . . . (Marie: Education Consultant]

The specific forms that women's feelings of intense responsibility for their children take flow partly from class-based cultural assumptions about children and their needs (Backett, 1982; Lopata, 1971) and partly from the material context in which they mother. The beliefs that children are emotionally fragile, for example, implies that their psychological security is contingent on the constant availability of their mothers. Parental images of their children's needs, Backett (1982) concludes, reproduce traditional gendered parenting behavior. At the same time, the skills and effort required to be constantly responsive and attentive to vulnerable others are not seen as real work but simply as a natural expression of emotional connections or of parental care (DeVault, 1991; Graham, 1983; Miller, 1976). Thus when things go wrong, mothers are blamed, or blame themselves, for not caring enough. The anxiety of maternal responsibility is exacerbated when mothers feel their behavior is determining for their children while at the same time they believe, as did many of the middle-class women in this study, that they should not "try to mold" their children. Beth, for example, came to feel that her *own* responses were perhaps the *only* things she really controlled as a parent:

[For me the worst thing is] worrying—anxiety, I guess, about the responsibility. I think people of my generation and education tend to overrate—I think we focus too much on our kids and the techniques and how we are going to raise them, you know. . . . I focus on them and worry about doing the right thing. I don't worry about *them* [the children], I mean, they can sort of do what they want. . . . And *who knows* what they are going to grow up like. But I worry about what I'm doing and what I'm saying a lot. (Beth: Management Board Officer)

THE WORST THINGS ABOUT HAVING CHILDREN: WORKING-CLASS WOMEN

Working-class women perceived fewer costs of having children than did middle-class women. What they saw to be those costs also differed.

Twenty-five percent of the working-class mothers said that, for them, there were no *"things"* about having children. Even when I probed, speaking in different ways about disadvantages or costs, many of the working-class women indicated they could not speak negatively about the experience of motherhood. At the same time, what some noted as things that didn't "even bother" them was suggestive of the difficulty many women had in separating the work of caring from the feelings of care. A married mother of a 6-month-old explained:

> [For me] I don't think there are any [worst things] about having a child. I can't even think of anything. I haven't had any bad experiences yet. I don't even care if I don't sleep at night, I'll get up. (Marg: Accounting Clerk)

So, although Marg had her sleep disrupted, she did not readily label such events as negative or personally costly.

For other working-class mothers, the demands of children were taken for granted, but they were not necessarily easy or without frustration: There were just "rough days."

> [For me] I don't think there are any disadvantages; [there are] just rough days. . . . It's hard working and then coming home, especially after you've had a hard day, and having to deal with this little person tugging on your leg, saying, "I want it." Some days are fine, some days are [not]. . . . You always feel bad after, you know, if you yell at them and you shouldn't have. Like, "Why did I do that?" That's the hardest. (Ramona: Bookkeeping Clerk)

Only 29% of the working-class women identified the work or the demands involved as one of the main disadvantages of having children; for half of these women it was lack of sleep, *not* the extra work, that was seen as the problem.

Women's evaluation of the demands of having children must be distinguished from their responses of satisfaction or frustration with this extra work (Boulton, 1983). One response is immediate, the other reflective. How women reflectively evaluate the work of caring for children depends on the social context and women's own expectations. Stack (1974), for example, showed that among the urban poor black families she studied, the high social and personal value attributed to children, together with the perception that children bring joy to life, meant that mothering work was not talked of primarily as a responsibility but as a cherished and much sought after *right*—a source of value.

In contrast to the middle-class women, only a minority of the working-class women (18%) talked about problems of "time" as a major disadvantage of having children. More puzzling, however, was that all the alone middle-class mothers, but only 9% of the alone working-class mothers mentioned problems of time as a major cost of children. This difference might be explained, perhaps, by the fact that alone working-class mothers got more help with their children from their families (see Chapter 8). It may also have been that, as several alone working-class mothers mentioned, they now had more *control* over their time and their lives and had less domestic work to do than they had when they lived with partners. Men, several of the alone working-class women pointed out, added to their workload:

[The advantages of being an alone mother are] not picking up after the husband, not worrying about whether his shirts are pressed, what are we going to eat for supper tonight, being able—I guess I've got a lot of freedom. (Cora: Word Processor)

Similarly, for Helen, a mother of two:

[The advantages of being an alone parent are] you do what you want to do. . . . You don't have to answer to [anyone]. . . . If you don't feel like doing the laundry or cleaning the bathroom [you don't]. . . . It's not quite as pressurized, because if you come home and you're tired and you don't feel like cleaning up this or that tonight, OK, fine, you don't. . . . Now it's [just] me and my kids. (Helen: Waitress/Cashier)

Many of the working-class women (43%) also said that restrictions and lack of "freedom" were among the worst things about having children. For them, however, freedom did not usually refer to personal freedom but, for example, to how their children restricted their opportunities to take better paid work that involved overtime—to earn an adequate income that would allow them to provide for their children's material needs. These mothers talked about the difficulty of juggling work and family schedules, and of the constant need to plan, as issues of freedom. Only 18% mentioned restrictions on "going out" or on their social life as major disadvantages of having children. The gendered organization of family work and caring is such, argues DeVault (1991), that women's lives are organized according to the needs, preferences, and schedules of others in ways that appear to be the outcome of women's personal decisions, management strategies, and emotional commitments. This leaves the gender and class privileges embedded in the organization of paid and unpaid work, of material and social resources, hidden from public view.

Few of the women in this study mentioned financial costs as among the greatest disadvantages of having children, but money was clearly a concern. For example, 55% of the alone working-class mothers and 41% of those with partners said that, if they were to do things over again, they would wait to have children until they were better off financially.

"I HATE IT WHEN I YELL AT HER"

Among the worst aspects of having children, about a third of the working-class women (36%) and almost half of the alone working-class mothers (46%) told me, were concerns about their own behavior as parents—in particular, issues of discipline and of responding to their children's inappropriate behavior. The problem was not simply one of guiding the child's behavior; it was also one of feeling all right about one's own behavior. Sue, for example, explained how bad she felt when she "yelled at her kids":

[The worst things are that] I get scared sometimes [that] something is going to happen to one of them . . . and wondering if you are giving them the right direction. I get very hyper and I might yell at them, and they might go to bed, and I think, "Oh, God, why did I yell at them?". . . You wonder what kind of impact you are having on your kids as they are growing up. (Sue: Legal Secretary)

Is it noteworthy that the working-class women spoke of "yelling" at their children, whereas the middle-class women did not? Might it be that the working-class women suffered greater stress, perhaps leading them to lose their tempers more often?[9] In effect, the working-class women's concern with discipline paralleled the middle-class women's concerns about responsibility. Both groups were worried about *their own performance as parents.* Both groups believed their children were affected by their behavior, but they looked to different forms of evidence to assess how they were doing as parents. As Kohn (1977) and Bernstein (1971) point out, parents socialize their children in class-specific ways. Middle-class parents' childrearing strategies, they argue, reflect a concern that children develop class-appropriate motivational structures; thus these parents use more psychological methods of socialization. Working-class parents, on the other hand, are often more concerned with behavior and use more direct means to ensure obedience.[10] Middle-class parents can assume the physical and economic security of their children in ways working-class parents cannot. Not surprisingly, working-class mothers often feel that to be good parents to their children and to keep them "out of trouble," they had to discipline the children (Rubin, 1976). For the working-class women in this study, discipline sometimes meant yelling at the children. But this way of responding to their children also made them feel bad.[11] The middle-class women, on the other hand, spoke less about behavior, perhaps because for them the "real" consequences of parenting were seen in more psychological terms. But they also worried:

[One of the worst things about having children is] you [always] have to be conscious of them. [It's] that ongoing responsibility—you can never forget their vulnerability. (Kim: Librarian)

Anxiety about how to respond to their children seemed even greater among women who, like Helen, were alone mothers and lacked social support for their parenting. Helen's children were 5 and 9 years old and presented her with issues not faced by parents of

younger children. She found it hard not to have someone with whom
to talk over difficulties.

> For me [the worst things], it's like knowing how to handle
> situations that come up. . . . And now, just lately, my daughter took
> something that didn't belong to her. . . . I didn't have anyone to
> discuss it *with*, you know . . . the discipline. Also, the way the
> situation is, you know. With me they want to get away with
> everything. With their father they don't. . . . I feel bad if I'm
> constantly [saying] "No, no, no; you can't, you can't, you can't."
> So maybe you give [in] a little bit more than you should. (Helen:
> Waitress/Cashier)

For almost half of those working-class women who were alone
parents, it was neither the work nor the time constraints that were the
worst things about having children; it was problems of discipline and
their anxiety about their own behavior as parents. The mystification
of the work of caring for others as not being real work that requires
adequate preparation, material resources, social support, and organizational responsiveness leaves women vulnerable to ambivalence and
anxiety, feeling they are not doing enough for their children or that
they are not doing it right. And it leaves women who do not have the
personal or material resources to approximate the ideals of good
parenting feeling like failures (DeVault, 1991). Few alone working-
class mothers have the resources with which to protect their children
from the consequences of social inequality.

THE NEGLECTED VARIABLE: THE CHILD

Although it is seldom emphasized in the sociological literature on
motherhood, I quickly learned that the women in this study did *not*
experience their own children as passive objects of their maternal care.
Children were seen as distinctive individuals and responded to accordingly. Participants recognized how their children's own personalities and moods affected the children's needs and thereby shaped
participants' everyday lives as mothers.

Some infants, I learned, were "easy babies," which usually meant
they slept well, and, more important, they slept continuously through
the night. Some babies fit in relatively harmoniously with their
mothers' lives; others decidedly did *not*. Wendy's baby did:

[So far] there haven't been any [worst things]. Well, the obligations—he is tiring; and [there's] much less freedom. That's about
it. It hasn't been that bad. Prior to going back to work I went
away for a week [with my baby]. He's really not that constraining.
So far he is quite portable. (Wendy: Researcher Advisor)

Katherine also recognized that her child had been a "good baby."

[The worst thing about having a child was] actually, the first week
[at home after the birth]. That's about it . . . because she's a really
good baby, from what I hear [about other babies]. She slept
through the night when she was 2 months old. She was a really
happy baby . . . always smiling. (Katherine: Bell Operator)

At the same time, however, Katherine suspected that *other*
women's difficulties were caused by their own behavior:

It's funny, like, you know, sometimes people say, oh, you know,
"The kid won't stop crying." They lose their patience real quick.
And I can't even relate to that. Like, I think, "How can you?"
Nothing she does bothers me. I don't get upset. (Katherine: Bell
Operator)

Women, DeVault (1991) points out, are culturally expected to
respond to the variability of others' demands such that caring work
looks like an extension of emotional attachment and feminine
personality rather than effort. Not surprisingly, La Rossa and La
Rossa (1981) found that mothers of young infants are more likely
than fathers to perceive their infants as interpersonally competent
and to interact and communicate with them accordingly. Fathers,
they report, are more likely to act toward their infants as things; the
fathers do not feel the infants need full attention when they are
with them. This difference, La Rossa and La Rossa (1981) conclude,
leads not only to different parenting behavior but leads men and
women to value parenting differently.

Irrespective of their perceptions of their children's individual
personalities, the working-class women in this study were less likely
than the middle-class women to see children as disruptive of their
lives or to see such disruptions as a problem. Middle-class women
were more likely to talk about the ways in which their children resisted
the order they attempted to impose on their children's lives; at the

same time, these mothers emphasized the importance of the child's psychological separateness or integrity from his or her mother.

Children's individual personalities also came to affect women's daily experience of motherhood in an indirect way. Children's behavior, for example, could be seen as reflections of their mothers' behavior. Tess explained that for her the worst things about having a child were not just the feelings of having lost control of her time but also the way others judged *her* by her son's very demanding behavior. Others, she believed, saw her either as an incompetent mother or as an oppressed woman, depending on their gender politics. For Tess, these judgements were worse than the exhausting work:

> I think [the worst thing about having a child] [is] the lack of control over your own time. . . . Even the very simple things in life [can become problems]. I think that the lack of control and the lack of understanding by other people of what you are going through. . . . [Most people] would think to themselves, . . . "Oh, but of course, the child is just spoiled. *Put on* their shoes. They are going to wear two shoes, and that's the way it's going to be. . . . After all . . . we should be able to control them." But I think it's because, fundamentally, we are not destined to be able to control them [children]. (Tess: Senior Policy Analyst)

Tess felt her identity was being evaluated by others on the basis of a little person whom she, Tess, did not control and should not expect to:

> But I find it very frustrating, because people think whoever he is and whatever he does, it's because of something I'm doing, and in essence, I can't control what he does most of the time. I can only keep him from harm or try to get some food down and try to make sure he gets some sleep. So, if he is screaming, it's not because of something I'm doing. Like I'm a *victim*, and you're looking at me like it's my fault. I can't control who he is. . . . [Nonparents] will *assume* there is something I could do about it and *assume* that . . . I'm not doing anything about it because I'm basically oppressed and I *want* to do it this way; like I don't realize how oppressed I am, and if I wanted to, I could do it differently. (Tess: Senior Policy Advisor)

Tess felt herself caught between alternative principles of organization: the rational world of adults around her, especially at work, and the nonrational world of her son. Women, Ferree (1987) points out, typically find themselves trapped in such contradictions. The organization of capitalist production, which is oriented toward the production of market value, she argues, conflicts with the organization of family work, which is oriented toward meeting the needs of those we care about. These contradictions, she stresses, produce much of the ambivalence women experience in combining work and family. Thus women's responses to the work of looking after children are tied to factors that extend far beyond the home and leave them mediating conflicting demands of social worlds organized according to quite different values and priorities.

RESPONSES TO FAMILY WORK

To understand the participants' everyday lives as mothers, I asked them how they felt about the daily activities of looking after children. Their replies were difficult to summarize both because of the nature of family work and the complex meanings it carries. If, following Boulton (1983), one separates women's *immediate* responses to the tasks involved from the deeper sense of meaning or purpose they often find in looking after their children, then it appears that many women do *not* find childcare tasks primarily enjoyable.[12] This finding does not imply, however, that women do not regard childcare as important and meaningful work.

Only 30% of the women in this study said they mainly received a great deal of pleasure or enjoyment from the routine tasks of looking after their children (Table 7.3). Ten percent said, with some qualification, that they found childcare routines primarily frustrating; and 42% said that their responses varied between frustration and enjoyment. Working-class women were somewhat more likely than middle-class women to say that they found looking after their children primarily enjoyable (38% versus 26%), but most often women described their responses as being situationally contingent. It all depended, they explained: It depended on factors internal and external to family work.

Family work is a mode of work with its own logic and organization (Ferree, 1987). It carries its own internal sources of pleasure and frustration (Boulton, 1983; Lopata, 1971; DeVault, 1987, 1991; Oakley, 1974). Mothers in this study experienced some tasks as

TABLE 7.3. Women's Responses to the Daily Work of Motherhood

	Middle-class women	Working-class women
Contingent on task, child, time available, mother's day at work, etc.	42%	43%
Mainly enjoy it a lot	26%	36%
Mainly frustration	3%	18%
Neutral	13%	3%
Other	16%	0%

Note. N = 31 for middle-class women, 28 for working-class women. Table built from responses to fixed-choice and open-ended questions.

inherently more enjoyable or frustrating than others.[13] Bath times, or time spent with children after supper, for example, were enjoyed by many mothers; but mealtimes were often very frustrating. Similarly, many women mentioned that their children's behavior shaped the way they experienced family work. An irritated or overtired child, for example, could make manageable tasks frustrating:

Sometimes I get irritated when I come home from work. . . . Some days I'm really irritated, and some days I'm all right. I guess it depends on how my oldest [two children] get on when they come from daycare. If they start screaming right away, then my night is ruined. It's their mood, not mine [that counts]. (Karen: Dry Cleaner's Shipping Clerk)

For women in this study, external factors—in particular paid work—frequently interacted with internal factors to make family work more or less enjoyable. Paid work, for example, imposed industrial time constraints on parents, constraints of which their children were delightfully oblivious and of which, on occasion, they were downright subversive:

Every day is different. . . . Some mornings he is cooperative, he wants to get up. Other days we clearly operate on different clocks. . . . Often there are trials and tribulations around getting organized, or he'll get dressed OK, but then he won't put his coat on, or he won't put his shoes on, or . . . he wants to go into his room to find something to bring with him. . . . So you never know. It can take anywhere between 5 minutes to an hour to get him out of the house. . . . [How I feel] depends on where I am at that day—if I'm not pressured [it's not too bad]. (Nina: Director, Nonprofit Organization)

For some of the mothers, it was often the combination of irreconcilable demands, not the particular task or the fact of having outside employment, that produced frustration and irritation.[14] For others, it was the feeling that a partner was unwilling to "help" that heightened the frustrations of trying to do several incompatible tasks at once:[15]

[I get a lot of pleasure from looking after my children.] The only one [task] I find really frustrating is trying to cook supper when you have two children running around. A lot of [the] time [I'm on my own]. . . . Even if my husband is home he won't be with the children anyways. (Sally: Bell Service Assistant)

It is not surprising that many mothers said that the way they responded to family work "depended." They talked in terms of their children's moods, the specific tasks they had to do, the feeling of being rushed for time, support from their partners, or the kind of day they had had at work.

Although women may experience some autonomy and creativity in how they organize domestic work and may derive pleasure from meeting the needs of those they love, as Devault (1991) shows, family life is organized around variable needs and competing sets of priorities over which, in reality, women have little control. Having to be constantly responsive to the needs of others may threaten women's sense of psychological integrity (Lopata, 1971; Mandel, 1989). Thus, as is repeatedly stressed in feminist analysis, many of women's frustrations with family work are produced by the inequalities embedded in its social organization. Other frustrations are inherent in caring for young children, although, of course, the perception of appropriate care for children is culturally shaped. The difficulties of family work, however, are exacerbated when this work is interpreted by the standards and values of a marketplace economy that degrades its logic and meaning.

UNDERSTANDING RESPONSES TO FAMILY WORK

It is important not to interpret the responses of the women in this study to family work primarily in terms of the fact that they were working full-time outside the home. Studies of women who combine paid work and motherhood have often emphasized the role conflict, the chronic fatigue, and the lack of time these women experience. As Baruch et al.(1987) note, however, such research results may unwittingly support the hidden assumption that the stresses in women's lives are caused by their external employment. Family work itself can be inherently stressful, and the life of stay-at-home mothers may be distressing (Boulton, 1983; Oakley, 1974), sometimes leading to a depressed sense of self-worth (Rossi, 1980, p. 397), especially where there is little social recognition for the value of their work. There is also evidence to indicate that involvement in multiple roles may have some quite positive effects for women. Women who work outside the home tend to experience greater self-esteem, more control over their time, increased family power and marital satisfaction and, not unexpectedly, increased dissatisfaction with the traditional division of family work (Eichler, 1983, p. 188). Having outside work may help make childcare tasks less, not more, frustrating for mothers. It may even enhance women's personal fulfillment in mothering (Wearing, 1984, p. 136). Over half of Boulton's (1983) sample of stay-at-home or part-time employed mothers reported finding childcare to be a predominantly irritating task, but only 10% of the employed mothers in this study expressed the same opinion. For many of the women in this sample, childcare tasks, especially evening routines, provided much of the contact time they had with their children on weekdays, and women valued this contact. Fran, for example, explained that working outside the home made her less irritable with her children:

> Nowadays it's all right. . . . I [used to] get irritated by about 8:00 at night. . . . The little one has been getting up a lot at night . . . and that's when I get irritated. . . . Otherwise I don't get [irritated] anymore because [now that I'm working full-time] that's the only time I spend with them. (Fran: Lawyer)

For Fran, having paid work superimposed a legitimate structure on her day that limited the seemingly boundaryless demands of motherhood, thereby reducing this costly dimension of the role.

It is important to stress how difficult it is to conceptualize the nature of family work, such as looking after children. Early feminist studies of family work, for example, tended to adopt theoretical frameworks borrowed from the world of paid work to understand women's work in the home. While such approaches have been effective in revealing the hitherto neglected amount of *real* work involved in unpaid family labor, they leave the impression that the true meaning of family work is primarily that of an unpaid burden for women. This conclusion is a mistake. To treat family work as similar to paid work, and as a burden for which there is no economic recompense, misrepresents large parts of the reality of women's experience of what they do for their children and the significance of these activities for these women (Boulton, 1983; Devault, 1987; Ferree, 1987). Because family work is associated with love and embedded in family relations, its meaning for the women who perform it is both complex and contradictory (Thompson and Walker, 1989).

As we saw, mothers often do *not* find the actual tasks of family work enjoyable or fulfilling. At the same time, however, most, though certainly not all, women obtain rewards from family work because through it, they are meeting the needs of those for whom they *care* (Boulton, 1983; Devault, 1987; Ferree, 1987). Family work is experienced as part of a caring relationship, as part of being a parent, and not simply as "work"; yet it is also so culturally constructed as expressive of women's love that it is difficult for women not to do it and thereby risk the charge of "not caring" (Devault, 1987, 1991). So women's immediate response to childcare tasks, be it irritation or enjoyment, must be conceptually separated from the broader significance that the performance of those tasks *for* their children carries. Women may both value and resent family work (Thompson and Walker, 1989).

Women's family work has both personal and social significance, and the two cannot be easily separated. DeVault (1991, p. 91) explains how the day-to-day activities of feeding a family *produce family*: These activities join the disparate individuals, material, and interpersonal tasks through which family itself is constituted, thereby simultaneously producing the illusion that this form of social life is a "natural" one. Family work, DeVault (1991) emphasizes, has a dual character: that of physical labor and that of the production of sociability itself.

What is not always visible to women, however, is how the emotional and physical labor of caring for and about others is organized through relationships of gender inequality (Bartky, 1990;

DeValult, 1991; Graham, 1983). Thus family work may be expressive of love, but in practice it also expresses and reproduces hierarchical gender relations.

ALTERNATIVE IDENTITIES: CHILDLESS WOMEN AND STAY-AT-HOME MOTHERS

I talked to participants about their feelings and impressions of what other women's lives were like: women who had full-time jobs or careers but no children and the stay-at-home mother. These images offered imaginary "counter-selves," which functioned as reference points participants could use to interpret their own situation as "working mothers." Their responses suggest that participants saw their children as not only shaping who they were but also who they were *not*: Their responses expressed their images of the lives they had forgone by becoming mothers and by being "working mothers."

Both the working- and the middle-class participants had surprisingly clear impressions of the lives of women who had jobs or career but no children. Such women were generally seen as materially advantaged but psychologically disadvantaged, compared with women who were mothers. For many middle-class women, for example, the lives of these women were perceived as more "glamorous" than their own (63%)—the "good life" of leisure, eating out, and travel.

Working-class women in the study (68%) typically perceived such childless women as having "easier" lives—better jobs, more money, a better social life, able to buy and do what they wanted, and just "free to pick up and go." Indeed, from many of the women's perspectives, maternal status appeared to determine women's material lives much more than did social class.

The materially advantaged situation of childless women was not seen as preferable by the majority of the women in the study, but their responses were complex. Sixty-five percent of the middle-class women said they felt relatively lucky compared with such women— but 70% of the middle-class women *also* felt somewhat envious. Similarly, 64% of the working-class women said they felt relatively lucky—again, 56% of these women *also* felt some envy. However, none of the middle-class women and only 18% of the working-class women described themselves as being primarily envious.

But how did these mothers compare their lives with those of childless women? According to 52% of the middle-class and 56% of the working-class mothers, women who had children had psychological and nonmaterial advantages over those who did not. Laura, a middle-class mother, explained that although she recognized the advantages of not having children, because she had once had that life, she did not want to return to it. She felt privileged compared with nonmothers, but she did not want to appear condescending toward them:

> [When I see other women of my age who have full-time jobs or careers but no children] I guess it makes me remember when I had more time on my hands and not as much responsibility. But that doesn't make me feel I'd like to return there. . . . I really feel that where I am now is better than where I was, so I have to watch I'm not condescending. . . . I imagine they have more free time, more money to do traveling and stuff with, but I don't think they are happier. I see myself as being happier. I see them as still searching. (Laura: Accountant)

Most women in the study perceived their lives and identities as mothers as determiningly distinct from those of childless women. For Cora, an alone working-class mother of a 3-year-old, mothers looked like mothers—and childless women looked as if they spent a lot of time on themselves: like women who didn't have to lift a finger.

> No, [I have no response when I see women who have full-time jobs or a career but no children, but] I can usually pick them out, though, so I guess there is a response. . . . Most mothers usually look like mothers. . . . You can tell that they [these other women] usually spend a lot of time on themselves . . . because they look like they've never had to lift a finger in their lives. They have probably chosen career over family, that's all. I've nothing against it. [Their lives are] probably lonely. (Cora: Word Processor)

Although many women in the sample found much of the imagery of "the childless life-style" attractive, these attractions were negated by the perceived psychological or moral costs. Thus neither the appeal of childlessness nor the costs of childrearing subverted these women's role commitment as mothers. Several of the middle-class women pointed out that they had "had all that" but had given it up to have children, and many working-class women felt that they had foregone the possibility of attaining material advantage by having children. The heavy investment of having relinquished the "glamorous" or "easy" life functioned to reinforce rather than to threaten their commitment to motherhood. At the same time, because the conditions of participants' current lives appeared to them to be grounded in having had children rather than in the inequalities of social class and gender arrangements, they talked in terms of alternative life-styles and personal choices rather than of alternative social arrangements:

> Only occasionally do I feel envious—but not really; I don't feel envy, and I don't want to trade life-styles at all. I'm not in the least bit envious. But occasionally I think, well. . . . But I also sort of . . . wonder about them, too. I wonder if they have chosen their lives, if they are happy. In some cases I know they are happy, but they are not always [happy]. I also feel I don't have as much in common with them. . . . Somehow, having a child means that I am in a different life experience from [theirs]. (Joanne: Elementary School Teacher)

Perhaps because the participants saw motherhood as *so* determining of their lives and the material rewards of nonmotherhood as being so concrete, their commitment to motherhood did require ongoing ideological work to reduce the potential for cognitive dissonance. Central to this process was the way in which women "reminded" themselves of the sort of persons they *really* were, their claimed characters and identities. As Sally told herself and me, she was not "the type of person" to be bothered by the costs of childrearing or what she had forgone in having children:

> Well, I just feel that they have a bigger financial bucket to dip into and are able to do whatever they want to do and go on trips or buy material things. It doesn't bother me *too* much, because I'm [not] that type of person, but some other people might be more envious. . . . I feel that what I have is *more* than having material things. So I'm not envious of that because to me it's not important. (Sally: Bell Service Assistant)

In spite of participants' heavy personal and practical investment in motherhood and the socially irrevocable nature of the commitment, the potential for ambivalence was endemic to motherhood, although not in ways that were subversive of commitment. Because women held their lives to have been shaped by being mothers, childless "career women" symbolized the potential selves these women had *not become.* In earlier chapters I showed that women valued the selves they had become through motherhood; indeed, some felt it had saved them. At the same time, becoming a mother meant *not becoming* the person one could have been. Ellen saw both gains and losses in her choice:

> I'm aware that I'm different from them [women who have full-time jobs or careers but who don't have children].
> . . . It's like looking at myself a few years ago. . . . If I think they will never have children, ah, . . . they will miss something, but they will have an opportunity to do things that I won't have. I don't know. It's a funny feeling. . . . Either they will take a road, either the same road I took, or they will be pursuing the road I didn't take. (Ellen: Typesetter)

"THEY LOOK SO HAGGARD": CAUTIONARY IMAGES OF FULL-TIME MOTHERS

Even when women work full-time outside the home, the image of the full-time mother and homemaker can remain culturally powerful, embodying deeply felt beliefs about what family is and what good mothering entails. Among the women in this study, the domestic ideal of full-time mother often evoked quite strong positive and negative responses.

Sixty-five percent of the middle-class women said they felt relatively *lucky* compared with women who stayed home, though 39% also felt some envy, primarily about the time the full-time at-home mothers were believed to spend with their children. No middle-class mother described herself overall as envious of full-time mothers. Rather, they saw the image, but not the daily reality of domesticity, as attractive. Kim explained that, in spite of the fact that she would have liked more time to spend with her child, she felt fortunate to be working:

> It's a bit of a double-edged sword. . . . I feel envious in the sense that there is some time they are spending with their children . . . the quality of [that] time might be questioned, however. On the

other hand, I feel fortunate that I have a life of my own—sometimes just getting out and having your own job and group of friends is very important for a woman's self-image. (Kim: Librarian)

Most of the middle-class women held quite negative images of the lives of those mothers who stayed home full-time—and also of their own lives, were they to stay home. Indeed, 52% felt sorry for stay-at-home-mothers or indicated that staying at home was psychologically harmful to women. Many others questioned whether it was really these women's free choice; some of the middle-class women indicated they had "a problem" with women who decided to stay home. A small minority of the middle-class women saw the full-time mother's life as almost heroic, but for the vast majority it was clearly not a desirable option for women like themselves. An alone middle-class mother explained that she felt relatively lucky:

Yeah. [When I see women who stay home full-time with their children] I want to help them. I would like to unburden them to some extent because I find, for the most part, women I see who stay home full-time, usually they have more than one child, they look *haggard*. . . . I want to take them out to lunch. I think I am lucky that I can balance the two. (Della: Childcare Social Worker)

Working-class women were more likely than middle-class women to see the domestic ideal as attractive. More than a third of the working-class women (36%) said that stay-at-home mothers were relatively lucky compared with themselves, or that they felt overall envious of the stay-at-home mothers. But, like most of the middle-class women, many (43%) of the working-class women held very negative images of the lives of stay-at-home mothers or of their own lives were they to stay home. Women who stayed at home were seen as being in danger—in danger of not getting financial or social recognition for their work; of letting their minds or bodies "go"; of risking irritation, frustration, and boredom. A married working-class mother of two preschoolers explained:

I think that [staying home] they have a harder job than I do because they don't have as many breaks and don't always have the prestige or appreciation. They are probably doing the most important job in the world and yet people look down on it. I feel sorry [for them] because they are not gaining anything financially, because they are investing themselves in their children. . . . I feel sorry they don't get paid and people don't really look up to them. . . . I feel lucky because I'm able to have two worlds. They only have one, but I have two worlds, plus the financial benefits. (Sally: Bell Service Assistant)

Within the working-class sample, however, there was a clear division on the ideal of domesticity between those with and without partners. Almost half of those with partners (47%) said they envied at-home mothers, but only 18% of alone mothers did. Given the personal experiences of poverty and welfare experienced by alone mothers who had previously "not worked" (for pay), it is not surprising that few of the latter saw at-home mothers as being relatively lucky.

Despite the popular misconception that "working mothers" are a relatively recent phenomenon, many women, especially economically disadvantaged women, have long taken paid work to support their families. Wearing (1984), however, suggests that there has been an ideological shift—that working for pay is increasingly recognized as part of what a good working-class mother does *for her children* (Wearing, 1984), although it has not replaced the ideal of spending time with and caring for children. Many women in this study did not think in terms of choosing or not choosing to work. For some, their concern was to find and hold employment that would earn enough money to support their children. For others, indeed for most of the middle-class women, the "choice" in a sense was to add children to their lives: Work was taken for granted. The vast majority of the middle-class women already had strong personal and financial investments in work and career that they found rewarding. None wanted to be a full-time mother.

Ironically, despite middle-class women's financial contribution to their families' well-being, their work is often represented, both inside and outside the family, as something they do *for themselves* (Ferree, 1984, 1987), thus weakening their bargaining power in negotiating the division of family work. I return to these issues in Chapter 8.

MAKING SENSE OF WOMEN'S LIVES: AN OUTSIDER'S PERSPECTIVE

Competing images emerged from participants' descriptions of their everyday lives as full-time employed mothers. The first was an image of the work, the *endless* need for organizing and scheduling. This image reflected the many ways in which individuals and resources were stretched to make the demands of work and family fit into a world that is organized as though these demands were completely separate and taken care of by different people. Managing the competing demands of two worlds was especially difficult for those disadvantaged by societal gender and class arrangements—women located at the intersection of inadequate social support for mothering and low-paid work.

The other image was that of women whose lives were indeed objectively difficult but who felt their lives to have been enriched through having children and who derived satisfaction and self-esteem from caring for their children, as well as from being able to combine work and motherhood in their lives. For as Mandel (1989, p. 41) also found in her study of employed mothers, women had "developed a perspective on their lives that allows them to assess their choices as worthwhile." For the majority of the women in this study, combining work and motherhood involved *hard work*, but it also seemed to have provided them with a sense of personal competence and strength. Like the women in the studies by Hochschild (1989) and Mandel (1989), the women in this study talked repeatedly of the coping strategies and organizational patterns they had developed to make combining work and motherhood manageable. Participants in this study, as we have seen, did not merely respond to the multiple pressures and time constraints on their lives but engaged them in ways that were personally meaningful. However, although caring for children was meaningful for the women involved, the gendered organization of caring in society reproduces other meanings not visible to those engaged in caring work: It reproduces hierarchical meanings of gender and the devaluation of unpaid work.

SUMMARY

Participants in this study said that watching their children learn and grow and their feelings of connectedness with them were among the greatest rewards of being a mother. Rather than seeing this connect-edness with children as "costing" a loss of self or denial of personal identity, we need to understand that talk of connectedness represented the extent to which participants' sense of self, like all social identities, were generated and sustained through the social relationship of motherhood. Some mothers' accounts also suggested the ways in which natural or biological relationships can be interpreted symbolically to express significant social relationships, thus intensifying feelings of social connectedness between self and others—in this case, mother and child. Biology can come to symbolize unquestionable attachment, in turn making social connectedness appear natural.

There was less agreement on the costs of having children, although the images held by the women in the study about childless career women suggest that many participants retrospectively perceived having children as synonymous with a decision to give up the "glamorous" or "easy" life. Working-class women saw fewer costs to having children and were less likely than middle-class women to see the work involved and time pressures as disadvantages. Both groups talked equally often of their worries about how they were doing as parents. Even though these women loved their children, they did not necessarily enjoy the work of looking after them. Many mothers' immediate responses to family work were best described as situationally contingent.

Two images, that of stay-at-home mothers and that of childless career women, readily functioned as reference points by which the women in the sample could interpret their everyday lives. While the majority of these women saw their situation as "working-mothers" to be preferable to either of these options, these other images also conjured up some attractions for participants, making the potential for ambivalence endemic to being a mother. One might hypothesize that women in all three categories—employed mothers, stay-at-home mothers, and career nonmothers—are likely to experience some ambivalence about their own choices and to recognize the advantages these alternative identities and life situations hold for other women. The accounts of mothers in this study show how children were perceived as helping determine not just who these mothers were but, also important, who they were *not*. Given the nature of most women's personal investment in their children, however, potential "counterself" images were not deeply subversive of maternal commitment.

The image of mothers' everyday lives that emerges from this study is a dual one. On the one hand, there is an image of women's long hours of work; their lack of time; and the ongoing tasks of organizing, scheduling, and managing. The negative images participants held of the lives of stay-at-home mothers, however, show these women's investment in work outside the home. Only a minority saw mother-

230 ENGENDERING MOTHERHOOD

hood as exhaustive of a woman's identity. For most, being *only* a mother was psychologically dangerous or undesirable.

On the other hand, there was an image of participants' joy in their children, that caring for others—especially their children—was valued, and that woemn felt a sense of personal competence and self-esteem at having both paid work and motherhood in their lives.

On the other hand, I pointed to how the consequences of the low public value of family work and the inadequate societal support for caring for others, be they children, disabled, or elderly folk, are generally privately borne by women. These consequences were exacerbated in the case of low-income women. Perhaps it is time to abandon the implicit assumptions that paid work is somehow optional or secondary for women, that family work is not real work, and that the difficulties women face are merely the costs of their personal choices. We need instead to ask why the costs of parenthood are made so high and why these costs are expected to be privately born by women. What is particularly harmful in the current social organization of caring as being women's private responsibility is not simply that it places an unfair burden of work on women. It is also, as Devault (1991) points out, that women are expected to produce sociability at the expense of equality and that the social value of family and caring work is rendered invisible. The consequences are pernicious for women in that subservience and hierarchical gender relationships become constitutive of intimate and caring relationships: caring draws women into relations of subordination (Bartky, 1990; DeVault, 1991). It is pernicious for society in that social goods and the production of sociability itself are devalued.

8

Mothers and Other Parents: Parenting as a Gendered and Engendering Experience

This chapter looks at the *consequences*, rather than the causes, of the social organization of parenting in the home. It looks at the ways in which the everyday practice of being a mother, in particular the division of domestic or family work, helped produce a gendered experience of self as parent for the participants in this study. I show how everyday domestic practice reinforced the socializing impact that having children had on women's identities, which was discussed in earlier chapters. What seems remarkable about motherhood is that so many different socializing influences converged to reinforce women's commitment to maternal identity.[1]

Socialization, in particular the inculcation of societal values during childhood, is frequently invoked to explain the enactment of adult social roles and the embracement of gender–role identities. Empirically, however, the situation is usually more complex. Motherhood, as Rossi (1980) points out, is distinguishable from other primary adult roles in that there is cultural pressure on all women to assume the role, but anticipatory socialization is inadequate. And, unlike many other adult roles, motherhood is usually considered irrevocable.[2] Consequently the transition to parenthood often takes on the character of a crisis. Generally the concept of childhood socialization has limited explanatory power in accounting for adult behavior (Brim and Wheeler, 1966), but this limitation is particularly evident when we attempt to understand women's family and occupational roles during the contemporary period of social change (Gerson, 1985; Bernard, 1975). Indeed, the lack of societal consensus on women's roles is reflected in the feminist and nonfeminist composition of the sample in this study.[3]

Rather than explaining adult family role enactment in terms of early gender socialization, I look at becoming a mother as a process of situational adjustment (H. Becker, 1981)—a process whereby individuals take on the characteristics required by the situations in which they participate, whether or not they are formally socialized. I show how the social organization of family life helped produce, among the women in this study, the character and identity of mother: a gendered experience of self as parent and a distinct identity as mother. The nature of social situations, H. Becker emphasizes (1981, p. 310), not the individual's personality or beliefs, explains much of the personal change experienced in adulthood. Individuals come to align actions and ideas with situations. Of course, situations themselves are structurally organized. Thus the concept of situational adjustment allows a social explanation that captures both the contingency and determinacy of social life. Given the irrevocable nature of the role of mother, the pressures toward adjustment that exist in most social situations are greatly strengthened. We can, as Rossi (1980) emphasizes, have ex-spouses and ex-jobs, but not ex-children.

Yet the concept of situational adjustment cannot fully explain women's commitment to motherhood. Because the behaviors and perspectives acquired by situational adjustments may be only as enduring as the situation itself, the concept of commitment is needed to explain consistency in identities and behavior as individuals move from one situation to another. Commitment, H. Becker explains, is built up through investment:

> The committed person has acted in such a way as to involve other interests of his, originally extraneous to the action he is engaged in, directly to that action. He has staked something of value to him . . . on being consistent in his present behaviors. The consequence of inconsistency will be so expensive that inconsistency . . . is no longer a feasible alternative. (H. Becker, 1981, p. 314)

I talked earlier about the ways in which children became constitutive of women's valued sense of self. When women become mothers, their new maternal identities become implicated in many preexisting social relationships, whether of partner, daughter, friend, or other, in ways that come to support their new commitment to motherhood. Thus what sometimes began as a side bet (H. Becker, 1981, p. 315)—for example, becoming pregnant because a partner wanted children—can become a full-blown commitment to maternity. Indeed, we saw in earlier chapters how, even among those who had once been ambivalent about having children, a deeply valued sense of self became invested in motherhood. The more at stake in a role or relationship, the greater the commitment.

But why do men apparently not experience a similar process of situational adjustment to parenthood? In spite of considerable changes in ideologies of fatherhood, research continues to show a greater salience of parental identities for women than for men cross-situationally, whether in familial or nonfamilial situations. And this greater salience holds even when mothers work full-time outside the home (Hochschild, 1989; Thompson and Walker, 1989) and even when men feel themselves deeply commited to their children (Daly, 1991). Commentators have described many "new fathers," who have internalized the ideal of paternal involvment in their children's lives, as being technically present but functionally absent (Feldman and Feldman, in La Rossa, 1988). The participants in this study accounted for this gendered experience of parenting not simply in terms of different domestic work loads but in terms of gendered consciousness, gendered feelings of responsibility, and men's perceived greater ability to compartmentalize and segregate parts of themselves from their children. Experientially, in this study, this was part of what made a woman a mother rather than just a parent.

Using H. Becker's (1960) notion of commitment as investment, however, I want to argue that the issue is not simply one of *how much* is committed but *what* is committed *to*, in parenthood. The cultural terms of the parent contract are different for men and women. The women in this study, I argued earlier, knew (and so had to handle) the cultural associations of mother, morality, and responsibility for their children. Implicit in women's investment in parenthood is the belief that children's daily emotional and physical well-being is ultimately dependent on their mothers' caring behavior (Backett, 1982; Wearing, 1984). Cultural beliefs about children and their needs can altercast women into being mothers, not simply parents.

Although mothers are no longer expected to be physically present with young children at all times, the assumption that they continue to be accessible to their children and responsible for them persists, even when the women work outside the home (Wearing, 1984). Like doctors on duty, women are thus on call from their daycare centers and available to meet their children's needs, even at work. The belief that women are "ultimately responsible" for their young children endures (Bernard, 1975; Wearing, 1984); they are seen to be responsible for the preservation, growth, and social acceptability of their children (Ruddick, 1984a). Whatever the empirical meaning of maternal responsibility, when it is socially expected, I suggest, it is profoundly socializing for women, if not socially controlling. Men's full involvement in daily childcare responsibilities, on the other hand, has become culturally perceived as laudable but remains essentially voluntary (La Rossa, 1988). Children are not considered to be at risk for profound emotional or physical harm if their fathers are not fully involved in childcare. Indeed, men's parental commitment may increase their investment in their provider roles, rather than in their domestic roles (Bernard, 1981). Thus the costs or consequences of noninvolvement in childcare and family work are quite different for men and women; even when both are personally committed to parenthood, the stakes are higher for women.

So central are the associations of responsibility, morality, and caring to the dominant cultural meanings of mother that for a woman to risk seeing herself or being seen as irresponsible toward her children would be to risk far more than an inadequate role performance. The women in this sample recognized that, as a social role, motherhood has low public value, but for them it was of high personal and moral worth (Wearing, 1984). Thus for a woman to be remiss in feeling responsible for her child would implicate her whole moral character.

THE DIVISION OF FAMILY WORK
AMONG MIDDLE-CLASS COUPLES

The term "parent" is replacing the terms "mother" and "father" in popular and academic usage. "Parent" is a gender-neutral word, but in this study the women's experience of parenting was not gender neutral. Eighty-four percent of the middle-class women and 82% of the working-class women were quite clear that parenthood was a *gendered* experience. Men and women may both be parents, I was told, but they *act, think,* and *feel* differently as parents. What, then, were these differences?

The participants grounded their claims to a distinctly female experience of parenthood in the gendered social organization of their households, in particular the division of domestic work; in their feelings of responsibility; and in the different or special awareness or consciousness they had of their children (see Table 8.4). Research supports their accounts. Family or domestic work remains primarily women's work (Michelson, 1985; Hochschild, 1989). Even when men do participate in family work, what they do, how and when they do it, and how they experience it differ from women's experiences (Thompson and Walker, 1989). Contrary to what one might expect, research evidence suggests the division of domestic labor is not directly determined by a woman having outside employment, by what she earns relative to her partner, by the time she has available, or even by the egalitarian beliefs held by a couple.[4] Perhaps more puzzling are the findings that many women are not openly dissatisfied with unequal gender arrangements (Baruch and Barnett, 1986a; Rosen, 1987).

As my main research interest focused on identity, I was more interested in understanding how women *felt* about the division of family work, rather than in documenting precisely who did what in the family. However, I did collect data on women's accounts of the division of family work. I began by distinguishing between childcare and other family work, such as laundry and cooking, home repairs and maintenance, and managing family finances, which I refer to as "other household work." The findings were somewhat unexpected (Table 8.1).

The middle-class women in this study described more sharing of family work than has been reported in many other studies.[5] A third of those with partners (34%), for example, said their partners did half (or more) of the childcare work, and another 26% said their partners did approximately 40% of childcare. Put another way, only 25% of the middle-class women said their partners did less than 30% of childcare work.

Loretta was one of the third of the middle-class women who felt their partners shared family work *equally*: She and her partner had decided on it before having children.

I'm very satisfied [with the division of family work]. It's something we've both really worked at. It's something I really value. . . . I feel it's unusual and that even makes you value it more. If you ask me how I feel about women who work full-time and

TABLE 8.1. Respondents' Descriptions of the Domestic Division
of Childcare Work in Two-Parent Households

	Middle-class women	Working-class women
Mothers did less than half	4%	0%
Mothers and partners shared equally	30%	0%
Mothers did 51%–60%	26%	18%
Mothers did 61%–70%	15%	35%
Mothers did 71%–80%	22%	23%
Mothers did 81%–90%	3%	18%
Mothers did 91%–100%	0%	6%

Note. N = 27 for middle-class women, 17 for working-class women. Table constructed from responses to fixed-choice questions.

have a husband who doesn't contribute, I have very strong feelings toward that. . . . We spent a long time in the first few years of our marriage working this out. (Loretta: Elementary School Teacher)

Kim also said she and her partner shared family work equally. She explained that although to an outsider it might look that her partner did *more* household work than she did, she compensated by contributing more emotionally to the children. Like Loretta, Kim emphasized the commitment to equal participation in family life:

[I am very satisfied.] We believe strongly that both parents should participate as fully as possible in the children's lives. We both have full-time jobs; our situations are very similar in that way. . . . If you were to look at this [check sheet], it would indicate that my partner does certainly much more than I do in terms of the household tasks. . . . [But] in terms of having two babies of this age, there is a certain tendency for them to want their mother, which is unavoidable. And that can be very, very emotionally draining. . . . I think there is a tendency to try to compensate for that; for example, when we come home from work, Karl will generally prepare the food. And I'm sort of with [the children]. (Kim: Librarian)

For some, however, "joint participation" is a better description of how women think about family life than of empirical practice.

"MY HUSBAND IS VERY INVOLVED":
DO EGALITARIAN BELIEFS PRODUCE
PARTICIPATORY PARTNERS
OR WISHFUL-THINKING WIVES?

Reports of fathers' involvement in childcare do not necessarily indicate a shift to egalitarian family arrangements. Backett (1982, 1987) and Hochschild (1989) show that claims to parental sharing are likely to be overstated among couples such as middle-class professionals, who are committed to the ideals of gender equality. Distortion and denial, La Rossa and La Rossa (1981) point out, seem to be a key strategy in the smooth transition to parenthood among professed egalitarian couples. And, as Hochschild (1989) and several women in this study state, fathers' involvement often means that men take over some of the more enjoyable aspects of parenthood. Men often take responsibility for playtime with their young children, whereas mothers' interaction time is more often characterized by caretaking work.[6] This situation may result in women devoting proportionately more of their time at home to housework and proportionately less of it to time with their children (Hochschild, 1989, p. 9),[7] thus displacing women from one of the more rewarding parts of motherhood: spending time with children.[8] Fathers' "involvement," therefore, is not always positive for mothers.

In light of evidence from other studies, it would be easy to suspect that many of the accounts of the middle-class women in this study were egalitarian wishful thinking. But such a conclusion does not easily fit the consistency with which the middle-class women described male involvement in family work. For example, many women reported that their partners were as likely as they themselves were to take time off from work when their children were sick. A third of those women with partners who said their partners shared childcare equally also reported, on an itemized checklist, that their partners shared other household work equally. Another 7% said their partners compensated for doing *less* childcare by doing *more* housework. Those who said their partners shared family work equally were also the most likely to say they were satisfied with the division of both childcare and other household work (Table 8.2).

There was no simple relationship between inequality in the division of family work and participants' expressed *dis*satisfaction. Not surprisingly, women whose partners shared family work, but did only about a third of it, were less likely to say they were satisfied with the division of family work, but they did not necessarily describe themselves as dissatisfied. Similarly, few of the 26% of the middle-class women whose partners did less than 30% of the childcare said they were satisfied; at the same time, less than half (43%) described themselves as dissatisfied. It seemed easier for women whose partners shared family work to say they were satisfied than it was for those with unequal family arrangements to say they were dissatisfied. As Thompson and Walker (1989, p. 859) point out, the cost of expressing such dissatisfaction may be an increase in family conflict while producing few practical gains. Expressed dissatisfaction undermines the belief in the jointness of family life. It is often safer and easier for couples to engage in "glossing" (La Rossa and La Rossa, 1981) or "family myths" (Hochschild, 1989) to bridge the gap between the reality and the ideals of shared parenting.

Sixty-three percent of the middle-class mothers were satisfied or very satisfied with the division of childcare; 22% were dissatisfied; and 15% were neutral or somewhat satisfied (Table 8.2). At the same time, 56% were satisfied with the division of other household work, while 30% were dissatisfied (Table 8.3). Overall, 41% of the middle-class women said they were satisfied or very satisfied with the division of both childcare and other household work, and 37% said they were dissatisfied with one or both of these arrangements.

For many of the participants however, the principles of equity, reasonableness, or fairness, rather than equality often guided their evaluation of the division of family work and hence their expressed satisfaction or dissatisfaction. That is, women judged arrangements in terms of, for example, whether they were perceived as reasonable or fair, inevitable in the context of family history, necessary in terms of their children's perceived needs, reasonable in terms of the parents' skills, and legitimate in terms of the parents' willingness to be involved. A minority of the women explicitly stated they were satisfied with

TABLE 8.2. Mothers' Satisfaction with the Division of Childcare

	Middle-class women	Working-class women
Satisfied or very satisfied	63%	35%
Neutral or somewhat satisfied	15%	30%
Dissatisfied	22%	35%

Note. N = 27 for middle-class women, 17 for working-class women. Table constructed from responses to fixed-choice questions.

TABLE 8.3. Mothers' Satisfaction with the Division of Other Household Work

	Middle-class women	Working-class women
Satisfied or very satisfied	56%	41%
Neutral or somewhat satisfied	11%	41%
Dissatisfied	30%	18%
No answer	3%	0%

Note. N = 27 for middle-class women, 17 for working-class women. Table constructed from responses to fixed-choice questions.

the division of family work because it was equal and that they and their partners had worked hard to achieve this equality. For most, the notion of legitimacy rather than equality permeated women's accounts.[9] Although most of the middle-class mothers described themselves as feminists, some inequality in the division of family work was not necessarily seen as illegitimate. In many cases it was the symbolic meaning of their partners' participation or nonparticipation that counted.[10]

Many middle-class women gave sophisticated reasons for why inequality was not necessarily illegitimate and therefore was not grounds for open dissatisfaction. Some referred to the ways in which motherhood was socially organized, in particular the institutionalization of maternity (rather than parental) leave to care for infants. As Backett (1982) points out, mothers' early specialization in postpartum childcare means they gain or are attributed greater expertise and skill—a pattern that then becomes the perceived reason for women's continued responsibility. It seems to "just happen," as Fran explained:

I think it all depends on your husband. I *have heard*, and I do know, of a *few men* who actually do [share the] work. But there aren't many of them. . . . I think it stems from the fact that the woman, if she is breast-feeding . . . you are usually off work for a certain number of months. And you get into the habit of doing everything there is to be done and you just continue it. And when you go back to work, the daycare fees come out of your paycheck. . . . I think that's where it starts. I don't think it is particularly *deliberate* on anybody's part. I think it just happens. (Fran: Lawyer)

It was not simply the acts of giving birth and breast-feeding that grounded the participants' subsequent greater responsibility for their children; it was also the social practice of mothers, but not of fathers, to "stay home" with newborn infants.

> Women take the major responsibility for the child. . . . Certainly for me there has been more responsibility. . . . Typically, I mean, women bear the children, you breast-feed the child, so you build up this initial responsibility at that time, and that generally carries on. And because I had stayed home. . . . Men don't usually stay home. (Tannis: Counselor)

Others pointed not so much to the differential socializing effects of early parenthood but to men's own early socialization to explain their lesser participation in family work:

> [It's the] socialization of males and females. Women have different expectations of themselves, and men have different expectations of women. The difference between me and my spouse . . . [is that] I take responsibility. (Beth: Management Board Officer)

Many middle-class mothers' day-to-day experience jarred with their intellectual understanding of their world. A minority made references to biology to explain the gap between expectation and experience, between what they believed intellectually and the gendered parenting they experienced:

> It has to do with how we are socialized . . . but I [also] think men's and women's nervous systems are different. . . . [They] react differently. . . . It's hard to break the traditions. You might know it intellectually, but . . . (Patricia: Community College Teaching Master)

A feminist consciousness or intellectual awareness of the dangers of traditional gender roles does not mean they are easily avoided:

> And it's because men are socialized differently [from] women, so that there are different expectations of their roles. And as much as one loves to be equal, it's very difficult to not fall into those [ways]. And sometimes you just have to decide, "This may be stereotypical, but. . . . " (Sandra: Civil Servant)

Some once-plausible explanations of men's lesser participation in family labor no longer worked for these middle-class women. Only 7% cited men's paid work as a reason for their unequal involvement in childcare. Even in these cases, the explanation lacked legitimacy, as these women were *not* satisfied with the division of family work.

For many of the middle-class mothers, the division of family work acquired a form of *de facto* legitimacy, not because it approximated their ideals but because in practice it seemed beyond their own, and even their partners', control. Like the "new fathers" in Daly's (1991) study, male partners might appear willing but unable to share equally. Thus, even to feminist women, the symbolic significance of inequality was depoliticized by circumstances.

"I WOULD LIKE MORE HELP, BUT MEN ARE A PAIN": WORKING-CLASS COUPLES AND THE DIVISION OF FAMILY WORK

In this study, the working-class women with partners described a more unequal division of family work than did the middle-class women who had partners (Table 8.1). None of the working-class women said a partner shared childcare equally, and only 18% credited their partners with doing 40% or more of the childcare work.

Working-class women are sometimes portrayed as more traditional than middle-class women and therefore more accepting of an unequal division of labor in the home. This was not the case among participants in this study. Only 35% of the working-class women with partners were satisfied with the division of childcare, and only 41% felt satisfied with the division of other household work.[11] Only 18% were satisfied with both. Yet, although most were not satisfied, only 47% of the working-class women were openly *dis*satisfied, whether with the division of childcare or with other household work. Others often described themselves as neutral (see Tables 8.2 and 8.3). Lisa was clearly dissatisfied:

Oh, yeah. [It's different for men and women.] OK. This is good. Now, *he* gets home. *He* sits. *He* eats. *He* gets up and goes to the living room. What do I do [when I come home]? I have to make the lunches for tomorrow. If the dishes [aren't done], if I didn't have time to do them in the morning, I do them then . . . and

I've got to make the dinner . . . and she's nagging at me and she's destroying the place. And he thinks it's great. . . . I wish he would spend more time with her. (Lisa: Data Entry Clerk)

Again, responses to the division of family work did not neatly reflect the existence of either equality or inequality in the division of family work. Chris, a mother of a preschooler, described herself as feeling neutral about the fact that she did far more domestic work than her partner:

I'm not very satisfied with [the division of domestic work. [I feel] neutral [about it]. Well, I can't expect more from him because he wouldn't do it. (Chris: Clerical Worker)

Like the middle-class women, the working-class women interpreted the division of family work according to whether it was seen as legitimate, or fair. "Legitimate" did not mean the mothers were satisfied, but it did inhibit dissent. It deprived these women of publicly or personally credible grounds for voicing dissatisfaction and also functioned to make the reality more acceptable. For these working-class mothers, typical legitimating explanations included the belief that other men did *less* work at home; feeling they had some control in the (unequal) division of labor; feeling more personally competent or more willing to do the work; and the belief that men are by nature inherently nonmaternal.

Becoming neutral was one way these women coped with a situation they had little power to change. Karen, a mother of three preschoolers, explained that she no longer cared that her husband did not share with family work:

Most [men from his ethnic background], the man is free all the time to do what they want. I can't put on my coat like how he does and go through the front door. . . . At first I didn't like it at all, but like, it's an everyday thing to me now. So I don't really think about it anymore. (Karen: Dry Cleaner's Shipping Clerk)

We can see from Table 8.1, however, that many of the working-class men did in fact participate in family labor.[12] But the widespread belief among the working-class women that men generally did little domestic work appeared to reinforce rather than challenge the inequality in family work. The belief in men's nonparticipation lowered women's expectations, encouraged a sense of powerlessness, and discouraged attempts to negotiate alternative arrangements. As Stephanie put it, she was *grateful* that her husband watched the baby while she cooked dinner or did the laundry. Comparing herself to women whose husbands "didn't lift a finger," she was satisfied:

> [I'm just] thankful that he *does* help. There are some husbands who won't lift a finger. He [my husband] watches him [the baby] while I make the dinner or do the laundry. It doesn't bother me [that I do most of the domestic work]. (Stephanie: Clerical Worker)

As argued in the previous chapter, we must not assume that family work is always burdensome or that it is culturally acceptable for women to acknowledge that caring for a loved one can be burdensome. Domestic work is often presented both to and by women as a "labor of love" (Luxton, 1980). As Barb explained, because she loved looking after her child she felt moderately satisfied with doing two-thirds of the work involved:

> [I'm somewhat satisfied.] I love doing it, but there are times! . . . [My husband] does a lot. He does a lot more than a lot of men I know. (Barb: Clerical Worker)

Like many middle-class women, many working-class women also offered explanations that justified the persistence of traditional domestic arrangements. Participants' beliefs about male incompetence, for example, functioned to reaffirm the inequality in the division of domestic labor, making it appear easier for women to perform tasks themselves. Ramona, for example, said she was neutral about the fact that she did 80% of the childcare tasks. Since her partner had turned all the baby's clothes pink in some laundry misadventure, she said she felt she could not trust him with certain responsibilities. At the same time, Ramona's partner's overt willingness to "help" makes him symbolically appear involved in family work and made the division of labor acceptable[13]:

> Sometimes you wish he would do just a little more, just to help you out. . . . I would say I am neutral [about it] because . . . if I

ask him to do something, he would do it. . . . [On the other hand] if I do it, I know it's done [and done properly]. (Ramona: Bookkeeping Clerk)

It is difficult to know if men's apparent incompetence was their way of avoiding family labor or women's way of maintaining control over valued territory (Boulton, 1983). However, as La Rossa and La Rossa (1981) point out, mothers of infants have good cause not to trust male partners who, by distancing themselves from family work (or embracing instead the breadwinner role), fail to acquire the skills and knowledge necessary to care for young children. Pam, for example, described herself as moderately satisfied with the 70% share of childcare tasks she performed: It was *easier* than having her partner do more.

I like to make sure things are done the way I want—not because I wouldn't like him to do more; it's because if I want things done a certain way, it's easier to do it [myself]. . . . I would like *more help*, but men are a pain. (Pam: Clerical Worker)

Family work, as Kranichfeld (1987) argues, can be an important source of power and value that women may be reluctant to lose. At the same time, as Ferree (1987) points out, many women are discouraged from struggling for greater domestic equality because they feel it is not worth their while to jeopardize what domestic control they do have to get just a little "help." Whatever its complex source, men and women find themselves trapped in a pattern of gendered interaction they and their partners reproduce on a daily basis (Backett, 1982; La Rossa and La Rossa, 1981). Sue, for example, said she was only moderately dissatisfied with doing 90% of the childcare work in her home because she was "quicker" at it. However, she also felt that her partner sabotaged her attempts to increase his minimal participation:

I don't mind doing the basic responsibilities. I have a routine, so I just go ahead and do it. Sometimes, when I have [something on] . . . I say, "Listen, Tuesday night I'm going out," . . . and he comes home late from work, which *always* happens when I am going out. I get angry. . . . That's the time I become dissatisfied. (Sue: Legal Secretary)

"LIKE IT'S A FAVOR!": MEN'S PARTICIPATION IN DOMESTIC WORK

It was obvious from talking to these working- and middle-class women that the division of family work was far from resolved. Its negotiation was complex, subtle, and ongoing in most households and, from the women's perspective, seldom equal (Hochschild, 1989). A woman risks the material well-being of her children if she jeopardizes her marriage by making what may be seen as excessive demands on her partner (Ferree, 1984). Apart from economic dependence, women remain dependent on men and their good will for down time from childcare (La Rossa and La Rossa, 1981) in a cultural context where men's help is seen as a favor men confer on women rather than a right women can demand.

Part of the difficulty in understanding the negotiation of family work lies in the fact that men and women come to family situations saying they believe in one set of gender ideals while they are *also* deeply committed to other gender ideals and the identities that go with them (Hochschild, 1989). Thus a couple who claim to believe in egalitarian family relations can find themselves negotiating the division of family labor from two very different sets of assumptions. Ellen's partner Sam, for example, came from a very traditional background but was committed to being an "involved father" and to equality. Ellen was aware that Sam was proud of his contribution to family work and that he felt himself different from other men in this respect. However, if Sam felt he was doing Ellen a favor by his involvement, Ellen did not see it that way. She resented defining Sam's participation as a favor, for this definition carried the reciprocal expectation of gratitude in exchange. *She* defined his participation as a responsibility—as merely expected behavior. Although both were overtly committed to equality, the couple's definitions of family reality clashed. With bitterness Ellen described two very different perceptions of being "equal."

> OK, he plays with her a lot. He plays with her more than a lot of fathers I have seen. . . . He takes her to school, he picks her up. He often dresses her in the morning, but I pick out the clothes and make sure the clothes are ready. I often feel that he has a lot of the fun. Like he does a lot of the fun and I do a lot of the work. . . . [Around the home I do] all of the cleaning . . . all those little

minor tasks—they don't seem to count or add up to anything. There is not much recognition for that. (Ellen: Typesetter]

"Equality" made Sam feel he was doing Ellen a favor, she said:

> But if you [Sam] make a meal—that's wow! That's five stars! And also he'll make [most of] the meals. But I'll hear about it, like it's a favor more than a neutral division of labor; like, "I'm doing something that should be *your* job. . . ." It's not, "Well, that's good, we are sharing it together." It's he is doing some of "my work," right? That feeling is there, even though we both "agree" that it is all equal. (Ellen: Typesetter)

Structural constraints also limited the working-class women's negotiations. Shift work or overtime absolved some of the men from responsibility for family work. For others, this justification had lost its legitimacy, but their partners had not lost their power:

> [I'm] very dissatisfied. It's always been myself that has to go out and find daycare. . . . He works shift work. If he is on 4:00 to 12:00 [P.M.] he only has one child to look after [in the morning]. When I come home I have *both* of them. . . .
> And it's always been I'm the one that takes time off [if children are sick]. He has established he is the *main* breadwinner—I'm the "incidental extras" [to him]. . . . He is very firm that *I'm* the one [to take time off]. Once, I'd gotten a verbal warning and he took time off. . . . [But he says] I'm the mother, it's my duty. (Judy: Apprentice Woodworker)

Several women explained how family responsibilities had forced them to take lower-paying jobs that did not involve shift work. At the same time I was told, because their partners earned more money, it was expected that these women would stay home from work with sick children.[14] The pattern becomes circular. Unlike the middle-class mothers, most of the working-class mothers with partners (65%) said that mainly it was they who stayed home with sick children.

Despite the persistence of inequality in family work, however, it seemed clear that traditional accounts of family reality, of men's and women's domestic and paid work roles, had lost much of their plausibility.

MIDDLE-CLASS WOMEN: MOTHERHOOD
AS ULTIMATE RESPONSIBILITY

Bernard (1975, p. 45) explains that the sexual division of labor in society is not a *consequence* of sex differences but is often the *cause* of these differences. For the middle-class women in this study in particular, the perceived differences between male and female parenting went beyond the division of domestic labor to differences, mothers said, in men's and women's feelings of responsibility and consciousness of their children (Table 8.4).

Feelings of responsibility are central to the socializing effects of becoming a mother (Wearing, 1984; Ruddick, 1984a; Backett, 1982; Bernard, 1975). Middle-class women in this study felt that, because of these feelings, they and their partners had *qualitatively* different relationships with their children. Over half (58%) said that mothers felt a sort of "ultimate responsibility" for their children—a type of responsibility, they thought, men did not feel:

I think ultimately the responsibility falls to most women—to 99% [of women]. Although men are helpers, when it comes down to it you are the one who's thinking [about the child] . . . who *really*

TABLE 8.4. How Being a Parent Is Different for Men and Women

	Middle-class women	Working-class women
Parenting is different for men and women	84%	82%
No difference/not in my case	10%	4%
Other	6%	14%
Women do more or most of the work	61%	82%
Women feel ultimate or more responsibility for children	58%	54%[a]
Women have a different consciousness or special awareness of children	60%	43%

Note. N = 31 for middle-class women, 28 for working-class women.
[a]For the working-class women, the notions of doing more work and feeling more responsibility were closely associated. Thus the figure of 54% who mentioned responsibility is an underestimation of the extent to which feelings of responsibility distinguished men's and women's experience of parenthood in the eyes of the working-class mothers.

feels for the child and really the only person in the world who is caring for him. (Tess: Senior Policy Advisor)

Beth, for example, whose partner did 40% of the childcare work, explained how being a mother was different:

> I take responsibility. I assume the leadership role in the home. What I am not doing, I am monitoring and making sure someone else is doing it. . . . For example, if I'm doing the laundry, or whatever, and he [my husband] is with the kids, I will notice when their [bed]time comes around. I will notice and go out and initiate the bed routine. If I leave it to him, he will do something which I think is very irresponsible. I take responsibility, I initiate, and I monitor. He does not feel that way [responsible]. I think he leaves that for me. (Beth: Management Board Officer)

For Rachael, whose partner did approximately 30% of the childcare work, responsibility was also an issue of priorities:

> I think we [women] feel more responsible. . . . I think that the [paid] job is not as important for some women—is not the only important [thing]. I think a man would rate it, quite honestly, as number one priority. And that's the difference anyway in my relationship—and I think number two [for a man] would be the children. *For me*, and for [other] women, or whatever, number one would be the children. . . . Our priorities are different on that. (Rachael: High School Teacher)

I showed earlier that middle-class women often attributed gendered parenting not just to their cultural beliefs about mothers' responsibility but to the practical social organization of childcare following the birth of a child. Such social arrangements differentiate men's and women's early experience of parenting and typically lay the ground for the gender-differentiating and traditionalizing effects of the couple's transition to parenthood (La Rossa and La Rossa, 1981), creating "his and her" transitions (Cowan et al., 1985). Becoming parents differentially socializes men and women. Peter and Loretta, as feminists, had consciously tried to avoid these differential socializing effects: They shared family work right from the birth of the child. Unlike many women, Loretta saw little gender difference in her own and her partner's experiences of parenting; she attributed her greater tendency to worry to her personality[15]:

> [For men and women the experience of being a parent] varies enormously with the type of relationship you have. In our case [the difference] is more personality—I tend to be a worrier. . . . I don't see a lot of relationships where the father is as involved in the childrearing as the woman. In my case, I don't think there is a difference. Peter took holidays when I came home from the hospital. (Loretta: Elementary School Teacher)

What was surprising was that even when middle-class women said they shared family work equally with their partners, more than half still felt that parenthood was a gendered experience. Perhaps for these women, in spite of their claims, family work was not shared equally; perhaps the work was shared but the ultimate responsibility was not. What is clear, however, is that these women claimed distinct identities as mothers rather than simply as parents.

For some, biology provided at least one intuitively plausible basis on which to ultimately ground their claims to distinct maternal identities. Jenny and her partner, for example, shared family work equally, but they did not share parental identities. Jenny felt that in a sense her pregnancy had made her child feel like a physical extension of her self, thus providing grounds for the establishment of a special social relationship:

> Yes. I think having had the child in the womb as part of one's body for 9 months has a strong impact as being an extension of the self—a physical extension of the self. I think it's a gut-level difference. I think the child has more experience of the mother in that same way as well. It is more familiar with the mother physically . . . and I think it lasts. (Jenny: Executive Secretary)

One does not have to posit biology as the cause of experience to understand how many women can come to build social realities on the symbolic meaning they attach to biological relationships. We can understand that women interact with their born and unborn children according to the meaning they ascribe to biology and a biological relationship. Indeed, the physical experiences of pregnancy, birth, and breast-feeding confront women with events in their lives of which they must make sense:

Absolutely [parenthood is different for women]. I say this as someone whose husband, I feel, is very involved. . . . The breast-feeding, the fact that you carry the child in the first place and you have to go through the pregnancy, the labor, and the delivery. No matter how active your partner is, no matter how cooperative your partner is, you're the one whose body is going through this invasion, which for me is how it feels. . . . Certainly you feel you are being taken over. It's just another thing you have to deal with, whether you react to it positively or negatively. It's still something you have to deal with . . . the sheer physical involvement. . . . (Nina: Director, Nonprofit Organization)

Making sense of their bodies, therefore, becomes part of the process by which women make sense of themselves.

Biology, however, was not among the most common grounds for supporting the claims to a distinct maternal identity among the middle-class women in this study. Sixty percent of the middle-class mothers with partners felt that women have a special "consciousness" of their children that men do not have. Kim, who emphasized that her partner shared childcare equally, explained the difference this way:

[I am] always *conscious* of the children, but [with men] I don't think there is as conscious a stream there as with women. (Kim: Librarian)

The difference is not simply one of workload, as Kate, whose partner did 40% of the childcare, emphasized:

Yes, [there is a difference]. . . . My husband is an incredibly involved father. He's just fantastic. But I know I'm the one who's always keeping track [of things for our daughter]. . . . I'm more conscious of her and her *life*, I suppose, than he is. Anyone I've ever seen, it's been that way. (Kate: Social Worker)

Mary Lynn's consciousness of her child was a source of tension between herself and her partner Frank. Although her partner shared childcare equally, Mary Lynn felt that she had an awareness of her child Sam that her partner did not have. Her perception of Sam's dependency on her helped shaped her consciousness—a consciousness in which her son came first:

Yeah, [being a parent is different for men and women, for example] Frank has trouble with the fact that I say that right now, Sam [my son] comes first in my life, because he is so dependent. His interests have to come first, and come even above Frank's. And Frank has a lot of trouble with that, and to me, it's without question or without a moment's hesitation. That's the way it has to be. . . . Although Frank is tremendous with him and we share quite equally . . . I think it's at that philosophical level where he and I have the biggest differences, more than anything. (Mary Lynn: Policy Analyst)

Thus even when their male partners shared childcare, middle-class women still claimed a distinct identity and relationship with their children. Men could potentially learn to *behave* like involved parents, but they didn't *feel* or *think* like mothers, they concluded.

Indicative of their male partners' different consciousness, several women pointed out, was their ability to compartmentalize and segregate parts of themselves and their lives in ways women felt they did not, or could not, do. Penny's husband, for example, had agreed to provide childcare during her interview with me. For him, this meant he could read the paper at the same time. For Penny, it did not. Although they had "jointly agreed" on his temporary responsibility, for Penny it seemed her partner was not fulfilling his commitment when their little boy constantly joined us during the interview or was unsupervised in other areas of the home:

He's pretty good if I *ask* him to do something. But most men aren't tuned in. Their antennae aren't up. So he doesn't notice that Pete is restless because he is in the other room reading the Sunday paper. . . . It's a question of responsiveness and awareness. (Penny: Managing Editor)

Thus, if it exists as these women believed it did, men's greater ability to compartmentalize, as well as women's greater feelings of responsibility, may help women to understand why they have problems leaving their children to go back to work, while their male partners apparently do not.[16]

Although to the participants different kinds of consciousness appeared to be reflections of gender differences, these forms of consciousness, Ruddick (1984a) explains, be they maternal consciousness or scientific modes of thinking, are grounded in social relationships. Women's way of thinking about their children are thus grounded in the social relationships of mothering. For the participants in this study, ultimate responsibility for children was central to this social relationship. However, the middle-class women who had atypical parenting relationships provided insights into the relationship between gender, consciousness, and responsibility. Joanne, an alone mother, thought that parenthood could affect men and women in similar ways. She pointed out that her son's father, himself a single parent, took on full responsibility:

> When Tim's father comes to visit, I know I can walk out that door and I do not have to say a single thing to him about "Don't forget this, and don't forget that" and "Do this and do that." I don't ever have to mention it. . . . My way of thinking is, "If you can be a single parent, then you'll make a good parent." (Joanne: Elementary School Teacher)

Debbie and Suzette were a lesbian couple. Debbie was the biological mother of Matt, whom the couple had planned to have and whom they coparented. Debbie's experience led her to conclude that what people usually see as male–female differences in parenting are actually differences in the nature of social and emotional relationships with children:

> I have a peculiar situation and . . . yeah, I think it's different for mothers than it is for the other parent. Suzette is very involved with Matt, and she really cares about him. But I really notice that [I'm more aware of him]. . . . So it's not male and female. (Debbie: Accountant)

Debbie experienced parenthood differently from Suzette. For Debbie, the essential difference was not fundamentally about biology or gender but had to do with "socioemotional alertness":

> I know that it's just been this past year that it's been possible for me to read a book while he was in the room. It's just like constant alert, and that doesn't seem to be something that's shared by the other parent [Suzette]. The difference is not around the physical work of the child. But it's around that socioemotional alertness, I guess. (Debbie: Accountant)

Whatever its origins, the majority of the working-class women (82%) agreed with most of the middle-class women that parenting was a gendered experience.

"THEY LOVE THEM JUST AS MUCH, BUT . . .": WORKING-CLASS WOMEN AND MATERNAL IDENTITY

Working-class women (82%) in this study were more likely than middle-class women to say that differences in domestic workloads made men's and women's experiences of parenthood different (Table 8.4). But many also joined middle-class women in pointing out there were, in addition, differences in consciousness of, and feelings of, responsibility for children. However, many working-class mothers found it difficult to separate work and responsibility: In practice the two often meant the same thing:

> Very much, yes. [The difference is] responsibility. After work I know I have to come home because I have somebody waiting for me, whereas a man can do, or so he thinks, he can do whatever he wants. Like, no worries whatsoever. If I want to go anywhere, or, you know, stop for groceries, I know that Jessica is waiting for me . . . at the babysitters. (Renee: Truck Driver)

Half of the working-class women (50%) said mothers' and fathers' experiences differed because, they believed, either men's lives were not significantly changed by parenthood or the men continued to have far more "freedom":

> [Being a parent is different for a woman than it is for a man.] The woman gets all the responsibility of the child. The man can still do basically what he wants to do. (Chris: Clerical Worker)

Like many of the middle-class women, many of the working-class women explained that they had difficulty in identifying with men's apparent ability to compartmentalize and segregate their experiences. They did not deny that men could love children, but, like Barb, participants sometimes had problems understanding male love:

I suppose it varies with individuals, but through my personal experience, it seemed to be [that] to us [women] our children are *everything*. We will do everything we can to spend every spare minute we can with them. For men, they love them, but they will go and spend a whole day away golfing even though they have been the whole week at work. (Barb: Clerical Worker)

For Barb, men were "just different":

They are just different. They don't become as consumed with the child. They love them just as much, but it's different. I think men tend to put themselves first. . . . The woman always puts the child first. (Barb: Clerical Worker)

Implicit in many of the participants' descriptions of gendered parenting is an image of men as having less moral competence as parents of young children. Men are seen as *not* having undergone the same sort of moral transformations these women experienced. A working-class mother reflected:

I find men are . . . a little more selfish with their time. They think of [other things]. . . . I like to shut everything out and concentrate on her, whereas the guys, they still go on with their regular [lives]. Their lives really haven't changed much. Maybe . . . [that's because] they don't give their full attention. (Marg: Accounting Clerk)

Men's different behavior as parents implied not just a different consciousness but a lesser moral commitment:

I don't think they [men] see the responsibilities. The women concentrate on it 24 hours a day, thinking about what [the children] need . . . for the present and the future. Men just take it as it comes. I don't know who does a better job . . . [but] the responsibility [is] always on the woman for safety, too. They [men] are there for guidance and support but no responsibility, really. (Kathy: Accounting Clerk)

Unlike most of the working-class women who pointed to empirical divisions in men's and women's parenting, Val, an alone parent, emphasized potential similarities. A man, she reasoned, could be "just as good as a mother"—if he wanted to "get that close":

> No [it's not different]. . . . They have the same responsibilities. They have to do the same things. They have to provide for their child, just as I do. [But] some fathers *don't want to get so close* or attached to their kids as mothers do. If a father wants to, he *can* be just as good as a mother. (Val: Apprentice Mechanic)

The idea that their male partners had not undergone the same moral transformations into parenthood as had the participants themselves had important implications for these women's claims to maternal identity. Working-class women, for example, interpreted men's and women's unequal parental workloads as expressions of different male and female psychology. Men as fathers, it appeared, not having undergone moral transformation, were seen as being *less* responsible or *more* selfish than mothers. Thus working-class women felt they could not expect much more of their partners—that was just the way men were. Working-class women could only wish they would "help out more."[17]

For the middle-class women in the sample the situation was a little different. Middle-class women perceived their partners to be more involved in domestic work than did the working-class women. Middle-class women also believed men *should* and *could share* parenting responsibilities, if only they had been correctly socialized. Although many of the middle-class women claimed their partners were "incredibly involved," they also claimed a special identity as mother rather than as parent. Middle-class participants could not, however, base this claim to a special maternal identity on the fact that they did more domestic work as readily as the working-class women could. Fathers, after all, were either seen as sharing parenting or as being *expected* to do so. On what, then, was middle-class women's identities as mothers, rather than parents based? For these middle-class women, mothers were essentially distinct from fathers because although, for some lucky women, men might potentially learn to behave like mothers, they would never think and feel like mothers. The connectedness with their children that women established through the moral transformation of self occasioned by maternity was something men were *not* seen to share. By becoming the fathers, middle-class men were expected to undergo a behavioral, but not a moral, transformation.

WE SEEK EACH OTHER OUT:
SOCIAL WORLDS OF MIDDLE-CLASS PARENTS

To better understand the social context in which the participants in this study gained support for their maternal identities, I asked them to whom they talked about their children. Married middle-class women answered that they spoke mainly with partners and, to a lesser extent, with family and with friends who also had children. Other research also shows partners to be the primary validators of middle-class parental identities (Boulton, 1983; Backett, 1982) and that indeed couples often talk themselves into traditional gender roles through everyday family conversations (La Rossa and La Rossa, 1981).

Their public parental identities were more of a problem for the middle-class women. Indeed, their social worlds seemed to be divided into parents and nonparents. Laura explained the social divide:

> I think parents [have], like, their own club. It's a very large club. . . . [There are] people who have children and people who don't have children. You *really* don't understand until you have them. (Laura: Accountant)

Most of the middle-class women with partners (78%) said that apart from husbands and family they generally restricted talk about their children to conversations with other parents. They felt limited to their "own kind" for support and understanding:

> [I talk with other] parents in general. Wherever—like you have to seek each other out. . . . They really are the only people you can talk to. People who don't have a child [can't understand]. (Tess: Senior Policy Advisor)

The social world of parents, however, was not restricted to bona fide parents. Also included, it seemed, were soon-to-be parents (pregnant women and partners, if any); those aspiring to pregnancy or parenthood; and, at times, the involuntarily childless who could be considered parents—by desire, if not by deed. Problems arose where participants' social worlds did not shift with their changing identities. Having a child set Janette apart from her childless friends:

[The worst things about having a child are that] I don't have any friends who also have children. All my friends are single or just married, and it has kinda set me apart from that group. (Janette: Manager)

But she also thought her parental identity was a problem for her friends, whether they were voluntarily or involuntarily childless: Some she saw as envious, others as hostile.

I mean some of them [my friends] are single and *desperately* wanting to have children and I feel like when I invite them over, they are all looking at her [my daughter] *green with envy*. And there's the other ones who are sort of yuppie—and [it's], "God, this child is just going to spoil our dinner party." (Janette: Manager)

Becoming a parent did not simply mean that a woman acquired a new identity; it also meant that once-significant others lost their identities as friends. Some of the women talked about the demise of old friendships. "Old friends" with whom these mothers had been their "old selves" now seemed more distant; some "old friends" became childless ex-friends who, the new parents believed, were unwilling or incapable of sustaining the new world of meanings and restrictions that parenthood brought:

None of our friends have children, so that's been "different." [Yes, it has affected some friendships.] One pair of friends in particular . . . didn't seem to have any consideration for the fact that we had a [baby]. . . . They didn't show much consideration at all. We were angry. (Carolyn: Secretary)

Overt displays of parental identities were limited to other parents:

[I talk about my children with my] spouse and friends *who have children*. . . . People who don't have children are bored very quickly with stories of your children. (Susan: Social Worker)

But newly acquired parental identities do not always take precedence over older identities.[18] In contrast to the distance, indifference, or hostility some heterosexual women felt they experienced, Debbie, a lesbian mother of a 2-year-old son named Matt, explained that *her* friends, who were predominantly childless, had adopted Matt into their social world. Far from finding she had less contact with childless friends, as did most "straight" parents, since Matt's birth, Debbie and Matt had found themselves the objects of increased visiting and social contact.

Participants in this study developed ways of handling conflicts of identity. By selectively revealing their maternal identities, for example, middle-class mothers tried to keep their parental identities and work identities strategically separate. According to Hochschild (1989), professional and middle-class women feel that to be taken seriously in the occupational world, they must conceal their identities as mothers. Thus they disguise and misrepresent the various ways in which maternal obligations intrude upon their worlds of paid work, lest their occupational identities be contaminated by their maternal identities. At the same time, however, such strategies perpetuate both women's isolation from each other and the gender-biased culture of the middle-class workplace.

SOCIAL SUPPORT: THE SOCIAL WORLD
OF WORKING-CLASS PARENTS

Unlike the middle-class participants in this study, working-class participants did not mention their partners first when they described with whom they talked about their children. Male partners seemed to play a secondary role to women's female networks as validators of maternal identity. For working-class women like Sally, parental conversations were opportunities to provide male parents with the proper interpretation of family life, rather than occasions for its joint social construction:

> I talk [mostly] with other mothers—kinda reaffirm that it is *really all worth it*, even if it is hectic or whatever . . . not so much with him [my husband]. But I will tell him quite frequently that we are very lucky and we have good kids . . . and try to make him appreciate that way. (Sally: Bell Service Assistant)

In contrast to the middle-class women who were concerned with keeping their occupational and maternal identities separate, to the working-class women the workplace often provided a universe of discourse that validated their maternal identities:

[I talk about children] usually [with the] women at work. Tim [my husband], too, but women at work [more]. They've had children, so they can relate with you. Whereas men can relate with men, and, well, we know how that story goes.(Jackie: Secretary)

Working-class women mentioned their families as part of their parental support networks somewhat more often than did middle-class women, but the alone mothers, both working- and middle-class, mentioned their families most often. Also, alone working-class mothers (36%), but not alone middle-class mothers, said they got significant social support from other single mothers.

In general, the working-class women in this study got more help with their children from their families than did the middle-class women. Sixty-eight percent of the working-class, but only 29% of the middle-class, women said that they were given regular help by their own or their partners' families.[19]

Working-class women cited their own female kin as the primary source of familial help with their children. Help from in-laws was mentioned by 41% of the working-class women with partners and by 19% of the middle-class women with partners. So, while working-class women received less domestic help from male partners, they gained access to the support of their partners' female kin in ways the middle-class women did not. In some cases, this support from a partner's family continued after the couple had separated; in the case of Mary, it was provided even though she and her boyfriend Ken had never formally been "a couple." Although Ken and Mary had never lived together, Ken's mother provided free daily childcare for Mary's child by Ken. Among the working-class mothers, the alone mothers received more family help with their children than did those with partners.[20]

Middle-class women, on the other hand, were more likely than working-class women to *buy* help with domestic work. Twenty-six percent of the former said they employed a housecleaning person, and 16% employed a nanny who also provided some assistance with household work. In Toronto, such work is typically done by immigrant or working-class women. Middle-class men have long had their professional lives supported by unpaid or low-paid domestic and service workers. Whereas purchasing domestic labor facilitates the "balancing" of work and professional careers in middle-class women's lives in ways that may represent some challenge to the gender order of that class, it often does so at the expense of reproducing an unequal class and race order. And such purchase of domestic labor does little to validate the social worth of domestic and caregiving work. To say that it is middle-class *women* who purchase domestic labor, however, perpetuates the assumption that family work is women's responsibility only, rather than also being men's responsibility. This assumption misconstrues the exploitative social organization of caring and domestic work as a problem of women exploiting other women, rather than as a problem of class and race relations and inadequate public funding for daycare. The "problem" of domestic labor, paid and unpaid, reveals the limits of conventional liberal feminism when it strives for gender equality without addressing the broader context of race and class inequality.

SUMMARY

In this chapter we saw some of the ways in which parenting was a gendered and engendering experience. Mothers in this study did not feel their different experiences of parenting were merely a matter of different work loads; rather, they had to do with differences in men's and women's thinking and feeling as parents. Participants' feelings of responsibility for their children were central to the socializing effect of parenthood, allowing mothers to claim a distinct maternal identity and a distinct maternal consciousness, while attributing "different" ones to their partners as fathers. Even among the middle-class mothers whose partners either shared or were expected to share family work, women still claimed an identifiable maternal, rather than simply a parental, identity. Men, these middle-class women believed, could, with the right socialization, perhaps learn to behave like mothers, but they did not think and feel like mothers. For middle- and working-class women, male partners were not seen as having shared the moral transformation of self that was occasioned by the women's connectedness with their children. And not having undergone such a transformation, these men, as fathers, were considered by the women to be less responsible, less conscious of their children, or, to some of the women, more selfish than were the mothers. Mothers could, however, still hope for, and many expected, men's participation in family work.

Participants' talk of ultimate responsibility for their children not only reflected a gender difference in parenting but implicitly expressed a privatization of caring relationships and a privileging of genetic ties in the organization of social reproduction. In contrast, among the urban, poor black families studied by Stack (1974), the use of kin titles among those who had special caring relationships with each other constructed a notion of family based on social relationships, not simply on biology. Indeed, in some cases responsibility, not biology, conferred the rights of parenthood. For example, a young woman deemed not to be, or not able to be, a "responsible" mother might have her rights to (the valued relationship of) parenthood appropriated by grandparents or other kin. In this study, the role that feelings of ultimate responsibility for children played in the construction of maternal identity expressed not only a gendered experience of parenting but an ideology of privatized caring.

Talk of mothers' special connection with their young children is risky. On the one hand, the idealization of the mother–child relationship has exempted fathers from family work. Traditionally, many nonfeminist observers of family life have been quick to claim that mothers and fathers are different and therefore should be treated differently—in practice, unequally. On the other hand, while androgynous representations of parenting may support feminist demands for fathers' equal participation in family work, in the current context of gender inequality and empirical differences in practical and emotional responsibility for children, this strategy may backfire. In the *absence* of men's equal participation in caring for children, the denial of women's "special" relationship with children in the name of gender equality, Smart (1989) points out, may result in the increase of men's power as fathers without increasing their responsibilities. The men's rights movement, for example, has successfully used androgynous images of parenthood or a profathering rhetoric to disempower mothers, especially lesbian mothers, in child custody cases (Ehrensaft, 1990; Smart, 1989). Although "the new father" may value his children greatly and feel he should be highly involved, as Daly (1991) shows, such committed fathers succumb to a variety of interpersonal, policy, and structural barriers that leave them being and feeling somewhat marginal to the everyday work of caring for children. The paradoxical character of "the new father," Daly (1991) observes, is one of personal investment in the idea of being a father but the practical experience of being marginal. Not surprisingly, many men fall back on the older idea that being a good provider is being a good father.

We may like to locate images of parents and children in a context of love, nurturance, and mutual support, and some couples in this study tried hard to achieve such a context. But in the everyday world of inequality and gender politics, as Smart (1989) points out, children and family remain implicit sites of power relations.

9

Conclusion

Studying motherhood changed how I think and feel about motherhood. Before I began the study I knew that having children draws many women into relationships of inequality, oppression, and harm.[1] What I didn't know, and still find difficult to put into words, is how becoming a mother can provide some women with symbolic and relational opportunities for human experiences that, when experienced by men, have traditionally been called heroic[2]: that is, transformative of self and potentially redemptive of society. And I didn't know the potential that analyzing motherhood had to serve as the grounds for political challenge and social critique.

I find my analysis caught in that tension between androgynous and woman-centered visions within feminism that Ann Snitow (1992) describes: the tension between validating women's lives and an alternative ethic of caring on one hand and the desire to resist the oppressiveness of being female in a male dominated society on the other.

I began this study wanting to resist the devaluation of those qualities and activities culturally associated with being a mother. Looking back, it now seems to me this research was a little like looking at images of life in a mirror—I could feel safe in that a reflected image might protect me from the consequences of being myself drawn into maternity. Instead it drew me personally and intellectually into the enigmatic and multiple meanings of motherhood.

Of course there is no single meaning or experience of being a mother. And I have learned that dominant representations of motherhood have long arms, often warmly embracing—at other times cruelly marginalizing—and shaping my life, the lives of the mothers I studied, and the lives of those women who do not fit the culturally powerful images of mother.

It is hard to write about motherhood, any analysis of which may be read as much for its political implications as for its representation of women's experience. Surely I will sound either too positive or too cynical. Motherhood, as I have shown, has much to do with moral identities. And so I suspect that representations of motherhood, even in academic work, are often implicit representations of personal and collective identities. They are expressive of the sorts of things we think of as being important in society and the sorts of persons we like to think women (and men) are, or are capable of being.

Is it because I do not have children that I emphasize how motherhood "attaches" women to children (others) in culturally significant ways? Is it the symbolic meaning of children as culturally sacred objects and the perceived "special" nature of mothers' social bonds with them that carry the power to so deeply shape women's identities—the identities of those who do and do not have children, or who have them improperly? And what moral implications do children hold for men's identities?

In practice, some children are not culturally valued. And for many women, motherhood socially devalues rather than morally enhances them, as studies of young, nonwhite, unwed, or "maternally unorthodox" women show. "Other" women's motherhood, I argue, provides shadow images that shape the dominant meanings of motherhood and thus how motherhood is experienced in practice.

The notion of choice now seems to me hopelessly inadequate for understanding both motherhood and childlessness, though clearly the absence of choice in matters of fertility is both painful and harmful to many women. Motherhood is more unsettling, complex, important, politically challenging, and hope-inspiring a research issue than I had initially thought.

LOOKING AT THE PROCESS

The subjective experience of motherhood for the participants in this study was not primarily that of oppression: Motherhood did not mean the denial of self. Along with the increased work and, for some, a perceived economic disadvantage, motherhood provided opportunities for these women to claim personal growth and development and to constitute themselves as morally enhanced persons. Although motherhood is conventionally taken as "proof" of female maturity, its potential for fostering personal growth appears to be little recognized or valued. This neglect may be because the personal growth associated with motherhood is of a certain kind. Motherhood produces "womanly" persons—but womanly persons are little valued.

Understanding the process whereby women become mothers is crucial to interpreting the meaning of the outcome: the fact that most women become mothers. The data show how women's identities as mothers are better understood as products of experience rather than of gender-role conformity. For the women in the study, motherhood emerged from a whole series of separate processes and actions, as these women came to maternity by very different routes; for example, there were clear class-related patterns. Explanatory concepts such as motherhood mandate and gender socialization do not capture participants' experience or the complexity of the process involved. Some of the women had always wanted to have children, others had once wanted to remain childless, and still others had had little occasion to reflect on either option before they became pregnant. Some were attracted to an idealized image of "having a baby"; others had not been attracted by the role of mother but found it difficult to avoid. For some, children emerged as products of the dynamics of their relationship with a partner; some strategically negotiated their desired transition to maternity; and others rejected permanent childlessness, as opposed to embracing motherhood. Still others described their paths to motherhood as the unintended and unanticipated consequences of their relationships with men or of contraceptive risk taking. Participants in this study did not necessarily step easily or smoothly into the role of mother; for many, the path was tentative, unanticipated, unfamiliar, and beset with problems. Although eventually various routes led all these women to an outcome of giving birth, experientially the processes and meanings of their actions were different for the different women involved.

MOTHERHOOD AND ADULT IDENTITY

We saw how becoming a mother was tied to issues of identity in adult life but in class-specific ways. When middle-class women in this study talked about having their first children they frequently put forward their claims to maternal identities as *achieved* social *accomplishments*. A certain level of maturity, they held, had to be achieved *before* they were "ready" to have children. It took many years and the right relationship for them to achieve readiness. But not only did middle-class women feel they had to be "grown up" before becoming mothers, they had to be appropriately grown up. Borrowing from middle-class masculinist models of the individual, these middle-class women constructed personal achievement, not "womanhood," as a precondition for having children. However, what was not visible to these women who sought the appropriate circumstances for motherhood was the fact that the dominant social rhetoric surrounding valid claims to motherhood often carry class, race, and heterosexist priorities.

Working-class women in the study viewed motherhood differently. Many saw themselves as achieving adulthood *through* having a child. For alone young working-class women in particular, although their pregnancies were typically unplanned, becoming a mother became both expressive and instrumental action. Claiming motherhood became expressive of an identity, of an ideal self as a loving, caring, womanly sort of person. It also became a means of establishing that one was grown up, that one was an adult. Having a child expressed their claimed maturity and responsibility, both of which they valued highly.

Conventional constructions of young, alone motherhood as a social problem tends to focus attention on the individual characters of those who mother "improperly" and away from the social structural features of such mothers' lives, such as poverty, educational and employment disadvantage, and inadequate support for parenting. Moral panics over welfare mothers and teen pregnancies, as Nathanson (1991) and Solinger (1992) show, fuse race and class tensions in social struggles over the control of women's sexuality and reproduction. Early childbearing does not cause poverty. But, for women in this study, it functioned as one of the avenues through which structural gender and class inequalities were transformed into individual young women's private troubles.

We saw that for some of the middle-class women, having children had assumed quasi-religious functions of providing solutions to the meaning of life and of how to live as an adult. The nomos-building function of marriage in modern society has been well recognized (Berger and Kellner, 1977). However, the data show how some women's relationships with their children provided perhaps even more powerful opportunities both to locate individuals meaningfully in the world and to stabilize their identity. Children can fulfill such a quasi-religious function of making sense of women's lives partly because of the capacity biological relationships have for symbolizing social relationships and thus grounding what women find personally meaningful in a so-called natural order.

MOTHERHOOD AS ADULT RESOCIALIZATION

Becoming a mother was more than a process of giving birth. Although for participants in this study the processes of recruitment to motherhood varied greatly and were marked by clear class differences, I found evidence for the pervasive impact of gender in the remarkably similar patterns of subjective experiences of motherhood the participants described. Becoming a mother involved a process of resocialization in which women experienced themselves as profoundly changed. The middle-class women in particular described themselves as having been totally unprepared for, or overwhelmed by, the experience of becoming a mother. Women's descriptions of becoming a mother and of maternal love carried many of the mythological themes and functions we usually associate with romantic love. Motherhood and maternal love provided the symbolic resources by which adult identities and the meanings of women's lives were restructured. The experiences of self-change described by middle-class participants were dominated by themes of self-actualization and personal growth. Among the working-class women the central motif of self-change was that of settling down. Among both groups, participants felt they had not simply been changed through motherhood: They had been morally transformed.

I pointed to the ways in which specific symbolic links between motherhood and female morality that were historically associated with white bourgeois American Christian family life became embedded in culturally privileged models of mothering. But moral images of motherhood carry implicit counterimages of immoral women and bad mothers. Thus the production of gender and womanly character through the cultural resources of moral motherhood and "sacred" children may reproduce "classed" and "raced" gender identities.

The meaning of motherhood was also explored through the meaning of childlessness. For the majority of the participants in the study, the idea of permanent childlessness signified not merely the absence of children in their lives but also strong feelings of loss and incompleteness: It signified a disruption in the phenomenological experience of self. Similarly, following Simmel's (1984) analysis of love, we saw how women's feelings could be considered guides to the nature of the social bond between mothers and their children. In particular, women's emotions were seen as signals of the relevance of children to women's sense of "real self" and to the ways in which their children had become constitutive of self among mothers in this study.

MOTHERHOOD AS A GENDERED
AND ENGENDERING PROCESS

The greatest rewards of being a mother came from the special connectedness these women felt with their children and from the pleasure of watching their children learn and grow. However, the flip side of feeling connected—feeling responsible—was seen as one of the worst things about being a mother. The data indicate that it is a mistake to think of mothers' connectedness with their children as costing a loss of self or as a threat to the women's personal identity. Rather, for many of the women, connectedness with their children was the basis of their morally transformed selves. We need, therefore, to challenge universalizing models of human development that emphasize the unique importance of the role of separation, independence, and autonomy in the development of adult identities by asking instead *what kinds of identities* are produced by such processes and what social interests they serve.

On the one hand, the data appear to support recent developments in feminist psychology. These developments suggest that the experience of self and the nature of self–other relationships are gendered and that women, more than men, tend to define themselves through connectedness and personal relationships. On the other hand, as I pointed out, there is no such thing as "woman": gender identities are products of social relationships and situations—not traits of individuals. The women in this study felt themselves connected to specific "others" (their own biological children) in culturally appropriate ways—they did not necessarily feel connected to "others" in general. The commonly held concept of women's "capacity for relationship" disguises the ways in which women are hierarchically, rather than caringly, connected to others in racially and economically unequal societies. Gender identities, therefore, both conceal and express political and personal processes.

The data do not warrant the conclusion that "women's ways" are either innately different or morally superior to "men's ways." Rather, the data suggest that we need to understand how such "womanly ways" of representing or experiencing self are socially, rather than psychosexually or biologically, grounded. That is, men and women tend to experience themselves and self–other relationships in gendered ways because social situations are deeply gendered both in the structures that organize them and in the expectations we bring to them. I suggested that by regarding the emergence of "womanly" feelings and behavior partly as forms of situational adjustment, we can understand how the social organization of motherhood contributes to the social construction of gender differences. We saw, for example, how the everyday practice of being a mother—in particular, the division of domestic work in the home—helped produce the gendered character and identity that these women as parents recognized as their own: It produced mothers. Thus we can understand that becoming a mother was both a *gendered* and an *engendering* process whereby the women came to a new sense of self. In contrast to the diversity of the processes whereby these women came to give birth, they shared experiences that transformed their identities in similar ways. The women produced babies, but having those babies produced "womanly persons."

WHAT IS COMMITTED TO IN MOTHERHOOD?: ULTIMATE RESPONSIBILITY FOR CHILDREN

If the concept of situational adjustment helps explain the personal change these women experienced in becoming mothers, the concept of "investment of identity" helps explain the enduring nature of their maternal commitment. Thus, what sometimes began as a "side bet" (H. Becker, 1960)—for example, becoming pregnant because a partner wanted children—could become a full-blown commitment to maternity. The data showed how many women who had been ambivalent about having children later came to have a deeply valued sense of self vested in motherhood.

The analysis of the social organization of motherhood focused on the *consequences* rather than on the causes of inequality in the division of domestic labor. One such consequence was that it helped produce gendered parental identities: those claimed by mothers and those which mothers attributed to men as fathers. Consistent with other research findings, the data showed that most of the women in full-time employment continued to do more family work than their partners. But mothers in this study did not feel that the different experience of parenting was merely a matter of different workloads: They believed that what made mothers different from fathers were differences in men's and women's *thinking* and *feeling* as parents. Paricipants' feelings of responsibility for their children were central to the socializing effect of their parenthood, allowing these women to claim a distinct maternal identity and a distinct maternal consciousness.

Using Becker's (1960) notion of commitment as investment, therefore, we can understand the greater salience of maternal identity in women's identities. But the issue was not simply one of how much was committed but of *what* was committed to in parenthood: The stakes for men and women in parenthood are quite different. The cultural meaning of parenthood for women is that they, as mothers, have *ultimate* responsibility for their children. What is deeply transforming and engendering about this ultimate responsibility is that it implies the frightening responsibility for the life of one's child; the child's physical and psychological welfare is perceived as finally dependent on the mother's behavior.

Cultural ideals about maternal responsibility, however, can privilege some images of motherhood from which the experiences of those outside the dominant patterns of family life are excluded. Ultimate maternal responsibility for children is neither a universal experience nor a universal ideal. Even where such imagery has ideological dominance, responsibility without adequate resources means that, in practice, motherhood for many women involves a struggle simply to keep their children alive and fed.

Yet feelings of ultimate responsibility were profoundly socializing for the women in this study. For such women, the feeling of responsibility for their children is more than the expectation of a social role; it becomes constitutive of self, making the denial of such responsibility almost unthinkable. Thus for a woman to be remiss in feeling responsible for her child would implicate her whole moral character. Being responsible for her child is about being moral as a person; in this study, motherhood was associated with female morality. An analysis of this association allows us to understand one of the central paradoxes of women's experience of motherhood: that as a social role, motherhood has low public value, but, to women, it also has high personal value and moral worth. This paradoxical character of motherhood makes ambivalence almost endemic to being a mother.

It is important, however, to expose the sociopolitical significance that the responsibility for caring carries in the constitution of female identity and the dual implications of love and labor that it signifies. For the women in this study, the work of caring for family had high personal value. Thus family work can carry social and personal worth even though it is publicly accorded little value or recognition. What is particularly harmful in constructing the care of children as women's private responsibility is not simply that it places an unfair burden of work on women. There is harm also in that caring draws women into intimate relations that reproduce hierarchy and subordination; in that caring work and the production of sociability (DeVault, 1991) are rendered invisible and valueless; and in that alternative approaches to caring for children, whether they make use of extended kin, the community, nonbiologically related others, or societal responsibility, are considered inferior to privatized nuclear families and receive little social support.

MOTHERHOOD AND MORALITY

To understand the meaning of participants' responses to motherhood, it is important to understand the ways in which motherhood is evocatively linked to female morality and how it thereby carries the symbolic power to transform the self.

On the one hand, it might be argued that the essence of female morality is to be nurturing. Caring for others is perceived as quintessentially feminine, and women are socially allocated to roles and occupations that require nurturing personal qualities. On the other hand, women are nurturant and caring in many social roles. For example, they may be social workers, nurses, or the very best friends in the world, but none of these roles, nor the associated female qualities, in themselves carry the power to morally enhance female identity. Nor are they as deeply engendering in establishing a woman's identity as is motherhood. As the data show, through having children women came to recognize themselves as women in special ways. But, as I have emphasized, the impact of children on women's sense of self went beyond the experience of gender identity as a woman. Children became implicated in women's profound experience of themselves as persons, not just as women.

The cultural meanings of motherhood and female morality, I argued, provided, for the women in this study, metaphors through which individual biography and personal identity could be organized. In this sense, becoming a mother can become an essence-making process that produces and sustains meaningful distinctions between mothers and nonmothers, proper and improper motherhood, and reflects *not what people "truly" are* but idealized social representations— metaphorical claims about identities that construct caring as an individual personality trait rather than as a characteristic of specific relationships. Clearly, dominant cultural associations of motherhood and female morality conceal political relationships. Not only do all women not share such cultural meanings or have equal opportunity for their symbolic engagement, but the imagery may be used to regulate the motherhood of socially marginal women.

The essence of the experience of transformation in the participants' identities did not come from the social role of mother, which many of the women recognized as a devalued one. Rather, it came from the new *character* women acquired as mothers. Culturally, as we saw through these women's accounts, motherhood provided women with the symbolic resource for a moral transformation that could be independent of their *actual performance* as mothers. That is, these women might be more or less skilled as mothers, but being a mother was qualitatively different from being a nonmother. And the women in this study experienced being a mother as qualitatively *better*. Perhaps it is the cultural association with selflessness or self-sacrifice that has imbued motherhood with its sacred character; perhaps it derives from the role of "guardian of the innocent." Meanings of motherhood, I argued, are shaped by implicit meanings of children as culturally sacred objects—as symbolic keys to the future and a perfectible social order. Indeed, Rothman (1989) concludes that it is children (in the abstract), not motherhood or mothers, that are really valued in contemporary U.S. society.

What is clear, however, is that socialization into motherhood is not simply the internalization of the appropriate expectations and the development of adequate skills. Some women never develop successful mothering skills, but they still feel they are mothers. Indeed, research suggests that neither men nor women are adequately prepared for parenthood; for many it is experienced as a crisis. In having children, women do not simply step into the role of mother. What is really internalized in becoming a mother is the sense of day-to-day practical responsibility for one's children. And it is this feeling of responsibility that motivates women to acquire the skill of mothering. Women may be more or less successful in this respect. However, according to many of the women in the study, fathers do not share this feeling of ultimate responsibility and thus, being unmotivated to acquire the skills of parenting, have remained either incompetent or unreliable. It is the feelings of responsibility for children, therefore, that also endow motherhood with much of its sacred character. Thus we can understand how motherhood can be "morally uplifting" to women even when it is not valued socially and even when it is not skillfully performed.

MOTHERS' SELVES: SOME THEORETICAL
REFLECTIONS ON IDENTITY

I began this study by asking what the social reorganization of adulthood might mean for women's experience of motherhood. As we saw, being a mother was central to participants' sense of self. But it was not exhaustive of social identity. Unlike older definitions of motherhood as women's "master status," it was *motherhood as personal character and relationship* that was central to participants' identities. And this meaning of motherhood was central in ways that did not preclude the importance of occupational identities or require the sacrifice of self. What does this mean for theoretical understandings of identity?

The symbolic interactionist concept of identity is complex and requires clarification in order for one to understand the salience of *personal character* rather than *role* in mothers' experience of self. We need, for example, to appreciate the dual location of persons as objects of their own acts and of the acts of others in the process that is self. Similarly, as Hewitt (1976) points out, we need to distinguish between *situated selves* and *biographical selves* (see Appendix 3).

Most discussions of identity focus on role identity or social location as the key defining feature of self as object. However, to understand the processual and social nature of the self it is important that the analytical dimensions of qualities (character) and evaluation (esteem) not be overlooked. People do not regard themselves or others merely in terms of their respective social locations; they appraise themselves and one another in terms of qualities and characters they are deemed to have and in how these are evaluated (Hewitt, 1976, p. 79). Indeed, the qualities people are alleged to have by virtue of occupying a specific role may come to take on a greater significance than situated role identity in establishing biographical self. For example, a woman who is loving to her children may come to view herself (or be viewed by others) as an essentially loving person, regardless of the specific roles she situationally takes on.

I argued in Chapters 5 and 6 that motherhood could be perceived as a structured time for intense emotion in women's lives—an emotionally structured rite of passage in the transformation of female identity. We saw that motherhood did not simply express gender identity, as is often argued; it also allowed participants in this study to *achieve* a feminine identity as a loving, caring, responsible person. I argued that character assessment, rather than role or status as a mother, was important in establishing the identities these women claimed. And these identities were not simply gender identities as women; they were *gendered identities* and *gendered selves*: a feminized, adult sense of self as a person, not simply as a woman. What was vested in the women's commitment to motherhood was not simply the social identity of mother but the character of a caring, patient, responsible adult person—a positively valued character that is symbolically expressed for women through motherhood. In short, through motherhood women judge their worth not just as women but as persons. In a gendered society, of course, what makes women feel good about themselves is typically different from what makes men feel good about themselves.

Identities are established through the process of placement and announcment (G. Stone, 1981). They may be located in *interpersonal relationships*, in which personal names are central to identity; or in *structural relations*, in which title or social position provides the key information. Structural relations provide important bases for identities in modern societies, but as G. Stone (1981, p. 189) points out, since one's name usually outlasts one's occupational title, interpersonal relations probably provide a more important social basis for the *continuation* of identity. Motherhood, therefore, might be expected to provide an important basis for biographical rather than situated identity. The data suggest that was the case in this study.

REPRODUCING CULTURE
IN RECONSTITUTING THE SELF

Many women in the study did not set out to fill the role of mother,[3] but the majority did come to value the persons they became through filling that role. What women chose in becoming mothers (and many did not choose) was not the role of mother in the way we often think of that role. They did not choose to take on the romanticized cultural image of mother, be it saint, self-sacrificer, or morally transformed person. Rather, through a wide variety of routes, women took on the behavior or outcome of having a child. What became clear from the data is that participants in this study, once they had assumed the behavioral role of mother, found that the everyday living of that role led to perceived character changes such that their claimed identities did in fact come to approximate the cultural romanticized image of a what a mother is supposed to be. That is, once women stepped into the situation of being a mother, the social relationships and cultural definition of the situation, along with women's own responses, acted together to make the participants feel they were morally transformed persons. Although they did not set out to achieve this identity, women came to claim for themselves the romanticized identity of mother. However, it should be emphasized that it was character assessment rather than social position that mobilized this female role identity. It is ironic, therefore, that women can come to reproduce the romanticized image of mother, which in turn functions to produce much of the ambivalence and pressure women feel about motherhood.

As I analyzed the data I became struck by the ways in which women's stories of their transitions to motherhood were analogous to many Western European mythological themes of heroic quests.[4] Typically, the traditional hero's mythological journey involved a quest for adventure, honor, or truth. The hero's journey can be seen as a metaphor for a search for identity. The heroine's journey, on the other hand, can be seen as based on alternative imagery. Whereas the hero's path typically involved a worldly and often solitary quest, the heroine's, as represented by the women in this study, was an inner journey of self-change and moral development. Unlike the hero's defiance of social ties as he responded to the call to adventure and rode off to distant lands, the noble journey of these modern women is represented as one of self-discovery and deepened social commitment. Like much of human experience, these women's experience as mothers was open to the human capacity to mythologize the mundane and to confer on everyday life the qualities of the sacred. Thus, women's accounts both reflected and reproduced many of the mythological themes of human existence and romantic images of motherhood.

MOTHERHOOD AS IDEALIZED
SOCIAL CONNECTEDNESS

But what makes motherhood so compelling a social issue and not simply a personal one? Cultural meanings of motherhood, I suggest, provide guiding metaphors not simply for the construction of identity but for the representation of idealized social bonds. Motherhood symbolizes connectedness. Motherhood—indeed, parenthood—offers culturally restricted access to socially valued others (children), but it also regulates access to culturally restricted and socially scarce experiences of deep social attachment. Rather than construing that the women's discussions about motherhood referred to some essential difference between men and women, we can perceive women's accounts as representing challenges to socially dominant masculinist myths of the abstract, separate, autonomous individual of liberal political thought and market economic theory. There is no unitary experience of motherhood, nor is there a common difference among women. Perhaps what makes the experience of motherhood "different" is its potential to symbolize alternatives to the dominant social relationships of commodification, inequality, and exploitation. Participants' accounts of motherhood represented alternative metaphors of the self constructed through cultural resources of human connectedness, caring, and interdependence, rather than of detachment, independence, and competition: alternative ties that socially bind.

Motherhood is not a "woman's issue" both because men, too, can (and do) care and perform family work and because it raises broader questions about the nature of social bonds and social responsibility. In a capitalist market society, motherhood has the power to symbolize noncontractual social relationships among people. Thus, as Stanworth (1990) points out, both public controversies over the social meanings of motherhood and feminist concerns about the commodification of childbearing express deeply felt fears about the loss of motherhood in the *symbolic* sense—the fear that modern society is increasingly losing relationships of enduring commitment, care, tenderness, and compassion.

If meanings of motherhood can implicitly challenge dominant metaphors of social life, in real life we know that connectedness without autonomy has been oppressive for women. And caring in the context of structural inequality has been exploitative. Much caring work is done not simply by women but by women from socially subordinate groups. Indeed, the likelihood that political challenges to the commodification of human relationships may arise from women's experience of motherhood is limited by the broader social relationships of gender, race, and class inequality on the one hand and, on the other, by social practices that confine caring relationships to privatized nuclear families and genetic family ties. Historically, maternal–feminist movements have often failed to realize their goals partly because they did not challenge the structural relationships of power and inequality. Without such a challenge, the politics of caring are vulnerable to co-optation by those who invoke women's role as nurturers to build appeal for conservative political agenda.

Perhaps it is because I do not have children that I am sensitive to the negative consequences of privatizing and biologizing caring relations. Perhaps it is being an immigrant without traditional family close by that helps me see that privatized families inhibit rather than encourage the possibility of community connectedness. The socially transformative potential of motherhood lies not simply in the inclusion of men in family work. It lies in a transformation of social arrangements such that the activities of producing and sustaining social life and human connections and the quality of those human relationships for all society's members are valued rather than made subordinate to commodity production and individual achievement.

It is tempting to think that mothers as moral actors can make the world a better place. But making society more caring is a political project that is neither exclusively nor necessarily grounded in maternal identities. Social transformation is the responsibility of everyone— mothers and nonmothers, men and women.

Participants' Family Context: Marital/Partner Status and Children

MIDDLE-CLASS MOTHERS WITH PARTNERS

Alice, mother of a 6-year-old
Beth, mother of two children, a 4-year-old and a 2-year-old
Carolyn, mother of a 1-year-old
Cindy, mother of a 3-year-old
Debbie, mother of a 2½-year-old
Fran, mother of two children, a 1½-year-old and a 3½-year-old
Janette, mother of a 2-year-old
Jean, mother of a 4-year-old
Jenny, mother of a 1½-year-old
Jill, mother of two children, a 1½-year-old and a 3½-year-old
Kate, mother of a 1-year-old
Kim, mother of two children, a 1-year-old and a 2½-year-old
Laura, mother of a 1½-year-old
Loretta, mother of a 4-year-old
Margaret, mother of a 2½-year-old
Marie, mother of a 2½-year-old
Marilyn, mother of a 2½-year-old
Mary Lynn, mother of a 2-year-old
Nina, mother of a 2½-year-old
Patricia, mother of a 4½-year-old
Penny, mother of a 5-year-old
Rachael, mother of two children, a 1½-year-old and a 3-year-old
Sandra, mother of a 2-year-old
Susan, mother of two children, a 9-month-old and a 5-year-old
Tannis, mother of a 5-year-old
Tess, mother of a 1-year-old
Wendy, mother of a 6-month-old

MIDDLE-CLASS ALONE MOTHERS

Anna, mother of a 2½-year-old
Della, mother of a 4½-year-old
Joanne, mother of 2½-year-old
Rebecca, mother of a 6-year-old

WORKING-CLASS MOTHERS WITH PARTNERS

Barb, mother of a 2-year-old
Chris, mother of a 3-year-old
Ellen, mother of a 3-year-old
Jackie, mother of a 7-month-old
June, mother of a 2½-year-old
Karen, mother of three children, a 1½-year-old, a 3-year-old, and a 4-year-old
Katherine, mother of a 2-year-old
Lisa, mother of a 1½-year-old
Marg, mother of a 6-month-old
Pam, mother of of two children, a 1-year-old and a 4-year-old
Ramona, mother of a 2-year-old
Renee, mother of a 5-year-old
Rita, mother of two children, a 1½-year-old and a 7-year-old (she shared custody
     of the older with an ex-partner)
Sally, mother of two children, a 2-year-old and a 4-year-old
Stephanie, mother of a 9-month-old
Sue, mother of three children, a 3-year-old, a 7-year-old, and a 13-year-old
Judy, mother of two children, a 2-year-old and an 8-year-old

WORKING-CLASS ALONE MOTHERS

Cora, mother of a 3-year-old
Diane, mother of a 5-year-old
Helen, mother of two children, a 5-year-old and a 9-year-old
Kathy, mother of a 5-year-old
Kimberley, mother of a 5-year-old
Mara, mother of a 3-year-old
Mary, mother of a 6-month-old
Nancy, mother of two children, a 4½-year-old and a 9-year-old
Rose, mother of a 3-year-old
Tina, mother of a 3-year-old
Val, mother of an 18-month-old

APPENDIX 2

Participants' Education and Occupations

MIDDLE-CLASS WOMEN

Occupation	Education
Senior Policy Advisor	M.A.
Literacy Coordinator	B.A.
Social Worker	M.A.
Community College Teaching Master	B.A., working toward M.A.
Management Board Officer	M.A.
Elementary School Teacher	B.A. + postgraduate work
Coordinator of Language Studies	B.A.
Lawyer	B.A., L.L.B.
High School Teacher	B.A.
Director, Nonprofit Organization	M.A.
Librarian	M.A.
Childcare Social Worker	3-year diploma
Civil Servant	B.A.
Executive Secretary	Journalism diploma working toward B.A.
Education Consultant	B.A. working toward M.A.
Policy Analyst	B.A.
Flight Attendant	B.A. working toward M.A.
Managing Editor	B.A.
Secretary	B.A.
Marketing Manager	B.A. + Business Diploma
Counselor	Diploma
Graphic Designer	B.A. + B.Ed. Graphic Arts Diploma
Community College Teaching Master	B.A.
Accountant	B.A. (Commerce)
Accountant	Professional Certification

Occupation	*Education*
Research Advisor	B.A., working toward M.A.
Social Worker	3-year diploma
Counselor	3-year diploma
Elementary School Teacher	B.A.
Archivist	M.A.
Manager	Grade 13

WORKING-CLASS WOMEN

Occupation	*Education*
Apprentice Woodworker	Grade 12
Bell Operator	Grade 11
Accounting Clerk	Grade 12
Secretary	Grade 12 + secretarial program
Clerical Worker	Grade 12
Bell Service Assistant	Grade 12
Clerical Worker	Grade 13
Dry Cleaner's Shipping Clerk	Grade 11
Unskilled Factory Worker	Grade 10
Clerical Worker	Grade 12
Truck Driver	Grade 10
Bookkeeping Clerk	Grade 12
Typesetter	Grade 12 + apprenticeship
Secretary	Grade 10
Daycare Assistant	Grade 12
Data Entry Clerk	Grade 12 + 1 year clerical training
Legal Secretary	Grade 12
Clerical Assistant	Grade 10
Hotel Housekeeper	Grade 11
Accounting Clerk	Grade 9
Clerical Worker	Grade 13
Sheet Metal Worker	Grade 9
Hospital Dietary Aide	Grade 9
Word Processor	Grade 13
Apprentice Mechanic	Grade 12
Secretary	Grade 13
Clerical Worker	Grade 11
Waitress/Cashier	Grade 12

APPENDIX 3

Conceptualizing the Self

"THE PERSON AS OBJECT TO SELF"

	Situated self	Biographical self
Location	Sense of position in a particular situation	Cumulative sense of place relative to others
	Situated identity	Identity
Qualities	Image of self in a situation	Cumulative image of self
	Situated self-image	Self-image
Evaluation	Evaluation of self in a particular situation	Cumulative evaluation of self
	Situated self-esteem	Self-esteem

"THE PERSON AS OBJECT TO OTHERS"

	Situated self	Biographical self
Location	Others' view of a person's position in a particular situation	Others' cumulative sense of a person's place
	Situated social identity	Social identity
Qualities	Others' image of the person in a particular situation	Others' cumulative image of the person
	Situated image	Image
Evaluation	Others' evaluation of the person in a particular situation	Others' cumulative evaluation of the person
	Situated esteem	Esteem

From Hewitt (1976, p. 81). Copyright 1976 by Allyn & Bacon. Adapted by permission.

Notes

1. In 1986, for example, the average age at first marriage for women in Canada was 26, up by 3 years since the early 1970s (Adams and Nagnur, 1989, p. 25). Also during this period Canadian women's fertility reached an all-time low. Between 1960 and 1980, women's fertility dropped from 3.9 to 1.7 children per woman (Eichler, 1983, p. 37). The crude birth rate fell from 27 per 1000 in 1960 (Eichler, 1983, p. 36) to 14.4 in 1987 (Statistics Canada, 1989).
2. The term "real self" is used here as a folk construct, not as a sociological concept. Turner (1981) argues that people appear to be turning to the personal or impulsive spheres of life to find what they claim are their "real selves."
3. Some recent feminist methodologists have argued that understanding women's subjective experience is the goal of feminist research, and they eschew social structural explanations as falsely objective (Stanley and Wise, 1983). Traditionally it is the sociologist's task to go beyond descriptions of subjective experience to analyze how social organization shapes personal experience. However, what constitutes the starting point for such sociological analysis has long been the subject of methodological debate between those who employ logicodeductive and those who use inductive research techniques (Glazer and Strauss, 1967). For a discussion of feminist methodology on this point, see Currie (1988).
4. For a review and critique of the sociological and psychological literature on motherhood, see Boulton (1983).
5. For a critique of how women's experience in general has been excluded

from the social construction of knowledge, including sociological knowledge, see Smith (1975). See also Jessie Bernard's (1973) now classic article on her four revolutions in sociology.

6. For a critique of the oversimplification of both psychoanalytic understanding of socialization and the "oversocialized" concept of the individual in Parsonian sociology see Wrong (1961).

7. My discussion of feminist analysis here is limited to North American feminism.

8. For a controversial application of economic decision-making theory, see Gary Becker (1981). Becker applied a utility maximization model of economic decision making to women's fertility behavior. Decisions about children, he argues, are motivated by economics. Women have fewer babies if the opportunity costs of their time—the income they forgo if they stay home—go up. Fertility has declined, he argues, because the rise in women's earning potential has made babies relatively more costly.

9. Jacobson and Heaton (1991), using American National Survey of Families and Households data collected in 1987 and 1988, estimate that only 3.5% of men and 2.8% of women were voluntarily (permanently) childless. Only unmarried men and women aged over 35 had rates higher than 10%.

10. The proportion of childless ever-married Canadian women aged 25 to 29 increased from 14% in 1961 to 30% in 1981. Among those aged 30 to 34, the proportion of childless ever-married women increased from 9% in 1971 to 14% in 1981 (Burke, 1986, p.7). However, it is not yet clear how much the changes in fertility patterns reflect a move to increased voluntary childlessness and how much they reflect deferred childbearing (Burke, 1986).

11. For a discussion of the use of "moral" as pertaining to the sphere of both identity and ethics, see Chapters 5 and 6.

12. This does not mean, of course, that many women did not act in mother-like ways to children who were not theirs by birth. As the work of Stack (1974), Solinger (1992), and others show, clearly they did.

13. Kaufman (1985), for example, has shown how women who returned to orthodox Judaism used traditional Jewish values and practices to enhance their own power and control in the family. Paradoxically, even elements of a traditional patriarchal culture can be sometimes employed by women to achieve nontraditional, personally empowering ends.

CHAPTER 2

1. Although the approach to data analysis was inductive, the use of semistructured interviews as a data-gathering strategy was less inductive than that more commonly used in grounded theory research employing,

for example, unstructured interviews or participant observation. This made it more difficult for me to shift the focus of the research from its original conceptualization to the issues of greater salience to the women themselves. See Kleinman et al. (1994).

2. There is a history in family research of using categories of respondents differentiated by race and class. Komarovsky (1962), Rubin (1976), Boulton (1983), and Wearing (1984), for example, provide studies of white working-class women's experience of motherhood and family life that allow comparison with this study. For a fascinating study of the social organization of mothering and kin in a black, urban community, see Stack (1974) and also Dill (1993). For some reflections on sociological representations of "the black family" see Martin and Martin (1980). For feminist analyses of black women's experiences, see hooks (1989) and Collins (1993). Variations in white family patterns associated with different economic conditions have also been studied by social historians and, more recently, by feminist anthropologists. See, for example, Sacks (1984), Bridenthal (1982), and Tilly and Scott (1978).

3. Questions were adapted, in particular, from Gerson (1985), Boulton (1983), and Pistrang (1981).

4. On two occasions a partner was present for part of the interview, and I directed the interview so as to avoid those questions that might have raised sensitive issues or have been difficult to answer in that context.

5. For example, Komarovsky (1962) found major variations in expectations of marriage and in familial behavior between white working-class women and men who had finished high school and those who had fewer years of education. And Rubin (1976) distinguished between the "settled-living" life-styles of the steadily employed and the "hard-living" life-styles of the erratically employed white working-class families she interviewed.

6. For example, many researchers see employment or work involvement as a major divide among middle-class women (Bernard, 1975; Pistrang, 1981; Luker, 1984; Anderson, 1987).

7. See White (1983) and Duffy et al. (1989) for discussions of the problems of operationalizing full- and part-time work. Mothers of pre-schoolers are somewhat more likely than other women to work part-time. About a quarter of employed married women in Canada work part-time, and approximately a third of these women have preschool children (Duffy et al., 1989, p. 11).

8. I use the term "alone mother" rather than "single mother" because the latter is often used to mean "never-married." I avoid the term "single parent" because it implies that children living with alone mothers do not have other parents.

9. See also, for example, Furstenberg (1992), Geronimus (1992), and Zimmerman (1992).

10. Zimmerman (1992, p. 427) suggests that a third of unwed adolescent

mothers in the United States marry within 5 years of the birth of their children.
11. See also Eichler (1983, p. 205).
12. Sidel (1990, p. 127) points out that if one looks only at white teenagers' pregnancies, the national differences persist. The pregnancy rate among white adolescent women in the United States is still more than one-and-a-half times that of Canada.

CHAPTER 3

1. This is not to say that in having children women are acting irrationally. In contrast to my analysis, approaches such as Luker's (1975) analyze women's behavior around risking pregnancy in terms of rational choices, broadly conceived.
2. Woollett's (1991) British research on women with fertility problems shows how motherhood can symbolize adult identity, provide an opportunity for intimacy, and allow women to overcome a negative identity associated with infertility and childlessness. Responses to infertility, Woollett (1991, p. 58) notes, expose the often hidden importance attributed to biological and social aspects of parenthood. In contrast, couples who adopt may attempt to replace the conventional story of filial relationships with an understanding of parental relationship that emphasizes the *unimportance* of biology (Sandelowski et al., 1993).
3. Ironically, voluntarily permanent childless women may hold traditional attitudes that associate motherhood with full-time childcare. For such women, postponement provides a temporary way out of conflicting demands (Nave-Hertz, 1989), and permanent childlessness expresses, not a rejection of children per se, but a rejection of being *only* a mother (Veevers, 1980, p. 49).
4. Stanworth (1990, p. 292) argues that the notion that career commitment provides a justification for childlessness is not a viable one. It both reflects a narrow form of economism to see a career as displacing desire for a child and leaves women who do not have careers with no justification for childlessness.
5. Research on motivation for parenthood suggests that the common reasons people give for wanting children include children's importance as a means of achieving adult identity, of establishing a family or primary ties, and of self-perpetuation (Gormly et al., 1987; Woollett, 1991, p. 48). Fun and stimulation, it seems, are losing appeal as motives for having children.
6. The intent of these figures is not to speak to women's commitments to childlessness but to indicate that many women now reflect on both

having children and *not* having children. The "parenthood mystique" (Veevers, 1980, p. 40) that once made childlessness unthinkable may have lost credibility, but other cultural and social organizational processes encourage women to have children. Typically, in this study, such women indicated that, at an earlier time, they had thought they would personally choose permanent childlessness; didn't want children; felt they would be bad parents; or, in a minority of cases, felt social circumstances presented barriers to ever having children. For a discussion of the most common given motives for childlessness, see Houseknecht (1987, p. 377).

7. For Canadian national data on the relationship between age at first birth and educational attainment, see Grindstaff (1988) and Moore (1987, 1989). The middle-class women in this study had an average of 1.2 children; the working-class women had an average of 1.4 children.

8. This comparison refers only to women who planned their first pregnancies.

9. Woollett (1991) found that the infertile women she studied sought release from a social identity of immaturity, selfishness, and psychological defectiveness associated with childlessness.

10. From a report on U.S. census data: "Births Outside Marriage Increase" (1993).

11. For a discussion of how "working on one's relationship" has become a secular form of modern religion, see Bellah et al. (1985).

12. Women are often cautioned against postponing childbearing, by tales of "aging eggs" and images of self-inflicted infertility. But, according to Berryman (1991, p. 118) the notion held until recently that women in their 30s are too old for pregnancy is a 20th-century one that has had socially controlling implications for women who wish to pursue non-family roles.

13. As will be argued in Chapter 5, the social responses to different women's motherhood, of course, vary greatly.

14. Reproductive biology, of course, is also mediated by the resources of medical technology, the social organization of health care, individual economic resources, and so on. It is now possible, for example, for some postmenopausal women to become pregnant and give birth—although such an opportunity is not available to most women.

15. Feminist analyses show that the devaluation of nature and its identification with women have been dominant political and cultural themes in Western history (Merchant, 1980). Both, according to O'Brien (1981), emerged from men's experience of temporal discontinuity and their *disconnectedness* from others. Western men's historical responses to temporal and social disconnectedness, according to O'Brien, have been the invention of enduring patriarchal institutions and the creation of fathers' propoerty-like rights to children.

16. One could argue, of course, that children are becoming a scarce commodity. My concern in this chapter is primarily with the value of motherhood, rather than the value of children.

CHAPTER 4

1. For example, 24.7% of all mothers aged 40 to 49 in Canada in 1984 had been alone parents for part of their maternal careers (Moore, 1989, p. 342).
2. One could argue, however, that alone mothers experience powerlessness in ways that parallel the powerlessness traditionally associated with belonging to the working class. The traditional effects of working class, on the other hand, are ameliorated for working-class women in two-income families with stable employment (see Chapter 7).
3. See Gerson (1985) for a study of how the experience of work and work advancement affect women's orientation to motherhood and domesticity. In this study, for example, Stephanie's experience can be contrasted with Sally's. Stephanie, 26, was also older than most working-class mothers when she had her first child, but the timing of her pregnancy was determined by her recent marriage. Years at work for Stephanie did *not* translate into high work involvement; she had experienced little by way of promotions at work and had had no personal desire to return to the labor force after giving birth.
4. See also Grindstaff (1988) and Moore (1987, 1989).
5. However, given that the women at other times noted that they had perceived interaction between other parents and children as unappealing and parents as spending a good deal of time complaining about the disadvantages of having children, the image of other parents spreading "the good news about parenting" needs to be interpreted cautiously. Childless women may have *perceived* themselves to be missing out, but few of the women in this study suggested that other women had told them they were missing out. For data on the social world of parents, see Chapter 8.
6. This idea is developed in Chapter 5.
7. On the whole, the working-class women's accounts portrayed them as having a far more positive conception and greater emotional attraction to motherhood. With reference to many issues raised in the study, the working-class women were less articulate about their own feelings and responses. This reticence may reflect difficulties with putting thoughts about feelings into words or with less practice in being self-reflective and self-analytical. If not always capable of saying why they wanted children, these young working-class women emphasized the *strength* of their motherhood motivation.

8. See Government of Ontario (1988, 1989). Also see Eichler (1983, p. 209).

9. See Burke (1986) and Moore (1987). For a full discussion of the growing separation between marital and parental roles in Canadian families, see Eichler (1983).

10. However, Furstenberg (1992) suggests that declining family and community controls on nonmarital sexual activity and the lack of male investment in preventing pregnancy increase the risks of unwed adolescent women becoming pregnant and giving birth.

11. Presumably many pregnancies that were not so defined were terminated and thus excluded from this study.

12. See Moore (1989). Eichler (1983) argues that monolithic and conservative biases in social policy and the sociology of the family literature have led to the view that families composed of married couples and their children are the normal and desirable family arrangement. But growing up in a single-parent household is not statistically abnormal. It has been estimated that 45% of the children born in the United States in the mid-1970s will have lived in a one-parent household before they reach the age of 18 (Eichler, 1983, p. 14).

13. There are alternative sociological explanations for unwed motherhood. Some see unwanted pregnancies as the result of ignorance of contraceptive methods. Others, like Goode (1961), use Merton's concept of anomie to explain that, because of the lack of legitimate means to achieve the culturally defined goal of marriage, women use getting pregnant as a way of becoming attached to a man. Related to this type of explanation are those, somewhat like Rubin's (1976), that argue that for certain groups lacking the resources to realize the dominant goals and values of society, the range of acceptable values and behaviors becomes stretched or widened. So marriage and motherhood remain most valued, but unwed motherhood becomes a second best. Finally, the "culture of poverty" approach argues that the working class or poor in society are characterized by their own value system, or distinctive subculture, in which unwed motherhood is acceptable.

14. The number of out-of-wedlock births in Canada between 1951 and 1985 rose from 4% to 16% of all births (Moore, 1987).

15. The treatment of unwed mothers, as Solinger (1992) shows, is race specific. Although unwed motherhood was generally treated differently for black and white adolescents, for a period in the United States unwed pregnant adolescent black women became targets of social programs that sought to "elevate" the status of black women by ascribing to them the same neuroses as white women (Solinger, 1992, p. 214).

16. See also Horowitz's (1987) study of unwed Chicana mothers, in which the professed and perceived salience of motherhood in young, unwed

mothers' identities could be used to neutralize the potentially degrading identity of nonvirgin, or "loose woman," in a traditional, male-dominated environment.

17. The "whiteness" of this patriarchal image is clearly revealed in Jones's (1993) analysis of the wages of black female tobacco workers in North Carolina.

18. As with the ideology of the breadwinner role, the reality of what is at risk is quite different for different women—depending on their social locations.

19. This reframing of the challenge of young white women's sexual unorthodoxy as a problem of black teenage mothers on welfare happened at a time when the number of births to black, unwed, teenaged women was falling relative to that of whites (Nathanson, 1991, p. 66). See Chapter 2.

CHAPTER 5

1. The different meanings of the word "moral" were discussed in the introduction. Both meanings of moral, its ethical or evaluative sense and the moral themes of changing self-conceptions (or Goffman's [1963] notion of moral transformation), were pervasive in women's accounts of motherhood in this and the next chapter.

2. See, for example, the discussions of Gilligan's work in *Signs*, *11*(2), 1986.

3. See the discussion of Gilligan's work by Greeno and Maccoby (1986).

4. Oakley (1979, 1980a) refers to the sense of shock the new mothers in the British sample felt at the gap between reality and their expectations about motherhood. For Oakley's explanation of "why society conspires to pull the wool over mothers' eyes," see Oakley (1980b).

5. Mothers may not instantly (or even ever) "fall in love" with their children. Oakley, (1979) for example, interviewed a sample of British mothers at 5 weeks and again at 25 weeks after the birth of their children and found that 70% were shocked to discover that they did not feel the immediate maternal feelings they had expected to feel. Her study led her to conclude that "it is clear that the rush of maternal love is an exception, and not a general rule" (Oakley, 1980a, p. 96). Indeed, she found that up to two-thirds of the mothers expressed negative feelings or ambivalence in their relationship with their new babies (1980a, p. 99). She further argues that the label "postnatal depression" and related theories and treatments can be seen as a major ideological strategy within the medical model of childbirth that is geared toward transforming maternal ambivalence and dissatisfaction into "nonproblems" (1980a, p. 99).

6. Workers in the field of psychology, which as a discipline has long

claimed an interest in emotions, are also experiencing a renewed interest in this area. For a criticism of sociology's failure to deal adequately with particular emotions—for example, grief—see Lofland (1982); and for a critique of an overly emotional interpretation of love, see Cancian (1987).

7. For a review of the interpretations of maternal love see Boulton (1983). For an analysis of the political functions of the recent interest in maternal bonding theory, see Arney (1980). For a controversial analysis of the biosocial origins of maternal love by a leading sociologist in women's studies, see Rossi (1977). On the ideological functions of maternal love, see Wearing (1984) and Oakley (1980a, 1980b).

8. See Hochschild (1979, 1983). See also *Social Psychology Quarterly, 52*(1), March 1989. This issue is devoted to the study of sentiment, affect, and emotion.

9. There is a debate among historians of the family and ethnographers of childhood as to whether what we recognize as parental love and maternal love are universal phenomena or are products of unique material and historical circumstances such as the rise of bourgeois society and declining infant mortality (L. Stone, 1972; Badinter, 1981). For a historical analysis of changing conceptions of love in American society, see Cancian (1987). My concern is not whether maternal love is or is not universal; rather, it is to look at the meaning and function of love, and the role that the rhetoric of love played, in the lives of the women interviewed.

10. See Mills and Kleinman (1988), who cite the work of Dutton and Aron (1974), for example, which shows a connection between vulnerability and falling in love.

11. Images of the nature of children and so of appropriate parental relationships, vary by class and sociohistoric period (Zelizer, 1985; L. Stone, 1972; Aries, 1962).

12. There are different understandings of myth and mythology among sociologists. Berger and Luckmann (1966, p. 110), for example, see mythology as representing an archaic form of legitimation: a level of thinking where there is least need for theoretical, analytical or critical thought. Swidler's (1980) use of the concept, however, seems closer to Campbell's (1988) conceptualization. In this view, mythology is neither primitive nor naive. On the contrary, myth represents metaphorical thinking: Myths are a means of expressing *insight*, not merely legitimations. Myths point to what are variously called metaphysical and spiritual realms of human experience and as such are present in all societies, albeit in different forms.

13. See Smith-Rosenberg (1975). See also the review articles on Gilligan's *In a Different Voice* in *Signs, 11*(2), 1986.

14. For a broader discussion of this theme see, J. Campbell (1988).

CHAPTER 6

1. Backett (1982) also found that middle-class parents emphasized that nothing can really prepare one to cope with being a parent and childrearing. She also found that only the experience of rearing one's own children was seen as a source of truly relevant knowledge.
2. The tendency of working-class men and women to blame themselves or their lack of education for the economic disadvantages they experience in class society has been widely reported (Rubin, 1976; Komarovsky, 1962). Interestingly, if the working-class women did link their "private troubles" to wider social processes, it was gender inequalities, not class structures, that they invoked to help them analyze their situation.
3. At other stages of the life cycle one could well expect these other selves to gain more importance as the relationship between self and child changed. For the working-class mothers of young children whom I interviewed, however, the experience of motherhood as a "settling down" and a form of moral reform showed that motherhood represented the symbolic departure from earlier self-conceptions and the emergence of new ones, rather than self-sacrifice.
4. For a fuller discussion of these themes, see Chapter 5 and Swidler (1980).
5. Although both groups talked about motherhood in moral terms, there were class differences in the way children were involved in how the two groups of women made sense of life. For example, 42% of the middle-class women, but only 11% of the working-class women, spoke about the "transcendent" changes they felt motherhood had made in the meaning and purpose of their lives and in their relationship to humanity or the universe. Another 6% of the working-class women said they would feel in some way disconnected from the future by not having children.
6. Broder (1994) points to the shift in the social worth of children evidenced in the decline of foundling homes and baby wheels for unwanted infants in 19th-century Europe. These practices were designed primarily to protect the social and moral worth of women and their families; the relatively low social worth of children, especially illegitimate children, no doubt explains the apparent indifference to the extremely high death rates in foundling homes.

CHAPTER 7

1. For an overview of some recent attempts to theorize gender so as to avoid the problems of essentialism, see Alcoff (1988). See also Gerson and Peiss (1985).

2. Cahill's (1987) symbolic interactionist analysis of gender identity formation in early childhood argues the opposite: that same-sexed parental
identification is the effect, not the cause, of gender identity. Sexually
differentiated patterns of caregiver–infant interaction, in particular the
use of sex-designated labels, she argues, are central to gender-identity
formation. Children respond to themselves as significant others respond
to them, and they learn to have their identity validated by behaving in
ways that will elicit gender-identity-confirming responses from others
and from themselves (Cahill, 1987).

3. I want to distinguish my use of the term "connectedness" from the
notion of "bonding" as used in "bonding theory." According to bonding
theory, "bonding" between mother and child is a natural and biologically based process that occurs at about the time of birth in a "normal"
mother and forms the basis of her motivation to care for her child.
Problems are considered to arise when the bonding process has been
impeded or prevented. This biologically based bond, it is suggested, may
subsequently develop into a social bond between mother and child.
Although the approach is associated with psychology rather than with
sociology, Alice Rossi (1977) published a challenging article aimed at
sociologists entitled "A Biosocial Perspective on Parenting," in which
she argues there are endocrinological and genetic factors in women that
facilitate bonding. In reply, Boulton (1983) suggests that women may
feel motivated to look after young children in their care, but one cannot
assume, as bonding theory does, that if they love (have bonded with)
their children they will find childcare enjoyable. "Love," she notes, may
be differently expressed and may be intertwined with other emotions.

Arney (1980) argues that bonding theory is deeply flawed metho-
dologically. Its widespread adoption, he claims, has been based on the
political interests of those involved in the medical organization of
childbirth and in childcare policy rather than on scientific evidence.
Bonding theory, he points out, was adopted by medical interests to
provide them with a scientific basis for responding to pressure from
women's groups for changes in childbirth practices and to the threat
from the "natural birth" movement. By appearing to reform medical-
ized childbirth for "scientific" rather than for political reasons, medicine
met some of women's demands but retained its authority as based in
science. Arney argues: "By expanding the medical domain to include
the social relations of parents and infants, medicine preserves institutionalized relationships between physicians and patients. Hospital practices are reformed to protect the interests they embody" (Arney, 1980,
p. 562). Indeed, he concludes that bonding theory is a modern-day
social–psychological–biological version of maternal instinct theory that
supports the idea that mothers are the only proper attendants for young
children.

In the area of social policy, nonbonding between parent and infant has been proposed as the cause of major social ills and criminal activity. Thus women are implicitly ascribed the biological capacity for solving social problems, if only they would bond adequately with their children.

4. See Note 6 in Chapter 5.

5. Most studies show that marital satisfaction between couples falls significantly after they have children. See Cowan et al. (1985).

6. In-depth interviews allow us to learn about the identities these women claim, but they provide less reliable data about day-to-day behavior and the extent to which the ideals the women expressed were realized in practice.

7. Interestingly, Pistrang (1981, p. 111) found that mothers who stayed home full-time complained more often about lack of "time for themselves" than did women who worked outside the home. The reason, Pistrang suggests, is that working mothers experience work as scheduled time away from the demands of their children.

8. Ruddick (1984) explains that maternal responsibility may be a powerful and positive resource for women but that it can also be a burden and a source of oppression. It depends, she points out, on whether maternal practices in a society reflect the interests of women and children or whether they are shaped by social forces antagonistic to these interests. Similarly, Chodorow and Contratto (1982) point out that the excessive sense of maternal responsibility from which many women suffer is the flip side of the myth of maternal omnipotence: the belief that mothers, and only mothers, are all powerful and totally determining of the "outcome" of their child. Our cultural perceptions of maternal responsibility, combined with little control and few objective resources for evaluating the outcome of one's actions, can lead to maternal anxiety (Oakley, 1974, 1980b).

9. There is some evidence to suggest that employed working-class women do indeed suffer from greater stress than their middle-class counterparts. Common features of working-class women's work are a lack of control over the work environment, a lack of opportunity for advancement, and underutilization of their skills—all of which are likely to be associated with greater stress (Mansfield, 1982, p. 7). Similarly, Waldron (1980, p. 444) points out that for women who have paid employment, the benefits in terms of well-being may disproportionately be in favor of women of higher socioeconomic status because of the difference between the sorts of jobs they and working-class women hold.

10. Disciplinary practices are related to occupational structure, explains Kohn (1977). And different socialization strategies prepare children for class-related occupational positions that emphasize self-direction on the one hand and obedience to authority on the other.

11. Rubin (1976) talks about the class-specific nature of parents' concern with disciplining their children. Middle-class parents, she argues, have a sense of control in the world and believe they can act to provide for their children's futures. For working-class parents, she argues, the future seems uncertain and far less subject to their control. For the latter, the concern is not which school their child will attend but whether the child will finish school at all; it is not what occupation the child will choose when she or he grows up but whether she or he will grow up without getting into trouble—or getting badly hurt. Working-class parents, Rubin argues, feel that only by constant vigilance over their children's behavior can they gain some control and ensure their children's futures (Rubin, 1976, pp. 85–86).
12. Boulton (1983, p. 58), for example, reported that over half of her sample of mothers of preschool children found childcare a profoundly irritating experience.
13. For a breakdown of what tasks women like most and least, see Oakley (1974). Men's family work does not seem to be as great a source of distress for them as family work is for women. But this observation is partly explained by the fact that men and women do different family work under different conditions. When men and women perform the same family work under the same conditions, their responses are very similar (Baruch and Barnett, 1986a; Thompson and Walker, 1989).
14. Similar reports come from other studies of working mothers. Waldron's (1980) review of stress and employment among working mothers concluded that it is not simply the combining of paid work and family roles that leads to increased stress levels for women. Indeed, paid employment has been shown to have physical and mental health benefits for women (Waldron, 1980). However, certain *combinations* of family and work roles are associated with an increased risk of stress and ill health for women. For example, clerical workers who have three or more children and are married to a blue-collar husband were found to suffer higher rates of coronary heart disease than other women (Waldron, 1980; Baruch et al., 1987).
15. Baruch et al. (1987) point out that although many studies show employment to have positive mental health benefits for women, these observations may be more the case for women who have partners who share family work.

CHAPTER 8

1. There are far more social pressures aimed at ensuring that women become mothers than there are at ensuring that women be skilled and competent parents (Rossi, 1980; Bernard, 1975).

2. An exception is the way those women who gave children up for adoption often lost the social identity of mother—whatever their personal claims to a maternal identity.

3. The majority of the middle-class mothers (77%) identified themselves clearly as feminists, and another 13% gave "yes and no" replies. Only 21% of the working-class women said they were feminists, 25% were clear that they were not, and most of the others did not understand the term.

4. For overviews of the research on the division of family or domestic work, see Thompson and Walker (1989) and Gerstel and Gross (1987).

5. Hochschild (1989) has estimated that among the mostly middle-class couples she studied, 20% of the men shared family work equally, 70% did less than half but more than a third, and 10% did less than a third.

6. See studies of fathering discussed in La Rossa (1988). See also Thompson and Walker (1989).

7. Oakley (1974) and Wearing (1984) have pointed out that even women who mother full-time, however, spend far less time directly interacting with their children than is commonly believed.

8. Research indicates that men's participation in family work tends to be restricted to certain areas, in particular to childcare. Thus women devote proportionately more of their time to household tasks and less to childcare, which both men and women find more rewarding (Thompson and Walker 1989; Hochschild, 1989).

9. The notion of legitimacy is similar to the ideal of "fairness" in the family arrangements discussed by Backett (1982) and La Rossa and La Rossa (1981). However, the women in this study judged the division of family work less in terms of fairness than in terms of whether the arrangements were reasonable, understandable, or inevitable, *under the circumstances.* Thus the notion of "legitimate" refers to neither right nor wrong in any abstract sense but to a pragmatic assessment of reality.

10. See also Kessler and McCrae (1982). Male nonparticipation in family work can be expected to have specific symbolic and political significance for women who hold feminist views.

11. For example, women who were more "traditional" in that they would have preferred to stay home than be employed, did not have a more unequal division of childcare than others.

12. Some studies suggest that working-class men may do relatively more family work than middle-class men in two-income families (Luxton 1983; Ferree 1984, 1987).

13. Backett (1987) found that even when men are not actively involved with their children, they can be passively involved by showing interest in the information about the children their wives constantly provide, by appearing willing to "help," and by claiming they would like to be more involved—if only circumstances and time would permit.

14. The pattern was far from simple. Who stayed home also depended on a couple's employment benefit package and who was entitled to take paid sick time, for example. In this study, middle-class women, in contrast, frequently talked about checking to see who had flexibility in a schedule in deciding who stayed home with sick children. Middle-class jobs usually offer better "benefits" in terms of sick time, so the men's and women's relative earnings would have been less important.

15. When parents do share childcare truly equally, differences in mothering and fathering behavior seem to decline (Daniels and Weingarten, 1988; cited in Thompson and Walker, 1989, p. 861).

16. Eighteen percent of the middle-class women raised this example when talking about the difference between men's and women's experience of parenthood. Men, it seems, are more likely than women to keep family and paid work as separate spheres of life (Gerson, 1985; Zussman, 1987).

17. Of course, men and women may have very different expectations about how much "help" women can expect. Men's "help" is also often interpreted as indicative of their commitment to their partners (Thompson and Walker, 1989; Boulton, 1983) and so has symbolic and practical significance.

18. Several of the women in this study mentioned, for example, that they had again become close to their families after having children.

19. Another 14% of the working-class women and 10% of the middle-class women said they got occasional help—babysitting once a month, for example.

20. We must not assume that this situation is typical for all alone mothers. Alone mothers with family support might have been overrepresented in this study because they were more likely than alone mothers without support to be able to hold full-time jobs and stay off welfare or Mothers' Allowance.

CHAPTER 9

1. The relationship between poverty and motherhood in Canada, for example, has been well documented in the National Council of Welfare's 1990 report.

2. The term "heroic" carries masculinist connotations. But in using the term I want to emphasize that women's lives can offer as significant models of valuable human experience as do men's. If I think about it this way I find it encouraging that women's heroic activity is the stuff of everyday life rather than an exceptional endeavor.

3. Working-class women in this study were somewhat more likely than middle-class women to have held romanticized images of the role of mother and to have found the role and the role identity attractive.

4. See Swidler (1980) and Campbell (1949, 1988). There has been an increase in popular interest in mythology, occasioned in part by the work of Joseph Campbell. The use of the terms "heroic journey" and "mythology" in this chapter follow Campbell's usage. The image of heroic adventures to which I refer are those drawn from Western European cultures, but Campbell and others influenced by Jung suggest that these myths may express universal archetypes common to all cultures.

References

Acker, J. (1988). Class, Gender, and the Relations of Distribution. *Signs*, *13*(3), 473–497.

Adams, O., & Nagnur, D. (1989). Marrying and Divorcing: A Status Report for Canada. *Canadian Social Trends*, *13*(Summer), 24–27.

Alcoff, L. (1988). Cultural Feminism versus Post-Structuralism: The Identity Crisis in Feminist Theory. *Signs*, *13*(3), 405–434.

Allen, J. (1984). Motherhood: The Annhilation of Women. In J. Trebilcot (Ed.), *Mothering: Essays in Feminist Theory* (pp. 315–330). Totowa, NJ: Rowman & Allanheld.

Anderson, M. (1987). Longing for Liberation or Satisfied with the Status Quo? In M. Deegan & M. Hill (Eds.), *Women and Symbolic Interaction* (pp. 179–190). Winchester, MA: Allen & Unwin.

Aries, P. (1962). *Centuries of Childhood: Social History and Family Life*. New York: Knopf.

Arney, W. (1980). Maternal–Infant Bonding: The Politics of Falling in Love with Your Child. *Feminist Studies*, *6*(3), 547–568.

Atkinson, C. (1991). *The Oldest Vocation: Christian Motherhood in the Middle Ages*. Ithaca, NY: Cornell University Press.

Baber, K., & Allen, K. (1992). *Women and Families: Feminist Reconstructions*. New York: Guilford Press.

Backett, K. (1982). *Mothers and Fathers*. New York: St. Martin's Press.

Backett, K. (1987). The Negotiation of Fatherhood. In C. Lewis & M. O'Brien (Eds.), *Reassessing Fatherhood: New Observations on Fathers and the Modern Family*. London, UK: Sage.

Badinter, E. (1981). *Mother Love: Myth and Reality*. New York: Macmillan.

Bartky, S. (1990). *Femininity and Domination: Studies in the Phenomenology of Oppression.* New York: Routledge.

Baruch, G., & Barnett, R. (1986a). Consequences of Fathers' Participation in Family Work: Parents' Role Strain and Well-Being. *Journal of Personality and Social Psychology, 51,* 983–992.

Baruch, G., & Barnett, R. (1986b). Role Quality, Multiple Role Involvement, and Psychological Well-Being in Midlife Women. *Journal of Personality and Social Psychology, 51,* 578–585.

Baruch, G., Biener, L., & Barnett, R. (1987). Women and Gender in Research on Work and Family Stress. *American Psychologist, 42,* 130–136.

Becker, G. (1981). *A Treatise on the Family.* Cambridge, MA: Harvard University Press.

Becker, H. (1960). Notes on the Concept of Commitment. *American Journal of Sociology, 66,* 32–42.

Becker, H. (1981). Personal Change in Adult Life. In G. Stone & H. A. Farberman (Eds.), *Social Psychology through Symbolic Interaction* (pp. 307–316). New York: Wiley.

Becker, H. (1993, October 19). *Coincidence.* Landsdown Lecture, University of Victoria, British Columbia.

Belenky, M., McVicker Clinchy, B., Rule Goldberger, N., & Mattuck Tarule, J. (1986). *Women's Ways of Knowing: The Development of Self, Voice and Mind.* New York: Basic Books.

Bellah, R., Madsen, R., Sullivan, W., Swidler, A., & Tipton, S. (1985). *Habits of the Heart.* Berkeley: University of California Press.

Berger, B., & Berger, P. (1983). *The War over the Family: Capturing the Middle Ground.* Harmondsworth, Middlesex, UK: Penguin.

Berger, P. (1977). *Facing up to Modernity: Excursions in Society, Politics and Religion.* New York: Basic Books.

Berger, P., & Kellner, H. (1977). Marriage and the Construction of Reality. In P. Berger (Ed.), *Facing Up to Modernity: Excursions in Society, Politics and Religion* (pp. 5–22). New York: Basic Books.

Berger, P., & Luckmann T. (1966). *The Social Construction of Reality.* New York: Doubleday.

Bernard, J. (1973). My Four Revolutions: An Autobiographical History of the ASA. *American Journal of Sociology, 78*(4), 11–29.

Bernard, J. (1975). *Women, Wives, Mothers: Values and Options.* Chicago: Aldine.

Bernard, J. (1981). The Good Provider Role: Its Rise and Fall. *American Psychologist, 36*(1), 1–12.

Bernstein, B. (1971). *Class, Codes and Control.* London, UK: Routledge & Kegan Paul.

Berryman, J. (1991). Perspectives on Later Motherhood. In A. Phoenix, A. Woolette, & E. Lloyd (Eds.), *Motherhood: Meanings, Practices and Ideologies* (pp. 103–122). London, UK: Sage.

Best, J. (1990). *Threatened Children: Rhetoric and Concern about Child-Victims.* Chicago: University of Chicago Press.

Births Outside Marriage Increase. (1993, July 14). *The Globe and Mail*, p. A8.

Blishen, B., Carroll, W., & Moore, C. (1987). The 1981 Socioecomonic Index for Occupations in Canada. *Canadian Review of Sociology and Anthropology, 24*(4), 465–488.

Blum, L., & Vanderwater, E. (1993). Mothers Construct Fathers: Destabilized Patriarchy in La Leche League. *Qualitative Sociology, 16*(2), 3–22.

Blumer, H. (1969). *Symbolic Interactionism*. Englewood Cliffs, NJ: Prentice Hall.

Boulton, M. (1983). *On Being a Mother*. London, UK: Tavistock.

Boyd, M. (1986). Socioeconomic Indices and Sexual Inequality: A Tale of Scales. *Canadian Review of Sociology and Anthropology, 23*(4), 457–479.

Breytspraak, L. (1984). *The Development of Self in Later Life*. Toronto: Little, Brown.

Bridenthal, R. (1982). The Family: The View from a Room of Her Own. In B. Thorne & M. Yalom (Eds.), *Rethinking the Family: Some Feminist Questions* (pp. 235–245). New York: Longman.

Brim, O., & Wheeler, S. (1966). *Socialization after Childhood: Two Essays*. New York: Wiley.

Broder, S. (1994). Illegitimate Mothers. *Women's Review of Books, XI*(7), 25–27.

Burke, M. (1986). The New Norm. *Canadian Social Trends*, Summer, 7–10.

Burke, P., & Franzoi, S. (1988). Studying Situations and Identities Using Experimental Sampling Methodology. *American Sociological Review, 53*(4), 559–568.

Burke, P., Stets, J., & Pirog-Good, M. (1988). Gender Identity, Self Esteem, and Physical and Sexual Abuse in Dating Relationships. *Social Psychology Quarterly, 51*(3), 273–285.

Cahill, S. (1987). Directions for an Interactionist Study of Gender Development. In M. Deegan & M. Hill (Eds.), *Women and Symbolic Interaction* (pp. 81–98), Winchester, MA: Allen & Unwin.

Campbell, E. (1985). *The Childless Marriage: An Exploratory Study of Couples Who Do Not Want Children*. London, UK: Tavistock.

Campbell, J. (1949). *The Hero with a Thousand Faces*. New York: Meridan Books, World Publishing.

Campbell, J. (1988). *An Open Life*. New York: Larson.

Cancian, F. M. (1987). *Love in America: Gender and Self-Development*. Cambridge, UK: Cambridge University Press.

Caplan, P. (1985). *The Myth of Women's Masochism*. New York: Signet.

Chodorow, N. (1987). *The Reproduction of Mothering*. Berkeley: University of California Press.

Chodorow, N., & Contratto, S. (1982). The Fantasy of the Perfect Mother. In B. Thorne & M. Yalom (Eds.), *Rethinking the Family*. New York: Longman.

Collins, P. (1993). The Social Construction of Black Feminist Thought. In

L. Richardson & V. Taylor (Eds.), *Feminist Frontiers III* (pp. 21–30). New York: McGraw-Hill.

Cowan, C., Cowan, P., Heming, G., Garrett, E., Coysh, W., Curtis-Bules, H., & Boles, A. J. (1985). Transitions to Parenthood: His, Hers, and Theirs. *Journal of Family Issues, 6*(4), 451–481.

Currie, D. (1988). Re-thinking What We Do and How We Do It: A Study of Reproductive Decisions. *Canadian Review of Sociology and Anthropology, 25*(2), 231–252.

Currie, D. (1993). Unhiding the Hidden: Race, Class and Gender in the Construction of Knowldge. *Humanity and Society, 17*(11), 3–27.

Currie, D., & Raoul, V. (1992). The Anatomy of Gender: Dissecting Sexual Difference in the Body of Knowledge. In D. Currie & V. Raoul (Eds.), *The Anatomy of Gender: Women's Struggle for the Body* (pp. 1–34). Ottawa: Carlton University Press.

Daly, K. (1991, May). *The Social Construction of Fatherhood*. Paper presented at the Qualitiative Analysis Conference, Carleton University, Ottawa, Ontario.

Davis, A. (1993). Racism, Birth Control, and Reproductive Rights. In L. Richardson & V. Taylor (Eds.), *Feminist Frontiers III* (pp. 346–358). New York: McGraw-Hill.

Davis, K. (1992). Toward a Feminist Rhetoric: The Gilligan Debate Revisited. *Women's Studies International Forum, 15*(2), 219–231.

Deegan, M. J. (1987). Symbolic Interaction and the Study of Women: An Introduction. In M. Deegan & M. Hill (Eds.), *Women and Symbolic Interaction* (pp. 3–15). Winchester, MA: Allen & Unwin.

Delphy, C. (1984). *Close to Home: A Materialist Analysis of Women's Oppression*. London, UK: Hutchinson.

DeVault, M. (1987). Doing Housework: Feeding and Family Life. In N. Gerstel & H. Engle Gross (Eds.), *Families and Work* (pp. 178–191). Philadelphia: Temple University Press.

DeVault, M. (1991). *Feeding the Family: The Social Organization of Caring as Gendered Work*. Chicago: University of Chicago Press.

Dill, B. (1993). "The Means to Put My Children Through": Childrearing Goals and Strategies among Black Female Domestic Servants. In L. Richardson & V. Taylor (Eds.), *Feminist Frontiers III* (pp. 100–109). New York: McGraw-Hill.

Douglas, M. (1970). *Natural Symbols*. London, UK: Barrie & Rockliff, Cresset Press.

Douglas, M. (1972). Environments at Risk. In J. Benthall (Ed.), *Ecology, the Shaping Inquiry* (pp. 129–149). London, UK: Longman.

Douglas, M. (1975). *Implicit Meanings*. London, UK: Routledge & Kegan Paul.

Drabble, M. (1965). *The Millstone*. Middlesex, UK: Penguin.

Duffy, A. (1989). The Traditional Path: Full-Time Housewives. In A. Duffy, N. Mandell, & N. Pupo (Eds.), *Few Choices* (pp. 44–73). Toronto: Network Basic Books.

Duffy, A., Mandell, N. & Pupo, N. (Eds.). (1989). *Few Choices*. Toronto: Network Basic Books.

Ehrenreich, B. (1983). *The Hearts of Men*. New York: Doubleday.

Ehrensaft, D. (1990). Feminists Fight (for) Fathers. *Socialist Review, 20*(4), 57–80.

Eichler, M. (1977). Women as Personal Dependents. In M. Stephenson (Ed.), *Women in Canada* (pp. 49–69). Don Mills, Ontario: General Publishing.

Eichler, M. (1983). *Families in Canada Today*. Toronto: Gage.

Eichler, M. (1988). *Families in Canada Today* (2nd ed.). Toronto: Gage.

Evernden, N. (1992). *The Social Construction of Nature*. Baltimore: John Hopkins University Press.

Ferree, M. M. (1984). Sacrifice, Satisfaction, and Social Change: Employment and the Family. In K. Sacks and D. Remy (Eds.), *My Troubles are Going to Have Trouble with Me* (pp. 61–79). New Brunswick, NJ: Rutgers University Press.

Ferree, M. M. (1987). Family and Job for Working-Class Women: Gender and Class Systems Seen from Below. In N. Gerstel & H. Gross (Eds.), *Families and Work* (pp. 289–301). Philadelphia: Temple University Press.

Fine, G., & Kleinman, S. (1979). Rethinking Subculture: An Interactionist Analysis. *American Journal of Sociology, 85*(1), 1–20.

Firestone, S. (1971). *The Dialectic of Sex*. New York: Bantam Books.

Fisher, J. (1989). Teaching Time: Women's Responses to Adult Development. In F. Forman (Ed.), *Taking Our Time: Feminist Perspectives on Temporality* (pp. 136–152). Toronto: Pergamon Press.

Foote, N. (1981). Identification as the Basis for a Theory of Motivation. In G. Stone and H. A. Farberman (Eds.), *Social Psychology through Symbolic Interaction* (pp. 333–341). New York: Wiley.

Forman, F. (1989a). Feminizing Time: An Introduction. In F. Forman (Ed.), *Taking Our Time: Feminist Perspectives on Temporality* (pp. 1–10). Toronto: Pergamon Press.

Forman, F. (Ed.). (1989b). *Taking Our Time: Feminist Perspectives on Temporality*. Toronto: Pergamon Press

Frazer, J. G. (1987). *The Golden Bough: A Study in Magic and Religion*. London, UK: Macmillan. (Original work published 1890.)

Furstenberg, F. (1992). Teenage Childbearing and Cultural Rationality: A Thesis in Search of Evidence. *Family Relations, 41*(2), 239–243.

George, L., & Bearon, L. (1980). *Quality of Life in Older Persons: Management and Measurement*. New York: Human Sciences Press.

Geronimus, A. (1992). Teenage Childbearing and Social Disadvantage: Unprotected Discourse. *Family Relations, 41*(2), 244–248.

Gerson, J., & Peiss, K. (1985). Reconceptualizing Gender Relations. *Social Problems, 32*(4), 317–331.

Gerson, K. (1985). *Hard Choices: How Women Decide about Work, Career, and Motherhood*. Berkeley: University of California Press.

Gerstel, N., & Gross, H. E. (Eds.). (1987). *Families and Work*. Philadelphia: Temple University Press.

Giddens, A. (1973). *The Class Structure of the Advanced Societies*. London: Hutchinson University Library.

Giddens, A. (1984). Hermeneutics and Social Theory. In G. Shapiro & A. Sica (Eds.), *Hermeneutics* (pp. 215–230). Amherst, MA: University of Massachusetts Press.

Gilligan, C. (1982). *In a Different Voice*. Cambridge, MA: Harvard University Press.

Gilligan, C. (1986). On *In a Different Voice*: An Interdisciplinary Forum. *Signs, 11*(2), 304–333.

Ginsberg, F. (1989). *Contested Lives: The Abortion Debate in an American Community*. Berkeley: University of California Press.

Glaser, B., & Strauss, A. (1967). *The Discovery of Grounded Theory: Strategies for Qualitative Research*. Chicago: Aldine Publishing.

Goffman, I. (1959). *The Presentation of Self in Everyday Life*. New York: Doubleday.

Goffman, I. (1963). *Stigma: Notes on the Management of Spoiled Identity*. Englewood Cliffs, NJ: Prentice Hall.

Goffman, I. (1987). The Arrangement between the Sexes. In M. Deegan & M. Hill (Eds.), *Women and Symbolic Interaction* (pp. 51–78). Winchester, MA: Allen & Unwin.

Goode, W. (1961). Illegitimacy, Anomie and Cultural Penetration. *American Sociological Review, 26*(6), 910–925.

Gormly, A., Gormly, J., & Weiss, H. (1987). Motivation for Parenthood among Young College Students. *Sex Roles, 16*(1–2), 31–40.

Government of Ontario, Ministry of Community and Social Services. (1989). *Ontario Child Health Study: Children at Risk*. Toronto: Government of Ontario.

Government of Ontario, Ministry of Community and Social Services. (1988). *Transitions: Report of the Social Assistance Review Committee* (Summary). Toronto: Government of Ontario.

Graham, H. (1983). Caring: A Labour of Love. In J. Finch & D. Groves (Eds.), *A Labour of Love: Women, Work and Caring* (pp. 13–30). London, UK: Routledge & Kegan Paul.

Greeno, C., & Maccoby, E. (1986). How Different Is the "Different Voice"? *Signs, 11*(2), 310–316.

Griffin, C. (1989). "I'm Not a Women's Libber, but. . . . ": Feminism, Consciousness and Identity. In S. Skevington & D. Baker (Eds.), *The Social Identity of Women* (pp. 173–193). Newbury Park, CA: Sage.

Griffin, C. (1992). Fear of a Black (and Working-Class) Planet: Young Women and the Racialization of Reproductive Politics. *Feminism and Psychology, 2*(3), 491–494.

Grimshaw, J. (1986). *Philosophy and Feminist Thinking*. Minneapolis: University of Minnesota Press.

Grindstaff, C. (1988). Adolescent Marriage and Childbearing: The Long-Term Economic Outlook, Canada in the 1980s. *Adolescence, 23*(89), 45–58.

Grindstaff, C., Balakrishnan, T., & Dewit, D. (1991). Educational Attainment, Age at First Birth and Lifetime Fertility. *Canadian Review of Sociology and Anthropology, 28*(3), 325–339.

Grindstaff, C., Balakrishnan, T., & Maxim, S. (1989). Life Course Alternatives: Factors Associated with Differential Timing Patterns in Fertility among Women Recently Completing Childbearing, Canada 1981. *Canadian Journal of Sociology, 14*(4), 443–460.

Grogan, R. (1992). Sleeping with the Enemy: Mothers in Heterosexual Relationships. *Feminism and Psychology, 2*(3), 495–497.

Hamner, J. (1993). Women and Reproduction. In D. Richardson & V. Robinson (Eds.), *Thinking Feminist: Key Concepts in Women's Studies* (pp. 225–249). New York: Guilford Press.

Harding, S. (1981). Family Reform Movements: Recent Feminism and its Opposition. *Feminist Studies, 7*(1), 57–76.

Hareven, T. (1977). Family Time and Historical Time. *Daedalus, 106*, 57–70.

Heise, D. (1989). Effects of Emotion Display on Social Identification. *Social Psychology Quarterly, 52*(1), 10–21.

Hertz, R. (1987). Three Careers: His, Hers and Theirs. In N. Gerstel and H. Gross (Eds.), *Families and Work* (pp. 408–421). Philadelphia: Temple University Press.

Hewitt, J. (1976). *Self and Society.* Boston: Allyn & Bacon.

Hochschild, A. (1979). Emotion Work, Feeling Rules, and Social Structure. *American Journal of Sociology, 85*(3), 551–575.

Hochschild, A. (1983). *The Managed Heart: Commercialization of Human Feeling.* Berkeley: University of California Press.

Hochschild, A. (1989). *The Second Shift: Working Parents and the Revolution at Home.* New York: Viking Penguin.

hooks, b. (1989). *talking back: thinking feminist, thinking black.* Boston: Southend Press.

Horowitz, R. (1987). Passion, Submission and Motherhood: The Negotiation of Identity by Unmarried Intercity Chicanas. In M. Deegan & M. Hill (Eds.), *Women and Symbolic Interaction* (pp. 251–264). Winchester, MA: Allen & Unwin.

Houseknecht, S. (1987). Voluntary Childlessness. In M. Sussman and S. Steinmetz (Eds.), *Handbook of Marriage and the Family* (pp. 369–395). New York: Plenum Press.

Jacobson, C., & Heaton, T. (1991). Voluntary Childlessness among American Men and Women in the Late 1980s. *Social Biology, 38*(1–2), 79–93.

Jones, B. (1993). Race, Sex, and Class: Black Female Tobacco Workers in Durham, North Carolina, 1920–1940, and the Development of Female Consciousness. In L. Richardson & V. Taylor (Eds.), *Feminist Frontiers III* (pp. 211–216). New York: McGraw-Hill.

Kahn, R. (1989). Women and Time in Childbirth and during Lactation. In F. Forman (Ed.), *Taking Our Time: Feminist Perspectives on Temporality* (pp. 20–36). New York: Pergamon Press.

Kaufman, D. (1985). Women Who Return to Orthodox Judaism: A Feminist Analysis. *Journal of Marriage and the Family, 47*(3), 543–552.

Kerber, L., Greeno, C., Maccoby, E., Luria, Z., Stack, C., & Gilligan, C. (1986). Viewpoint: On *In a Different Voice*: An Interdisciplinary Forum. *Signs, 11*(2), 304–333.

Kessler, R. C., & McRae, J. A. (1982). The Effect of Wives' Employment on the Mental Health of Married Men and Women. *American Sociological Review, 47*, 216–227.

Kessler-Harris, A. (1993). The Wage Conceived: Value and Need as Measures of a Woman's Worth. In L. Richardson & V. Taylor (Eds.), *Feminist Frontiers III* (pp. 183–197). New York: McGraw-Hill.

Kleinman, S., Stenross, B., & McMahon, M. (1994). Privileging Fieldwork over Interviews: Consequences for Identity and Practice. *Symbolic Interaction, 17*(1), 37–50.

Kohn, M. (1977). *Class and Conformity: A Study in Values* (2nd ed.). Chicago: University of Chicago Press.

Komarovsky, M. (1962). *Blue Collar Marriage*. New Haven: Yale University Press.

Kranichfeld, M. (1987). Rethinking Family Power. *Journal of Family Issues, 8*, 42–56.

Laqueur, T. (1990). *Making Sex: Body and Gender from the Greeks to Freud*. Cambridge, MA: Harvard University Press.

La Rossa, R. (1988). Fatherhood and Social Change. *Family Relations, 37*(October), 451–457.

La Rossa, R., & La Rossa, M. (1981). *Transition to Parenthood: How Infants Change Families*. Beverly Hills, CA: Sage.

Lasch, C. (1979). *The Cult of Narcissism: American Life in an Age of Diminishing Expectations*. New York: Warner Books.

Laslett, P. (1971). *The World We Have Lost*. London, UK: University Paperbacks.

Lofland, L. (1982). Loss and Human Connection: An Exploration into the Nature of the Social Bond. In W. Ickes & E. Knowles (Eds.), *Personality, Roles and Social Behavior* (pp. 219–242). New York: Springer Verlag.

Lopata, H. (1971). *Occupation Housewife*. New York: Oxford University Press.

Lopata, H. (1993a). The Interweave of Public and Private: Women's Challenge to American Society. *Journal of Marriage and the Family, 55*(1), 176–190.

Lopata, H. (1993b). Career Commitments of American Women: The Issue of Side Bets. *The Sociological Quarterly, 34*(2), 257–278.

Luker, K. (1975). *Taking Chances: Abortion and the Decision Not to Contracept*. Berkeley: University of California Press.

Luker, K. (1984). *Abortion and the Politics of Motherhood*. Berkeley: University of California Press.

Luxton, M. (1980). *More than a Labour of Love*. Toronto:Women's Educational Press.

Luxton, M. (1981). Taking on the Double Day. *Atlantis*, 7(1), 12–22.

Luxton, M. (1983). Two Hands for the Clock: Changing Patterns in the Domestic Division of Labour. *Studies in Political Economy*, *10*, 27–44.

Lyons, N. (1983). Two Perspectives: On Self, Relationships, and Morality. *Harvard Educational Review*, *53*(2), 125–145.

Maccoby, E. (1990). Gender and Relationships: A Developmental Account. *American Psychologist*, *45*(4), 513–520.

Machung, A. (1989). Talking Careers, Thinking Job: Gender Differences in Career and Family Expectations of Berkeley Seniors. *Feminist Studies*, *15*(1), 35–58.

Maines, D. (1981). Recent Developments in Symbolic Interaction. In G. Stone & H. A. Farberman (Eds.), *Social Psychology through Symbolic Interaction* (pp. 461–478). New York: Wiley.

Maines, D., & Hardesty, M. (1987). Temporality and Gender: Young Adults' Career and Family Plans. *Social Forces*, *66*(1), 103–120.

Mandel, N. (1989). Juggling the Load: Employed Mothers Who Work Full-Time for Pay. In A. Duffy, N. Mandel, & N. Pupo (Eds.), *Few Choices* (pp. 17–43). Toronto: Garamond Press.

Mansfield, P. (1982). Women and Work: A Proposal for Women's Occupational Health Education. *Health Education*, September/October, 5–8.

Maroney, H. (1986). Embracing Motherhood: New Feminist Theory. In R. Hamilton & M. Barret (Eds.), *Politics of Diversity* (pp. 398–423). London, UK:Verso.

Martin, E., & Martin, J. (1980). The Black Family: An Overview. In A. Skolnick & J. Skolnick (Eds.), *Family in Transition* (3rd ed., pp. 468–478). Boston: Little, Brown.

Matthews, R., & Matthews, A. (1986). Infertility and Voluntary Childlessness: The Transition to Nonparenthood. *Journal of Marriage and the Family*, *48*(3), 641–649.

McCall, G., & Simmons, J. (1978). *Identities and Interactions* (rev. ed.). New York: The Free Press.

McDaniel, S. (1989). A New Stork Rising?: Women's Roles and Reproductive Changes. *Society/Société*, *13*, 6–14.

Mead, G. H. (1962). *Mind, Self, and Society* (C. Morris, Ed.). Chicago: University of California Press. (Original work published 1934.)

Merchant, C. (1980). *The Death of Nature: Women, Ecology and the Scientific Revolution*. New York: Harper & Row.

Michelson, W. (1985). *From Sun to Sun: Daily Obligations and Community Structure in the Lives of Employed Women and Their Families*. Totowa, NJ: Rowan & Allanheld.

Miller, J. B. (1976). *Towards a New Psychology of Women*. Boston: Beacon Press.

Mills, C. W. (1981). Situated Actions and Vocabularies of Motives. In G. Stone & H. A. Farberman (Eds.), *Social Psychology through Symbolic Interaction* (pp. 325–332). New York: Wiley. (Original work published 1940)

Mills, T., & Kleinman, S. (1988). Emotions, Reflexivity, and Action: An Interactionist Analysis. *Social Forces, 66*(4), 1009–1027.

Moore, M. (1987). Women Parenting Alone. *Canadian Social Trends*, Winter, 31–36.

Moore, M. (1989). Female Lone Parenting over the Life Course. *Canadian Journal of Sociology, 14*(3), 335–352.

Morrison, T. (1987). *Beloved*. New York: Knopf.

Murgatroyd, L. (1982). Gender and Occupational Stratification. *Sociological Review, 30*, 574–602.

Nathanson, C. (1991). *Dangerous Passage: The Social Control of Sexuality in Women's Adolescence*. Philadelphia: Temple University Press.

National Council of Welfare. (1990). *Women and Poverty Revisited*. Ottawa: Minister of Supply and Services.

Nave-Hertz, R. (1989). Childless Marriages. *Marriage and Family Review, 14*, 239–250.

Nicolson, P. (1993). Motherhood and Women's Lives. In D. Richardson & V. Robinson (Eds.), *Thinking Feminist: Key Concepts in Women's Studies* (pp. 201–224). New York: Guilford Press.

Nock, S. (1987). The Symbolic Meaning of Childbearing. *Journal of Family Issues, 8*(4), 373–393.

Noddings, N. (1984). *Caring: A Feminine Approach to Ethics*. Berkeley: University of California Press.

Oakley, A. (1974). *The Sociology of Housework*. New York: Random House.

Oakley, A. (1979). *From Here to Maternity: Becoming a Mother*. Harmondsworth, Middlesex, UK: Penguin Books.

Oakley, A. (1980a). Normal Motherhood: An Exercise in Self-Control? In B. Hutter and G. Williams (Eds.), *Controlling Women: The Normal and the Deviant* (pp. 79–106). London, UK: Croom Helm.

Oakley, A. (1980b). *Women Confined: Towards a Sociology of Childbirth*. Oxford, UK: Martin Roberton.

O'Barr, J., Pope, D., & Wyer, M. (1990). Introduction. In J. O'Barr, D. Pope, & M. Wyer, (Eds.), *Ties That Bind: Essays on Mothering and Patriarchy* (pp. 1–14). Chicago: University of Chicago Press.

O'Brien, M. (1981). *The Politics of Reproduction*. London, UK: Routledge & Kegan Paul.

O'Donnell, L. (1985). *The Unheralded Majority: Contemporary Women as Mothers*. Toronto: Lexington Books.

Parliament, J. (1989). Women Employed Outside the Home. *Canadian Social Trends*, Summer, 2–6.

Pateman, C. (1989). *The Disorder of Women: Democracy, Feminism and Political Theory.* Cambridge, UK: Polity Press.

Phoenix, A. (1991a). Mothers under Twenty: Outsider and Insider Views. In A. Phoenix, A. Woolette, & E. Lloyd (Eds.), *Motherhood: Meanings, Practices and Ideologies* (pp. 86–102). London, UK: Sage.

Phoenix, A. (1991b). *Young Mothers.* Cambridge, UK: Polity Press.

Pistrang, N. (1981). *Women's Work Involvement and Experience of New Motherhood* (Ph.D. Dissertation, University of California, San Francisco, UMI Dissertation Information Service, Cat. No. 8201146). Ann Arbor: University Microfilms International.

Pistrang, N. (1984). Women's Work Involvement and Experience of New Motherhood. *Journal of Marriage and the Family, 46*(2), 433–447.

Pollert, A. (1981). *Girls, Wives, Factory Lives.* London, UK: Macmillan.

Pruett, K. (1987). *The Nurturing Father: Journey toward the Complete Man.* New York: Warner Books.

Rains, P. (1971). *Becoming an Unwed Mother.* Chicago: Aldine-Atherton.

Rapp, R. (1978). Family and Class in Contemporary America. *Science and Society, 42,* 278–300.

Reitsma-Street, M. (1991). Girls Learn to Care; Girls Policed to Care. In C. Baines, P. Evans, & S. Neysmith (Eds.), *Women's Caring: Feminist Perspectives on Social Welfare* (pp. 106–137). Toronto: McClelland & Stewart.

Rich, A. (1976). *Of Women Born: Motherhood as Experience and Institution.* Toronto: Bantam Books.

Rich, A. (1980). Compulsory Heterosexuality and Lesbian Existence. *Signs, 5*(4), 631–660.

Rosen, E. (1987). *Bitter Choices: Blue Collar Women in and out of Work.* Chicago: University of Chicago Press.

Rosenberg, M. (1965). *Society and the Adolescent Self-Image.* Princeton: Princeton University Press.

Rosenberg, M. (1979). *Conceiving the Self.* New York: Basic Books.

Rossi, A. (1977). A Biosocial Perspective on Parenting. *Deadalus, 106*(1), 1–31.

Rossi, A. (1980). The Transition to Parenthood. In A. Skolnick & J. Skolnick (Eds.), *Family in Transition* (3rd ed., pp. 389–398). Boston: Little, Brown.

Rothman, B. K. (1989). *Recreating Motherhood: Ideology and Technology in a Patriarchal Society.* New York: W. W. Norton.

Rowland, R. (1987). Technology and Motherhood: Reproductive Choice Considered. *Signs, 12*(3), 512–528.

Rubin, L. (1976). *Worlds of Pain: Life in the Working-Class Family.* New York: Basic Books/Harper Colophon.

Rubin, L. (1984). *Intimate Strangers.* New York: Harper Colophon.

Ruddick, S. (1984a). Maternal Thinking. In J. Trebilcot (Ed.), *Mothering: Essays in Feminist Theory* (pp. 213–230). Totowa, NJ: Rowman & Allanheld.

Ruddick, S. (1984b). Preservative Love and Military Destruction: Some

Reflections on Mothering and Peace. In J. Trebilcot (Ed.), *Mothering: Essays in Feminist Theory* (pp. 231–262). Totowa, NJ: Rowman & Allanheld.

Russo, N. (1979). Overview: Sex Roles, Fertility and the Motherhood Mandate. *Psychology of Women Quarterly, 4*(1), 7–15.

Rowland, R. (1987). Technology and Motherhood: Reproductive Choice Considered. *Signs, 12*(3), 512–528.

Sacks, K. (1984). Generations of Working-Class Families. In K. Sacks and D. Remy (Eds.), *My Troubles Are Going to Have Trouble with Me* (pp. 15–38). Piscataway, NJ: Rutgers University Press.

Sampson, E. (1988). The Dabate on Individualism: Indigenous Psychologies of the Individual and Their Roles in Personal and Social Functioning. *American Psychologist, 43*(1), 15–22.

Sandelowski, M. (1990). Failure of Volition: Female Agency and Infertility in Historical Perspective. *Signs, 15*(3), 475–499.

Sandelowski, M., Harris, B., & Holditch-Davis, D. (1993). Somewhere Out There: Parental Claiming in the Preadoption Period. *Journal of Contemporary Ethnography, 21*(4), 464–486.

Schoenfeld, S. (1988). Re-reading a Canadian Classic: Crestwood Heights as a Study of the Invisible Religion. *Canadian Review of Sociology and Anthropology, 25*(3), 456–463.

Scott, J. (1988). Deconstructing Equality-Versus-Difference: Or the Uses of Poststructuralist Theory for Feminism. *Feminist Studies, 14*(1), 33–50.

Scott, M. & Lyman, S. (1981). Accounts. In G. Stone & H. A. Farberman (Eds.), *Social Psychology through Symbolic Interaction* (pp. 343–361). New York: Wiley.

Seccombe, K. (1991). Assessing the Costs and Benefits of Children: Gender Comparisons among Childfree Husbands and Wives. *Journal of Marriage and the Family, 53*(1), 191–202.

Shiva, V. (1989). *Staying Alive: Women, Ecology and Development.* London, UK: Zed Books.

Sidel, R. (1990). *On Her Own: Growing Up in the Shadow of the American Dream.* New York: Penguin Books.

Silverman, D. (1985). *Qualitative Methodology and Sociology.* Aldershot, UK: Gower.

Simmel, G. (1984). On Love (a Fragment). In G. Oakes (Ed.), *On Women, Sexuality and Love* (pp. 153–192). New Haven: Yale University Press.

Smart, C. (1989). Power and the Politics of Child Custody. In C. Smart & S. Sevenhuijsen (Eds.), *Child Custody and the Politics of Parenthood* (pp. 1–27). New York: Routledge.

Smart, C. (1992). Disruptive Bodies and Unruly Sex. In C. Smart (Ed.), *Regulating Womanhood: Historical Essays on Marriage, Motherhood and Sexuality* (pp. 5–32). New York: Routledge.

Smelser, N. (1980). Issues in the Study of Work and Love in Adulthood. In

N. Smelser & E. Erikson (Eds.), *Themes of Work and Love in Adulthood* (pp. 1–26). Cambridge, MA: Harvard University Press.

Smith, D. (1975). An Analysis of Ideological Structures and How Women are Excluded. *Canadian Review of Sociology and Anthropology, 12*(4), 353–369.

Smith-Rosenberg, C. (1975). The Female World of Love and Ritual. *Signs, 1*(1), 1–29.

Snitow, A. (1990). A Gender Diary. In M. Hirsch & E. Fox (Eds.), *Conflicts in Feminism* (pp. 9–43). New York: Routledge.

Snitow, A. (1992). Feminism and Motherhood: An American Reading. *Feminist Review, 40,* 32–51.

Solinger, R. (1992). *Wake Up Little Susie: Single Pregnancy and Race before Roe v. Wade.* New York: Routledge.

Spelman, E. (1988). *The Inessential Woman.* Boston, MA: Beacon.

Squier, S., & Ruddick, S. (1983). Book Reviews. *Harvard Educational Review, 53*(3), 338–342.

Stack, C. (1974). *All Our Kin: Strategies for Survival in a Black Community.* New York: Harper & Row.

Stanley, L., & Wise, S. (1983). *Breaking Out: Feminist Consciousness and Feminist Research.* London, UK: Routledge & Kegan Paul.

Stanworth, M. (1990). Birth Pangs: Contraceptive Technologies and the Threat to Motherhood. In M. Hirsch & E. F. Keller (Eds.), *Conflicts in Feminism* (pp. 288–304). New York: Routledge.

Statistics Canada. (1989, Autumn). *Canadian Social Trends.* Ottawa: Author.

Statistics Canada. (1990a). *Women in Canada: A Statistical Report* (2nd ed.). Ottawa: Ministry of Supply and Services.

Statistics Canada. (1990b). *Profile of Visible Minorities and Aboriginal Peoples, 1986.* Ottawa: Author.

Stokes, R., & Hewitt, J. (1976, October). Aligning Actions. *American Review of Sociology, 41,* 838–849.

Stone, G. (1981). Appearance and the Self: A Slightly Revised Version. In G. Stone & H. A. Farberman (Eds.), *Social Psychology through Symbolic Interaction* (pp. 187–202). New York: Wiley.

Stone, G., & Farberman, H. A. (1981). *Social Psychology through Symbolic Interaction* (2nd ed.). New York: Wiley.

Stone, L. (1972). *The Family, Sex and Marriage in England 1500–1800.* New York: Harper & Row.

Stryker, S. (1968). Identity Salience and Role Performance. *Journal of Marriage and the Family, 30*(4), 558–564.

Suleiman, S. (1988). On Maternal Splitting: A Propos of Mary Gordon's Men and Angels. *Signs, 14*(1), 25–41.

Swidler, A. (1980). Love and Adulthood in American Culture. In N. Smelser & E. Erikson (Eds.), *Themes of Work and Love in Adulthood* (pp. 120–147). Cambridge, MA: Harvard University Press.

Swidler, A. (1986). Culture in Action: Symbols and Strategies. *American Sociological Review, 51*(2), 273–286.

Thompson, L., & Walker, A. (1989). Gender in Families: Women and Men in Marriage, Work, and Parenthood. *Journal of Marriage and the Family, 51*(4), 845–871.

Thompson, S. (1994). Cruel and Unusual Punishment. *Women's Review of Books, XI*(10–11), 16–17.

Tilly, L., & Scott, J. (1978). *Women, Work and Family.* New York: Holt, Rinehart & Winston.

Turner, R. (1962). Role-taking: Process versus Conformity. In A. Rose (Ed.), *Human Behavior and Social Process* (pp. 87–106). Boston: Houghton-Mifflin.

Turner, R. (1981). The Real Self: From Institution to Impulse. In G. Stone and H. A. Farberman (Eds.), *Social Psychology through Symbolic Interaction* (2nd ed., pp. 203–222). New York: Wiley.

Valverde, M. (1991). *The Age of Light, Soap, and Water.* Toronto: McClelland & Stewart.

Veevers, J. (1980). *Childless by Choice.* Toronto: Butterworth.

Waldron, I. (1980). Employment and Women's Health: An Analysis of Causal Relationship. *International Journal of Health Services, 10*(3), 435–454.

Wearing, B. (1984). *The Ideology of Motherhood.* Boston: Allen & Unwin.

Weeks, J. (1981). *Sex, Politics and Society: The Regulation of Sexuality since 1800.* New York: Longman.

Weitzman, L. (1985). *The Divorce Revolution.* New York: Free Press.

Welter, B. (1966). The Cult of True Womanhood, 1820–1860. *American Quarterly, 18,* 151–174.

West, C., & Zimmerman, D. (1987). Doing Gender. *Gender and Society, 1,* 125–151.

White, J. (1983). *Women and Part-Time Work.* Ottawa: Ministry of Supply and Services.

Woollett, A. (1991). Having Children: Accounts of Childless Women and Women with Reproductive Problems. In A. Phoenix, A. Woollett, & E. Lloyd (Eds.), *Motherhood: Meanings, Practices and Ideologies* (pp. 47–65). London, UK: Sage.

Wrong, D. (1961). The Oversocialized Conception of Man in Modern Sociology. *American Sociological Review, 26*(1), 183–193.

Zelizer, V. (1985). *Pricing the Priceless Child.* New York: Basic Books.

Zimmerman, S. (1992). Family Trends: What Implications for Family Policy? *Family Relations, 41*(4), 423–429.

Zussman, R. (1987). Work and Family Roles in the New Middle Class. In N. Gerstel & H. E. Gross (Eds.), *Families and Work* (pp. 338–346). Philadelphia: Temple University Press.

Index